P9-COO-936

contents

Projects

Gratitude

So many people to thank. I'm a lucky girl and I know it.

First, thanks and massive hugs to the people at Interweave Press: Betsy Armstrong for signing me; Tricia Waddell for her amazing support; the team of Paulette Livers, Joe Coca, and Ann Swanson for taking my photographic wishlist and making it real; Karen Frisa for making the illustrations clear and correct; and my beloved editor with the softest shoulders, Ann Budd—thank you for sharing your experience and wisdom with me.

Thanks to Debbie Bliss, Suss Cousins, Fiona Ellis, Amy Swenson, Kay Gardiner, and Sally Melville for whispering their nonwool secrets into my e-mail box; to Linda Pratt and Susan Mills at Westminster Fibers, Jonelle Raffino at Southwest Trading Company, Lana Hames at Hemp for Knitting, Tina Newton (pandas!) at Blue Moon Fiber Arts, and Gina Wilde at Alchemy Yarns for their insight into the way yarn companies and manufacturers do what they do; to Susan Preston at Estelle for the 11th-hour Opal; to all the companies who contributed materials for the projects in this book—we couldn't have done it without you; to Dr. Sandra Gawchik, board-certified Allergist, Co-Director of the Division of Allergy and Immunology at Crozer-Chester Medical Center in Upland, Pennsylvania, Clinical Associate Professor at Thomas Jefferson University in Philadelphia, Pennsylvania, for speaking with me at length about fiber allergies and sensitivities; to all the designers in the book, especially Celeste Culpepper, Libby Baker, and Jenna Wilson, who conquered bigger challenges than any of us expected them to have to face; to Wannietta Prescod for brilliant knitting under fire; to Wendy Wonnacott for her help in naming the geeky thing; to Michael Cook for his input and feedback on the silk section; to Bette Hochberg for her brilliant books on fiber, which were essential in helping me figure out the science bits (and Cindy Howard-Gibbon for permission), and J. Gordon Cook for the raw science; to the readers of the Knittyblog for their input on what makes them itch and sneeze; to Denny McMillan for the pep talks; and to the Lettuce Knit s&b crew for the sanity breaks.

Special thanks to my Mom, Anne, for her input, editing, and guidance; to Jillian for talking me off the ledge more than once and always making me laugh; to Philly for paddling alone this summer without complaint and all the other sweet things he does; to Grandma, as always, for teaching me how. And to all the people who love Knitty, cheer me on, and read the stuff I write, thank you. I love my job.

Introduction

"Soft wool from the simple silly sheep can be as fine as a cobweb, tough and strong as string, or light and soft as down. There are scientific reasons why wool is the best material for knitting, and into these I will not go. I only know that it is warm, beautiful and durable . . .

For people allergic to wool, one's heart can only bleed. Synthetics are a marvelous substitute, but a substitute is all they are. The allergic must be grateful that they didn't live in the Dark Ages of fifty years ago when one kept warm in winter with wool, or froze to death in linen and cotton."
—Elizabeth Zimmermann, *Knitting Without Tears, 1971*

Elizabeth Zimmerman was right, of course. But she's also not right. (I would never call anything she did "wrong.")

I learned to knit a few years before Elizabeth wrote these words. Until the last decade or so, I'd have agreed with her wholeheartedly. But things have changed since 1971, and thank the sheep they have! Knitters who don't use wool (let's call them nonwool knitters) are no longer stuck knitting with rigid string or scrinchy plastic "yarn" substitutes. The fibers we knit with may not all be natural miracles like wool, but thanks to science and technology, they're still a miracle and are totally knitworthy for their own merits.

Knitting opinion has also shifted a little in recent years. Now there's room for knitters to love more than one fiber at a time without feeling sheepishly unfaithful. Silk, for example, does things that no other fiber can do, and for some reason, only in the last few years have we allowed ourselves to think about it as a serious fiber to knit with. For me, it's my current favorite.

Natural fibers like hemp and linen are as old as intelligent life on this planet (well, almost), and they're enjoying a resurgence in popularity as knitters realize that the beautiful, long-lasting end product is worth a little extra wrist action to produce. Technology has helped by softening the fibers enough to make knitting and wearing them much more enjoyable.

Yarn companies and scientists have brought wagonloads of new fibers to our needles in the last few years, so if we feel like knitting a little corn for breakfast, soy at lunch, and bamboo before bedtime, we can. Clever yarn gimmicks? Nope. Though these fibers are novel, there's nothing novelty about them. They're seriously yummy and worth getting to know and knit.

No fiber will ever duplicate everything wool does naturally. Scientists have spent more than a hundred years trying and the best they've done so far is . . . acrylic? Never mind. I've got a book full of gorgeous fiber to share with you, and none of it squeaks.

No Sheep for You is not about us against them; it's about having great stuff for everyone to knit with. I'm itching (excuse the pun) to get started. Join me!

A Little Song, a Little Dance, a Little Fiber in Your Pants

one

When I first talked about writing a nonwool knitting book, nearly everyone I asked assumed it would be about cotton. And it will be, no worries. But there is so much more available than just cotton for nonwool knitters, and there's no way I'm going to ignore all the other good stuff. There's a new appreciation among yarn manufacturers, designers, and knitters for ancient fibers like linen and hemp. And then there are the new fibers developed by progressive yarn companies (I love these guys) who aren't just taking whatever they can find—but working to create new fibers, yarn textures, and blends. This is what makes being a nonwool knitter in this century something to envy. If you're lucky enough to be able to knit with wool, too, then you have it all.

Okay, let's get into it. Every fiber we'll talk about and knit with is part of a group of similar fibers. Not every member of the group behaves the same as every other, but like any family, they've got stuff in common. You'll see.

So here goes, then. Time to dive headfirst into the nonwool knitting waters.

Cellulose Fibers

When you think of nonwool yarns, likely these are what you think of first–yarns made from plant fibers. These fibers belong to the cellulose group and come in two flavors: bast and seed.

Bast Fibers

In order for plants to stay upright, they need some kind of internal structure. That's lucky for knitters, because the structure that bast-fiber-producing plants have tucked safely inside their tall stems is long, fibery bundles. These fibers are made up of long overlapping cells that have thick outer walls that make them strong. Naturally occurring waxes and resins hold the cells together.

Flax fibers

Flax stem

Core

Bundle of fibers

Flax stem

How did anyone realize the stuff inside these tall plants would work as the raw material for cloth? Well, the stalks were tall and flexible, which meant they were useful on their own; think of how we use bamboo stakes in our gardens today. One source suggests they were used as windbreaks in fields or woven as barriers across streams to trap fish. And once those stalks got wet, then dried in the sun, over and over for weeks and months, the outer layers of the stalks would have broken down and people would have seen the long, shiny fibers inside. Either that or aliens told them how to do it. Okay, probably not aliens.

Although machines and chemicals do the job now, the process of getting the fibers out of the tough stalks follows the same steps as it did hundreds and thousands of years ago. It takes time and a lot of work. It starts with rotting the stems under controlled conditions (called "retting"), breaking up the outer bark into bits without hurting the inner fiber, "scutching" to separate these bark bits from the fiber, then "hackling" the fibers to align them and remove short fibers (called "tow"), leaving only the long, lustrous "line" fibers behind. The line is carded, which tidies up the fibers even further. *Now* it's starting to look knittable.

We're not done yet, though. The line fibers need to be spun, either wet (for a fine yarn) or dry (for a coarse one). Wet spinning also helps soften the resins and waxes, and that makes the spinner's job easier. Finally, we have yarn.

Should you ever wonder why bast-fiber yarns can cost more than cotton, this might help explain it. Even with modern techniques, producing bast-fiber yarn is a labor-intensive process. But the resulting fiber is worth it.

Hemp

Industrial Hemp and the Law

Canada is the only North American country that has legalized the production of industrial hemp and has a viable commercial hemp industry. There are pages and pages of regulations farmers must follow to make sure there's no funny stuff in the crop we'll end up knitting with. Industrial hemp can be grown in the United States, but only with a difficult-to-obtain multi-requirement Drug Enforcement Agency (DEA) permit.

A United States Department of Agriculture report released in 2000 said that there's no market for the stuff and Canada's producing more than can be used as it is. (I don't think they took knitters into consideration in this study . . . have they seen the size of our yarn stashes?) So right now, Canada is the only source of hemp fiber in quantity in North America.

Hemp: Deeply misunderstood, this one. Botanists have failed the textile industry, because for some reason, both the industrial hemp plant (which is the one we knit with; it has no narcotic properties) and marijuana are officially called *Cannabis sativa*. How is the layperson not supposed to get confused?

But the industrial hemp variety grows stalky and tall with few leaves and flowers and—by Canadian law (see box at upper right)—contains less than 0.3% THC (the stuff that makes you goofy). If you're foolish enough to smoke it, all you'll get is a headache. The other kind? It's short, stubby, mostly leaves and flowers, and has THC out the wazoo (in scientific terms, that means 3–20%).

Modern hemp fiber still has a vague mis-association with the goofy stuff, probably because hemp clothing is often sold in the same shops as rolling papers and incense. But as you can see, the two plants are merely cousins. Rest assured that the hemp yarn you're buying has nothing in it but good, clean fiber. In fact, hemp *is* a relatively clean crop. It is a hardy plant that doesn't need a lot of chemical intervention from the farmer to produce a profitable crop if grown in rotation. (If you plant it on its own in the same place every year, like any other crop it'll require chemicals to survive.)

Outer layer—
Bast fibers—
Shive—

Cross-section of hemp stem

Hemp plants grow 10 feet (3 meters) tall. The actual fiber length is hard to pin down, but multiple sources say it's somewhere between ¾ and 4¾ inches (2 and 12 cm).

Long fiber = happy knitting. Bast fibers like hemp can be stringy and coarse looking, and don't appear very finger friendly. But as I'll say more than once in this book, you need to get to know a fiber before you show it the door.

Depending on your preferences, you might find hemp anything from annoyingly inflexible to a wee bit stiff on the needles. But the charm of hemp comes in the endless washing-wearing-washing-wearing cycle of a garment. Hemp is strong so machine washing doesn't hurt it; each cycle just makes it softer. It can be machine dried—and loves it, in fact. And wearing? Would you be surprised if I told you that fabric knitted from hemp yarn has "sproing?" It does. Knit a big swatch and give it a tug. It doesn't just surrender to your touch; it bounces back where it wants to be and looks good all the while.

Hemp-loving designer Celeste Culpepper (see her Manly Maze sweater on page 81) tells me a hemp sweater won't wrinkle if you roll it and cram it into your suitcase, and if it gets wet, it won't mildew. (My reference texts agree.) Lana Hames, founder of the pioneering company Hemp for Knitting, tells me that when she first opened her business several years ago, she took the coarse-but-strong hemp twine she bought from Europe, skeined it, washed it, softened it, and then—no kidding—beat it against rocks by hand before she put her label on it. She has now developed a mechanized process that softens the twine and dyes it in rich, appealing colors, turning it into very knittable yarn. Her hemp is also mercerized (see more about mercerization on page 12), which improves its hand and helps the colors stay fast.

Not everything in the world of nonwools is about instant gratification. Knit a hemp something and fall in love with it a little more every time you pull it out of the dryer.

Linen: Linen has a reputation as hemp's more sophisticated sibling. At the time when hemp was the fiber of peasants, linen was the fiber of royalty. But really, they're not that different. In fact, the word "linen" was historically used to describe the fiber that came from both flax and hemp plants.

Flax

What we call linen today comes from the flax plant. It's almost all stalk and stands 3 to 4 feet (1 to 1.25 meters) tall with inconsequential leaves and pretty but unknittable blue flowers. It can be grown for its seed, which is popular in health food products (and very good for you, 'cause it's full of omega-3 fatty acids), yet strangely can also be pressed into very stinky linseed oil, which is used for finishing wood products.

Flax has been with us (that'd be civilization on earth) for a long, long time. Fragments of flax fibers and ancient spindle whorls have been found in archaeological digs in the Middle East and dated to 8000 B.C. The fiber has a natural luster thanks to those plant waxes I mentioned. It's two to three times stronger than cotton, really absorbent, and conducts heat away from the body. No wonder it's the fiber of choice in summer.

But it wrinkles. And it wrinkles because it's got near zero elasticity . . . how can it bounce back if it has almost no bounce? Never mind. It has so many other virtues, bounciness isn't required. It's elegant. It drapes beautifully. It holds color well. It makes you want to touch it. And it can last forever, if cared for properly.

But linen can be unforgiving when you're trying to create a perfectly smooth stockinette stitch fabric . . . so Sally Melville (author of the must-read *The Knitting Experience* series of books) advises us not to struggle. Instead, she says, "Use it in lace: (linen) shows off the stitches well but also lets the holes mediate the unevenness that it is sometimes prone to." Louet Sales, the North American distributor of Euroflax linen yarn, agrees. Their website says it's "more suitable for pattern knitting than for plain knits."

But what if you don't expect perfection in your stockinette? What if quirky is just what you wanted? Then knit on!

Like hemp, linen yarn may appear less flexible than other yarns you're used to knitting. And like hemp, the reward comes in the washing and wearing. Machine washable and dryable, absolutely. And again, like hemp, linen garments soften and become more wearable over time. In fact, you should notice a significant difference after your first washing of your finished linen piece. Don't hesitate . . . throw that baby in the washer and dryer. There's nothing to be scared of.

One more note on linen. It's a strong fiber, but it's not invincible. Repeated folding along the same crease lines may eventually cause the linen fibers to break. So store it with care. Change where you fold the piece each time, or slip in a few sheets of acid-free tissue paper between the layers to soften the line of the fold.

Seed Fibers

Though there are quite a few plants that produce their fiber in their seed pods, the only one knitters really need to know about

Is Your Fiber Behaving Itself?

How a fiber ultimately behaves is a combination of the brand of fiber you use (which includes where the fiber came from, how it was processed, and the final form of the yarn—chainette, tube, plied, whatever), how you knit it (your technique and your gauge), what kind of needles you use, what textures you knit into it, and how you want to use the finished product. Don't take anyone else's word on any fiber. When it comes to nonwools, it's all about getting to know each other before you can build a long-term friendship. For more on this subject, see Chapter Three.

is cotton. Other plants, like kapok and milkweed—even cattails—make seed fiber, but it's suitable only for stuffing or insulation. It can't be spun because it's too brittle and weak to hold together.

Cotton: Cotton dating back to 12000 B.C. has been found in Egypt and may have been used before flax. In India, cotton became the fabric of the people because it was affordable and practical to grow, spin, and weave. As far back as 1500 B.C., India was producing good-quality cotton goods from their primitive spindles and looms.

Cotton

So, how does it grow? We don't care about the stalk this time. Instead, picture a shrubby plant that eventually pops out delicate blossoms at the end of each stem. When this cotton flower is finished, it shrivels up and falls off the plant, leaving a seed pod behind. This pod

Merceri–Who?

Mercerization is a process used to improve the luster and smoothness of fibers and make them stronger and more able to accept dyes. The fiber is held under tension as a solution of caustic soda is applied. This makes the fibers swell, and fighting against the tension, they get smoother and shinier. Where'd the name come from? The guy who invented the process—John Mercer.

All About Naturally Colored Cotton

This naturally colored, very-soft yarn has been showing up in shops for several years, but how does the natural color get there? Remember the protoplasm in the center of the cotton fiber? Well, when the fiber dries out, the protoplasm dries into something called endochrome, and the nutrients that are in the endochrome are what produce the color—natural green, a whole selection of browns, and a variety of soft cream colors. As you wash stuff made of naturally colored cotton, the color deepens, too. It's a home chemistry experiment! The higher the pH (a measure of acidity) of the water you wash in, the deeper the color gets. Sally Fox, the developer of naturally colored Foxfibre® (a registered trademark of Vreseis Ltd.) cotton, recommends adding ¼ cup (60 milliliters) of washing soda to the washing machine to help it along. Or just wash as normal in hot water and machine dry several times—the color change is accelerated by heat. If you want to see how deep the color will get, boil the yarn before you start knitting. Sally also warns that the green color can change to tan over time when exposed to the sun.

is full of cotton seeds, each covered with microscopic hairs; those hairs are the cotton fiber. (The hairs exist to help the wind catch the seeds once the boll has popped open and disperse them over a wider area.)

The seeds continue to push more fibers out until what we've got is a very hairy seed indeed. Each hair is a hollow tube of cellulose fibers filled with a liquid called protoplasm that carries nutrients. The hair's only job at this point is to get longer. Once the hairs grow to their full length, it's time to thicken up.

So layers of cellulose are slathered on each fiber's inner walls, one a day, which makes them stronger. It's sort of like the growth of an inside-out tree—it builds strength inward, layer by layer.

Soon the seed pod is completely crammed full of seeds and long-and-thicker fibers, and eventually, it pops open at the top. Voilà, a cotton boll. After the boll bursts open, the fibers, formerly plump and round, dry out. What we're left with are fibers that look like long, very skinny raisins—irregular, oval, and shriveled on the outside. But the internal strength remains because of those layers and layers of cellulose along the wall of each fiber. The other really neat thing cotton fibers do as they dry is twist—in both directions, unpredictably, as many as 125 times per inch. This is as close as we're gonna get to the natural crimp in a (shh) wool fiber, and it's why cotton holds together when you spin it.

Cross-section of cotton fibers

The boll is mostly fibers, but the seeds are still in the way, and they have to be removed if we're going to be able to spin this stuff into yarn. Enter Eli Whitney's cotton gin, invented in 1793, a mechanized device that saws the seeds away from the fibers. Newer roller gins are gentler on the fibers than Eli's original vicious beast, but they still use saws to free the fibers.

In the 1960s, chemical modification added beneficial properties to the fiber itself like resistance to heat, improved absorbency, better dye absorption, and resistance to rotting. Transgenic crops (that's another term for "genetically modified") are now going one step further, building resistance into the DNA of some strains of cotton to eradicate the boll weevil—still a serious and continuing threat to cotton crops. Like organic gardeners do with their crops, cotton farmers also use the weevil's natural enemies to help fight them to reduce the use of insecticides. Of course, organic cotton farmers don't use insecticides or chemicals of any kind, but they can use transgenic seed and are big on the natural enemy approach.

Protein Fibers

There are two kinds of protein fibers that knitters use. Fibers like wool, alpaca, cashmere, and other woollies are made up of keratin. These fibers are naturally elastic, great insulators, and beautiful. In the nonwool world, the protein is fibroin, it comes from silkworms, and it is, as silkworm farmer Michael Cook so eloquently coined it, worm spit. (Visit his squirmy, shimmery site at wormspit.com.) Silk fibers are beautiful, great insulators, and precious . . . and for people who can't knit with wool, knitting with silk makes them care not a whit.

Silk

There are many types of silk, but for a knitter's purposes, they can be categorized into two groups.

Bombyx Silk: Bombyx silk comes from hand-raised *Bombyx mori* silkworms; it's also called "cultivated" silk. These silkworms are more domesticated than your average cat. After more than 4,000 years of being hand raised, they can't survive without constant human care. The dang things don't even fly once they've got wings. They walk. Bombyx silkworms are raised indoors under highly controlled conditions. The moment a silkworm hatches from its egg, it's got to be hand fed a steady diet of fresh, cool mulberry leaves for a month.

Bombyx

Tussah silk: Tussah is a word that's come to mean any member of a group of wild silkmoths. Although they're wild, they're still farmed, though more like sheep than the highly pampered Bombyx silkworms. Immediately upon hatching, tussah silkworms are placed on a leafy tree in the plantation by their caregivers, they eat the tree bare, and then are moved to the next tree. Vertical pastures, sort of. They mostly eat oak, som, or soalu leaves (the last two are trees that grow in India). Tussah moths are significantly bigger than Bombyx moths, and because of their diet, their silk is more darkly colored. There's another difference in the silk,

Tussah

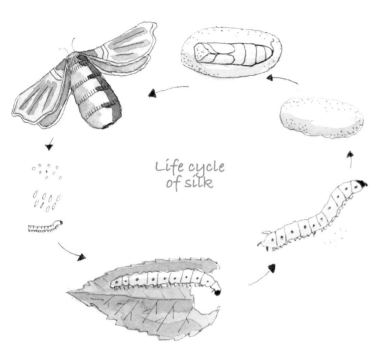

Life cycle
of silk

but this one is due to genetics. Tussah silk is thicker and coarser than Bombyx silk. Both are beautiful.

Okay, so we've got two different species of silkworm. When last we saw them, they were both eating and growing bigger, shedding their skins, and becoming progressively more caterpillary with each shed. Finally, each starts to wind a cocoon, which is where the spit comes in. The spit (fibroin) is secreted in a continuous filament from a pair of spinnerets located just below the caterpillar's mouth, and it hardens when it comes in contact with the air. Silky the caterpillar waggles his head from side to side as many as 150,000 times in order to surround himself in a bubble of his own silk. The fibroin is naturally coated in sericin, which is essentially bug glue. It holds the fibroin strands together so that the cocoon, when completed, is a safe place for the caterpillar to transform into a silkmoth. How much silk is in one cocoon? Between 275 and

1,640 yards (250 and 1,500 meters), all in one continuous strand. How's *that* for fiber length?

Now, at this point one of two things can happen:

Option One: The silkmoth is allowed to live out its natural life span. This means it spews enzyme goo on one skinny end of the cocoon, which dissolves the silk so it can work its way out of the cocoon, find a mate, do the wild thang, and then die. (Somewhere in there, the female of the species will have to lay her eggs.) These moths have no mouths (eek!) so there's no way they can live once their internal food supply runs out. They go to all this trouble, building the cocoon and mating, just to create the next generation. Nature is freaky.

From a silk standpoint, what's left after this curiously fixated lifespan completes itself is a cocoon with a browny hole in one end. This is usable silk, but it can't be reeled in one unbroken strand—and that's what produces the smoothest, finest, most valuable yarns. So it's not the norm in the industry, but it is available. If you're looking for silk raised this way, look for "peace" or *ahimsa* silk ("ahimsa" is the Sanskrit word that means "a reverence for life").

Option Two: The moth has its short life ended a few days earlier than normal, before it has a chance to break through the cocoon. The common word for this is "stifling." It's done with either dry heat or steam, and what's left is an undamaged cocoon with a little deceased bug inside. RIP.

Okay. So we've got cocoons. Now what? The most perfect ones get the hot water treatment. They're floated in a steamy bath that loosens the bug glue just enough for the end of the strand to be released. Brushes are used to help find the end. Patience is involved. We're talking about finding the end of a thread thinner than a human hair. Once the ends are found, a number of single filaments are grouped together and unwound from their cocoons all at once. This is called "reeling." (The twist is added later.) Reeled Bombyx silk makes the smoothest, shimmeriest, longest-fiberest stuff. The finished yarn can be as thin or thick as the reeler wants.

The less-than-perfect cocoons get used in a number of ways. If the moth didn't break a hole in one end, but the cocoon is irregular or a double cocoon (that's where the word "dupioni" comes from—it means double, or two cocoons attached together), it's spun into a lumpy-but-still-shiny yarn.

Cocoons that have a hole in one end can be fluffed up and then spun into strong but not-so-shimmery yarn, or they can be degummed and stretched out into lighter-than-air layers (called hankies or caps), which are amazing fun for handspinners (the people with hand-spindles or spinning wheels who make their own yarn).

So there you go. The source of one of the most beautiful natural fibers on this planet is a worm. Amazing.

Now, what about silk as a fiber for knitters? Until recently, it probably wasn't something the average knitter had a lot of experience with. You could find a lot of crunchy silk (like the stuff that's in Rowan's Summer Tweed—strong, drapey, and beautiful, but no shimmer whatsoever) but the smooth stuff was not very affordable or available. Suddenly, smooth silk yarns, plied or not, are showing up in every manufacturer's line.

How Do You Block Silk?

Because it stretches so much when it's wet, don't wet the piece before you block it. For lace, pin the piece into shape on a blocking surface and spritz thoroughly with water. Let dry. For a garment, lay flat, spritz or use a little steam, and coax it into shape. Let dry.

Be aware that the crunchy silks are more fragile than shimmery 2-ply, because they're not made with super-long filaments like reeled yarn is. A strand of reeled 2-ply would probably dig a groove in your hands before it'd break, so you can use some force as you pin it into shape. Crunchy silk, and some unplied smooth silks, on the other hand, will pull apart like candy floss with a too-firm tug. Handle gently.

photos: Amy R. Singer

Smooth silk

Crunchy silk

The biggest surprise of silk is that it is the perfect fiber for lace. The shimmery stuff blocks beautifully. Bonus: Because it doesn't have the sproing of wool, you can see what the lace pattern looks like *as you knit it*. If you drop a stitch or make an error, silk yarn makes it easier to find and fix because all the stitches aren't jumbled up on top of each other. (I will *not* provide a warranty to that effect, however. Use a lifeline—a contrasting yarn that wise lace knitters thread through all of the stitches on the needle every few inches.)

When it comes to lace, silk goes one step further: you can block it, and it REALLY DOES hold the blocking. Do you get what I'm saying here? You can make an entirely silk lace whatever, block it once, and have it look gorgeous for years. The actual dimensions of the piece may move about a little as you wear it—we *are* talking about a really slippery yarn—but the lace pattern stays true and visible and wearable for years.

And please . . . *do* block your silk lace. You might be tempted just to bind off and wear the thing, but even though you can see the lace pattern, it will look exponentially better after you block it. It adds a final touch of civilization to your work. Plus it makes the thing bigger. Yum.

But what about using silk in a garment? Absolutely doable . . . you just have to choose carefully. A 100% shimmery silk, heavily cabled sweater? I'd probably not knit that, though it would feel so sexy against my skin that I might not care that it was drooping as I walked out the door. But a tightly knit vest or hat, an intricate lace wrap . . . absolutely. The mosaic sweater with lace sleeves on page 55 is one designer's approach to taming silk. The natural inward pull of the mosaic pattern helps the sweater hold its shape.

If a shimmery silk is too much for you, look to the matte finish and greater tooth of the crunchy silks. I won't say raw because raw silk literally means it's still full of sericin (that's the bug glue, remember?), and the bug glue is rarely present in finished yarn. But yarns like Summer Tweed or Estelle's 100% Tussah silk yarn aren't slippery like spaghetti. They're cushy and drapey, with enough grab to do a better job of holding their shape than their slippery sisters. Crunchy silk tip: Jillian Moreno knit her Twist vest (see page 65) in Summer

Tweed tighter than the ball-band gauge so that the stitches would stay where she put them.

Still, silk yarn will never be Lycra, and we have to accept the trade-off—delicious drape, scintillating shimmer, exceptional warmth, and unequaled softness. Seems fair to me.

Manufactured Fibers from Natural Materials

In the early 1900s, a new category of fiber was created: created fiber. Seriously, though—until then, the only fiber available was what grew from the ground or out of the skin of animals. But scientists are a restless bunch, and their search for an artificial silk started us along a path we're still pursuing today.

Here's a very general description of the process by which we get fiber from something that used to be a tree or a food byproduct. Mulch the stuff up into chips or pulp (if necessary), and process it with heat and/or chemicals to turn it into a flowable liquid. The liquid is then forced through a bunch of tiny holes in a nozzle called a spinneret, which can create smooth, solid filaments to replicate silk or fuzzy, hollow filaments in any shape and configuration you can imagine. (Fuzzy makes things feel soft against your skin. Hollow means the fiber holds air, so it feels warm.) The stuff that comes out of the spinneret is either surrounded by fluid (for wet spinning) or air (for dry spinning) to cure it and make it into solid fiber. This stuff is then spun into yarn.

Spinneret

I know, that's pretty vague. That's because manufactured fibers, my friends, are the great secrets of the nonwool fiber world. Because each company is highly protective of their trade secrets, not a lot of production specifics are shared with the public. (You're going to see a lot of ®s and ™s in this section.)

Jonelle Raffino, president of South West Trading Company, has been in many of the mills that make these types of fibers and she tells me that each one uses different base ingredients, but reasonably similar processes, to go from raw material to finished fiber.

Jonelle also says that one of the big appeal factors of this category of yarn is that it's (for the most part) created out of the leftovers from the manufacturing process of a number of different annually renewable materials, like soybeans, corn, bamboo, and milk. This stuff would just get tossed out . . . instead it's made into really desirable knitting yarn. Works for me!

Rayon is the grandmama of this category of fiber, so let's start there.

Rayon

Rayon was the world's first man-made fiber, first commercially produced in 1905. A 1929 book produced by the Viscose Company called *The Story of Rayon* tells it all so in this case we don't have to speculate. Rayon—the generic name—is made, with the help of a lot of chemicals and technology, out of cellulose. Mostly chopped up tree bits, but cotton fibers can be used as well. The raw materials get ground up, purified, bleached, and then turned into what are called "cellulose crumbs." A lot of chemicals are required to make this happen. These get aged for two to three days, goop is added, and the crumbs are liquefied into a thick solution called "viscose" (aha!) that looks a lot like honey. Again with the aging. Then a vacuum removes

any bubbles from the solution so there are no blips in the fiber, and finally the stuff is pumped out through spinnerets (just like silkworms have, except these are made of metal) into solid-but-delicate fibers, which are then spun into yarn.

Whew. That's a lot of work. It was a big honkin' deal at the turn of the last century. Who ever heard of making usable fiber out of wee bits of leftover cellulose? Amazing. At first, rayon was called "artificial silk" because of the sheen and drape of the fabric it produced, but soon was valued for its own merits. Rayon can be found in almost every textile application, and some not so textile. Sausage casing? Yup.

What's the deal with the name? Is it rayon? Viscose rayon? Rayon viscose? Just viscose? Well, viscose is the process that makes rayon. As far as we knitters are concerned, viscose and rayon are different names for the same thing: manufactured fiber from cellulose.

Rayon is shimmery and slippery to knit with, but it has a big weak spot, literally. It absorbs moisture more easily than cotton. Get it wet and you can ruin it by looking at it sideways. Okay, maybe it's not that delicate, but if you casually stick it in the washer, be prepared for as much as 10% shrinkage. Or it might stretch instead. How fun! That's why you'll often find "dry-clean only" labels on garments that have rayon in them.

But the trade-off is the shimmer and the brilliance of color rayon provides. You'll often find it blended with cotton or other less showy fibers, and it's likely thanks to the rayon that the yarn's caught your eye. It adds drape to a stiff fiber and sparkle to a dull one. Tightly plied rayon yarns are resistant to pilling. Just read the yarn's label and in this case, don't ignore it. Handle rayon with care and she'll treat you well in return.

Bamboo

Bamboo

According to the International Network for Bamboo and Rattan, "A sixty-foot tree cut for market takes sixty years to replace. A sixty-foot bamboo cut for market takes fifty-nine days to replace." Can you say that bamboo is environmentally sustainable? I thought you could.

Bamboo, because it's naturally strong and flexible, is used to make everything from paper to furniture to flooring to houses to musical instruments to suspension bridges. Some bamboo bridges are strong enough to drive a car on. Unbelievable. And young bamboo shoots are mighty tasty in a stir fry.

The versatile bamboo is actually a giant, woody grass. It can grow to over 100 feet (30 meters) tall, but unlike bast fibers, plant height doesn't equal fiber length because the fibers aren't created until the bamboo is broken down into cellulose goop. Once spun, bamboo fibers are about $1/32$ to $1/4$ inch (1 to 5 millimeters) long.

Bamboo in yarn form can be softer than silk. The yarn is usually a bundle of very fine plies that are softly twisted together. It knits like a dream and the finished fabric is soft, it breathes, and it insulates.

Bamboo is starting to show up in other things we buy, like sheets and underwear. Why? Not only is it soft, but it is naturally antibacterial and keeps fighting bacteria (like the kind in perspiration) even after fifty washes, says BambroTex, a bamboo manufacturer in China.

The Mystery of Bamboo Yarn Revealed ?

Picture a whole bunch of pandas (big ones) sitting around in a loose circle of sorts with piles of bamboo all around them. They are laughing and hanging panda style, chewing away on their bamboo lunch. Every once in a while, one of 'em will utter a panda expletive and spit into the middle of the circle where there is a big basket. After this has been going on for a while, a small boy runs out from the bamboo forest and grabs the basket to take to the mill to be spun into yarn.

—Tina Newton, Blue Moon Fiber Arts

Corn

You've likely heard of Ingeo® (a registered trademark of NatureWorks LLC), but that's just one brand name for the fiber made from corn. To make corn fiber, plant sugars are extracted from corn and fermented. Scientific name for this goop: polylactic acid (PLA).

Jonelle Raffino tells me that she's handled a lot of corn fiber and she says it's not all the same. She now uses a fiber she prefers over the brand-name stuff, because it dyes more easily and produces a nicer yarn. I'd agree— South West Trading Company's "A-maizing" yarn is a

Corn

delight to knit with. It's a stretchy, soft tubular ribbon that makes a fabric totally suitable for anything that needs to retain its shape, and it's machine washable and dryable.

Corn fiber is also light, machine washable, UV resistant, wicks moisture away from the skin, and comfortable to wear. Downsides? Don't iron it. It'll melt at temperatures above 300˚F (150˚C). The Ingeo website (ingeofibers.com) says the fiber is naturally wrinkle resistant, so it doesn't need ironing.

Lyocell

Okay, so read the bit about rayon again. See the part where I say it's got a significant weakness? Manufacturers got all excited about their new rayon-producing technology and figured they could do better. So they kept working and the result is lyocell, born in 1992. Like rayon, lyocell starts as wood pulp. Unlike rayon, lyocell isn't trying to mimic silk, so extreme sheen isn't the goal; it's meant to be used as a substitute for (or blending partner with) cotton. You've probably heard of Tencel®—it's a brand name of a type of lyocell fiber.

The lyocell manufacturing process starts out like the viscose process, but veers off into its own unique technology after the raw materials are turned into pulp. As a result, lyocell is a significantly improved fiber. It's very strong wet *and* dry, soft, absorbent (which makes it feel pleasant against your skin), drapey, resistant to wrinkling and can be "fibrillated" as it's being processed to create a variety of appealing textures.

Modal

We've started to see a lot of modal in yarn in the last few years, and there's good reason for this. Modal is made with the viscose process and has been around longer than lyocell—since the 1930s. It was initially developed for products like conveyor belts and industrial tubing, which meant it needed to be stronger than its ancestor, the relatively fragile rayon. Modal is also engineered from wood—specifically beech this time. Lenzing says its brand of modal fiber is softer than cotton, more durable, and—unlike cotton—won't allow lime residue from hard water to build up on the fiber through repeated washings, so it stays soft. It's dimensionally stable and won't stretch or shrink when wet. The fiber has a smooth surface and is ideal for blending with other fibers like cotton.

Seacell®

I was first introduced to Seacell® (a registered trademark of Zimmer AG) by Handmaiden's Seasilk yarn. Seasilk is 70% silk, 30% Seacell and, in my opinion, softer than pure silk. Incidentally, the fiber also smells delicately of the sea—vaguely salty and fresh. So what is Seacell?

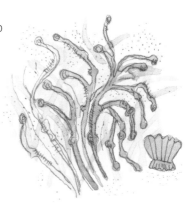

Seaweed

Seacell starts with the lyocell base (which means cellulose again) which has algae added to it. Seaweed, basically. Sounds like a crazy new invention? Not so much. The fiber properties of algae cellulose were discovered in 1883 by a chemist named E. C. Stanford.

Think of decomposed, stringy seaweed goop you may have stepped in on the beach—doesn't that sound like the raw material they make lyocell out of? Alginate-based fiber was even manufactured on its own for a while: in WWII, they made camouflage netting out of it. That version of the fiber wasn't very durable, though. We can now knit with this stuff, because they've fixed the durability issue. Seacell added to silk (that's the only way I've come across it so far) gives the yarn a little extra body and grab (but just a little). But here's the kicker: it's also good for you. I know, I know. According to seacell.com: "The seaweed extracts also promote the production of glucosaminoglycans, which not only accelerate the healing process of skin inflammations, but also protect the skin from free radicals" (according to a study by Alban Muller International). Um, okay.

Science aside, the stuff smells wonderful and is irresistible to touch and heaven to knit with. That's enough for me.

Soy Fiber (Soysilk®, a registered trademark of South West Trading Company Inc.)

The Ford Motor Company grew soybeans specifically to make fiber for car upholstery from 1939 to 1942. To advertise his company's progressive approach to seat covers, Henry Ford wore a suit made of soy fiber. Production of the fiber was transferred to another company in 1943 and stopped a few years later.

Soy beans

Modern soy fiber is made from a byproduct of the tofu manufacturing process. Soy, like most of the other fibers in this category, is soft, has great drape, and is breathable, absorbent, and wrinkle resistant. Like bamboo, it too is a natural antibacterial fiber.

Soy fiber is available in an increasing number of yarns. South West Trading Company has just released Pure—a 100% soysilk yarn that I had to keep touching because it looked so much like wool to me. It may not behave exactly the same, but I've never seen any other nonwool that looks this much like the sheep.

Synthetic Fibers

Synthetics might be considered the bad boys of knitting. They're the fibers we don't necessarily love, but sometimes can't live without. Science went kind of crazy with new fibers at the beginning of the 1900s. After the success of rayon—a manufactured fiber from natural materials—the next obvious step was to see what else scientists could make fiber out of.

Most synthetics are made from petroleum products. These fibers start as some sort of plastic material in the form of pellets, chips, or goop. The plastic is either heated or treated with chemicals to get it to flow so it can be forced through the nozzle of a spinneret. Out it comes on the other side of the nozzle looking like a fiber we'd recognize, requiring exposure to air, liquid, or chemicals to get it to firm up.

If you ask me, synthetics work best in blends with other fibers. Synthetic yarns can make our favorite nonwools behave better. Or differently. They give drape where there was none. They add bounce and stretch. They can reduce the threat of shrinkage to almost nothing. A good blend can be better than any of its ingredients on their own.

There are a few exceptions, of course. For example, Suss Cousins has just developed a new yarn called Love that's 100% Tactel® nylon and feels like 100% cashmere. Is it exactly the same as cashmere? Nope, but it's a lovely substitute. For this group of fibers, let's start with the first synthetic. It helps explain all the rest.

Nylon

You probably could guess that nylon was the first big thing in synthetic fiber. Remember all that talk of nylon stockings around WWII? Nylon was created out of the DuPont company's free-form research phase that started in 1928. The company took a rather unconventional approach and allowed Dr. Wallace Hume Carothers and his team to investigate anything they felt was worthwhile without a guarantee of a marketable product at the end. Their first target: long-chain molecules (we call them polymers today). There was messing about with atoms, there was the investigation of molecular structure, and eventually, there was the melting of plastics to see what would happen. I believe it went something like this:

> Scientist 1: I'm going to melt some plastic.
>
> Scientist 2: Well, I'm going to stretch it, then.
>
> Scientist 1: You mean the way you're always playing with your chewing gum? That's gross.
>
> Scientist 2: Shut up. Hey. Look. As this stuff stretches, it gets more lustrous, firms up, and looks an awful lot like silk or something. I wonder if I could knit with it?
>
> Scientist 1: It was my idea. Gimme that.

Nylon's first practical use was as brush bristles; that was in 1938. Nylon stockings followed in 1940.

During WWII, silk became impossible to find, but a similar lightweight, very strong fabric was still badly needed for wartime essentials like parachutes and tents. So all nylon production from 1942–1944 went into products for the war. Nylon helped fortify truck tires and ropes, too.

Nylon is about ten times stronger than cotton. It's also very elastic. It's these two traits that make it so valuable in knitting yarn. Add nylon to cotton and an inflexible yarn starts to have a little stretch and can

What's Microfiber?

Microfiber isn't a kind of fiber It's a description of how fiber is made—how fine it's spun. Microfibers can be made of acrylic, polyester, or nylon, with each having very different properties. But the key is that the fiber is spun very, very, fine—finer than a filament of silk.

last longer, too. Who wants to knit socks that will wear out in a few weeks?

It's not a very absorbent fiber, which means it doesn't get very saturated with water, so it dries quickly. But because it's not absorbent, it's a static electricity magnet. And keep it out of the sun because prolonged exposure makes it break down.

But, see, nylon, like most synthetics, is not that easy to pigeonhole. Because once scientists came up with the base formula, they didn't just stop. They kept tweaking the manufacturing process to achieve different finished results—more breathability, added softness, etc. All the good stuff we want in our knitting yarns.

For example, take Tactel® nylon. This stuff comes in eight different varieties that may be chemically related, but you'd never guess that by looking at the finished product. One variant goes for intense shine and gentle drape, another for "the shiniest brightness ever seen" with a smooth, luxurious touch and drape, and another "provides the ultimate in softness" and maximizes breathability when textured. Isn't science cool?

Acrylic

It's really hard to love acrylic. On its own, it's squeaky on the needles and feels kind of like the yarn equivalent of fingernails on chalkboard. It was created to replicate wool, and though it shares some of wool's characteristics, they're really nothing alike. One reason acrylic is a bit like wool is that it's one of the only synthetics to retain an uneven surface on the outside of the fiber, even when the openings in the spinneret it's squeezed out of are perfectly smooth and round.

Acrylic is resistant to moths, oils, and chemicals, it's washable, and it doesn't shrink. But the reason we keep it around is that it adds substance and elasticity to yarns like cotton that don't have much of it on their own.

But beware: ironing kills acrylic. People actually do say "I killed my acrylic by ironing it," though likely not at the dinner parties you attend. I hang out with weird people.

Leisure suit

Polyester

The technology that made polyester possible was developed at the same time and by the same team that discovered nylon. But research on polyester didn't ramp up until the 1950s.

Hang on. Do we really care enough about polyester to get into any kind of detail? I don't think so. It's polyester, for heaven's sake. It's just *there*, like that creepy relative of yours that won't go home after the family reunion. He probably serves some useful purpose, but it's been a long time since anyone can remember what it is.

Okay, that's not nice. How about this: Polyester fiber is strong, resists shrinking, stretching, mildew, and abrasion, and is the epitome of easy care.

Reality check: Type "polyester yarn" into a search engine and what comes up are the yarns Elizabeth Zimmermann wouldn't have touched with a really long pair of tongs: fuzzy, froofy novelties.

Spandex (Lycra®)

Now this stuff I love. As a hardcore nonwoolly, I've been forced to use fiber with absolutely no give for much of my knitting life.

I knew something had changed in nonwool yarns when I first heard about Cascade's Fixation—a cotton/Lycra sock yarn. Spandex is like an invisible friend that exists solely to keep your knitted thing in as close to original shape as possible. If I were in charge of the yarn world, I'd blend spandex with every single nonwool. It makes me giddy just thinking about it.

Spandex can be stretched up to 500% beyond its original size without breaking. It's even stronger and stretchier than rubber! Conveniently, because it's so often used in stuff that sits against skin, it's not significantly damaged by perspiration or the goop we put on our bodies. (Keep bleach away from it, though.) It can be dyed or it can be clear. It's a freaking miracle fiber! All hail spandex!

As yarn companies are beginning to notice that yarn with additional stretch built in is something that knitters want, we're starting to see more and more of it. Lycra and Elite are two brand names for spandex fiber, and more are likely coming. Be happy. Stretch is not the exclusive domain of woolly knitters. We may not come by our stretch naturally, but that just means we appreciate it even more.

Fiber Families, Substituting, and Your New Career as a Yarn Detective

In Chapter One, I talked about the different groups of fibers that make up the nonwool knitting repertoire. You can see that within each group the fibers differ in their exact natures, but they're similar enough that thinking of them as families will help steer you to the most suitable section of your LYS (local yarn store) for your next project.

So let's talk about the groups again and summarize what each is most likely to offer you when you put it on your needles. I think a chart is in order. By the way—in this chart, we're talking about the pure fiber itself, before it's spun into yarn.

Nonwool Fiber Families and Their Quirks

FIBER GROUP	FIBER STRETCH	FABRIC STRETCH	ON THE NEEDLES	AFTER WASHING	CARE	SHRINKAGE	BLOCKING
bast	minimal	some	stiff	drapey	machine wash and dry	negligible	takes well
seed	some	some	average to soft	can be drapey or stiff	machine wash; lay flat to dry; pat into shape	lengthwise depending on how tightly knit	see care blocking may not last
manufactured	significant	significant	can be slippery	drapey	handwash; lay flat to dry	negligible	takes well
protein	some	minimal	slippery to sticky	can be drapey or stiff	handwash; lay flat; iron damp if required	negligible	takes well
synthetic	Each fiber is constructed to have unique properties. See Chapter One.						

As I mentioned, the chart above refers to the fibers themselves, not spun and certainly not in yarn form. We've all seen stretchy (relatively speaking) 100% cotton yarns and others that are more suitable for tying up a bouquet garnis for your next pot of vegetable stock.

Why do we need to know this stuff? Well, if we find a pattern that was designed in exactly the nonwool yarn we want to knit, we don't, really. The designer has done the work for us already. (The designs in this book, for example.) But *most patterns are designed to be knitted with wool or other animal fibers, not nonwool yarns.*

If we want to substitute, how can we get as close as possible to the original look of the thing?

The Secret to Successful Sheepless Substitutions

All you need to do to substitute yarns in a pattern is match the gauge, right? *Not even close.* When you're swapping nonwool for wool, matching gauge is only the first step of the process.

Now, I'm not saying that all wools (or all animal fibers) are the same as each other. But when you swap one wool yarn for another, matching gauge alone is often enough to get you a result that you will be happy with. That's not the case with nonwools. We've talked about *why* nonwools are different, so let's get on with *how* to successfully use them as substitutes.

There are *three* things you need to match to get a successful yarn substitution: gauge, texture, and weight. Okay, so gauge we know about. But the other two may not be aspects you're used to thinking about when it comes to yarn swapping.

Texture

How a knitted fabric looks and feels depends a great deal on the texture of the yarn you're knitting with. Is it smooth or fuzzy, drapey or structured? If you knit a cardigan in soft, shimmery bamboo that was designed for toothy-almost-scratchy Shetland wool, how could it possibly be anything like the original?

Weight

Amy Swenson, the designer behind Indiknits.com and co-owner of Make One Yarn Studio in Calgary, says she looks at how she substitutes yarns. She looks at the weight of the yarn the pattern was designed for and then tries to match it with one that has a similar texture. Her shop actually lists each yarn's specific weight per meter along with stitch gauge to make the swapping easier.

Think about it. Let's say we're knitting that cardigan that was designed for toothy-almost-scratchy Shetland wool. The gauge measures 4.5 stitches to the inch in stockinette stitch and weighs 0.54 grams per yard. If you substitute a really gorgeous ribbon yarn that knits to the same gauge but weighs 0.2 grams per yard, the finished sweater may be the same size as the original, but will it have the same drape and body? How could it? Not possible.

With practice, you'll start to notice almost automatically what it is about the yarn used in the original design, especially its texture and weight. And then you can seek out a substitute that will match it as closely as possible.

Here's something else that will help you get a better handle on what each fiber is really like when the lights are off and no one's watching.

Encyclopedia Periwinkle, Yarn Detective

This is my new favorite hobby. It's amazing what you can learn by lightly dissecting a paid-for ball of yarn. (Don't be doing this in the yarn shop to stuff that's not yours. Bad form.)

I have held and fondled and knit with Rowan's Calmer for several years without ever taking the time to pull the strands apart. And when I did, it became instantly apparent just *why* it's so different than other cotton/acrylic blends. Got a ball? Play along!

Comparison of Properties of Knitting Yarns

PROPERTY	MOST								LEAST
FIBER STRENGTH	linen	hemp	silk	nylon	polyester	cotton	acrylic	wool	rayon
RELATIVE WEIGHT	cotton	linen	rayon	hemp	polyester	wool	silk	acrylic	nylon
ABRASION RESISTANCE	nylon	linen	acrylic	cotton	coarse wool	silk	fine wool	rayon	
ELASTICITY	wool	silk	rayon	cotton	linen				
ABSORBENCY	wool	linen	hemp	silk	cotton	nylon	acrylic	polyester	
HEAT TOLERANCE (IRON TEMPERATURE)	linen (450°F)	cotton (425°F)	rayon (350°F)	silk (300°F)	wool (300°F)	acrylic (300°F)	nylon (250°F)	polyester (250°F)	
HEAT RETENTION	silk	wool	cotton	linen					
RESISTANCE TO PILLING	silk	linen	cotton	wool	acrylic	polyester	nylon		
RESISTANCE TO SUNLIGHT	acrylic	polyester	linen	cotton	rayon	nylon	wool	silk	
RESISTANCE TO WRINKLING	wool	silk	cotton	rayon	linen				

Data compiled with permission from Fiber Facts by Bette Hochberg, © 1981, 1993

I love a good chart, and this one is a doozy. (Thank you, Bette.) Why is wool in the list? That's so you can see where nonwools fit in the fiber hierarchy. For example, see where wool sits in elasticity? Sure, it's the most elastic. But what's right behind it? Silk. When stretched 2%, wool fibers recover 99% of their original shape; silk fibers recover 92%. Stretch the fibers more, or hold them in a stretched position for a while, and it will take longer for the fibers to recover . . . and they likely won't recover as much.

Case Study: Rowan Calmer

Calmer is the yarn that made even passionate wool lovers notice something sheep-free. It's 75% cotton and 25% acrylic microfiber. Ever look at it closely? Let's do that.

photo: Amy R. Singer

Okay, it's made of two textured plies. Look even more closely, and you'll see that each ply is a slightly irregularly twisted chainette. That gives the yarn a subtle grabby texture. You mean like wool has naturally? Now you're getting it. Let's tug one of the plies—look how much give it has! That's due to the added acrylic microfiber and the way it's spun. Clever, those people at Rowan. Without a sheep in sight, they've created a yarn that does much of what wool does, and—best of all—doesn't do the one thing you hope never happens to your favorite handknitted sweaters. It won't felt.

Case Study: Organic Cottons

Take a look at Blue Sky Organic Cotton—fluffy like a cotton ball, soft and gentle on the hands as you knit. Now grab a skein of Pakucho organic cotton—it feels soft, but it's more streamlined, has less fluff, and makes a tidier knitted fabric. Both are pure organic cotton, so what's the difference in this case? Time to dissect!

Both are plied yarns, but they're nothing alike. The Blue Sky is made of two thickish, softly spun plies. The Pakucho is made up of five gently twisted strands of tightly twisted 2-ply yarns—that's 10 strands in total.

Each individual ply of the Pakucho is more tightly spun than the two soft plies in Blue Sky. So the extra structure in the Pakucho gives a more elegant finished fabric, and the relaxed, soft twist of the Blue Sky gives you a softer, easier fabric.

Very few of us get to design yarn, but the more we knit with all different kinds, the more we learn about how it works. Spend a little time pulling apart balls of your favorites and you'll understand them even better.

photo: Amy R. Singer

Top: Blue Sky
Bottom: Pakucho

How to Knit Things Designed for Wool Without Any Wool at All
It's absolutely possible. You just have to choose carefully.

CABLES	pick a yarn with some tooth and stretch; pay close attention to yarn weight: cables + heavy yarn = droopy sweater; knit tightly
DURABILITY	choose a bast fiber or pure, tightly spun cotton; knit tightly
EASY CARE	choose a blend that includes a synthetic; check the yarn label . . . if it says "hand-wash" or "dry clean only"; keep looking
FAIR ISLE/ INTARSIA	pick something with tooth so it will hold together at the color changes; easy care; pay close attention to yarn weight—you're working with multiple strands, so extra weight will just make the sweater droopier
FELTING	You're out of luck. Sorry. There's no nonwool equivalent to knitting something and then shrinking/fuzzing the begeebers out of it to turn it into a solid fabric.
SOFTNESS	pick something loosely spun; look for silk, a silk blend, or bamboo; try one of the new synthetic yarns designed to mimic cashmere or merino
STITCH DEFINITION	pick a smooth, tightly spun yarn; knit it snugly
STRETCH	pick a yarn built to stretch, like something with added Lycra, spandex, Elite, or certain stretchy synthetics; add ribbing where you need stretch
WARMTH	use silk or a silk blend; choose a yarn with built-in air space (fuzzy and/or hollow)

Learn to Love Your Geeky Thing

THREE

I can imagine that you're sick-sick-sick of hearing about how you have to knit swatches. Who ever says, "I spent the weekend knitting swatches and it was a ball!" Feh. How does that sound like fun? Well, I think we're all looking at it the wrong way.

When it comes to nonwool knitting, the reason you knit a little something before you knit the bigger something is to learn more about the yarn than just gauge. Otherwise you end up knitting a whole sweater to learn the same lesson. So fine, then. Call a swatch something else. No one likes the word anyway. Swatch sounds too much like "homework."

The Mistress of the Geeky Thing

When I first met Jillian Moreno, I watched her leave every yarn shop we visited with a bag full of single balls of all the yarns she liked. One single ball. What could possibly be the point of that?

Jillian isn't limited to nonwools, but she really loves getting to know her yarn before she commits herself to knitting an actual wearable. Sometimes she knits geeky things just to knit them. To meet the yarn, shake hands, and get to know what it does for a living. How it behaves in polite company, what kind of needles it likes, how well it plays with others.

On a recent vacation, Jillian's only travel knitting was a long tubular geeky thing. A sock tube. She brought all her new sock yarns along, a variety of needles, and knitted until she found which needle size worked best with each yarn. And then—and this is why Jillian is smarter than most of us—she marked each yarn and its corresponding preferred needle size on a little tag that she attached to the tubular geeky thing.

A wasted vacation's worth of knitting? Sez who? Jillian can now pick up any of those yarns and know instantly which size of needle to grab and not have to second-guess herself. During the trip, she got to enjoy hours of knitting in a car with her husband and two young kids without having to follow a pattern. I call that efficient and enjoyable time management. I'm proud to know her. Plus, she's fun at parties.

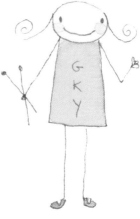

Hanging around my friend Jillian has helped me think differently about this whole process. I've watched her knit little samples just to get to know the yarn and how it'll work in real life, not just in her knitting dreams. She invests a little bit of time at the beginning and it pays off. The things she knits aren't really swatches; they're "**G**et to **K**now **Y**ou" things. GKY things. Geeky things. (Hey, it's my book. I can push the limits of acronym construction if I want to.) Geeky things they are, then.

If you don't care about the finished product, and all that matters is slipping strands of yarn through your fingers and around your needles, then skip this chapter. If it's okay that the stuff you knit doesn't turn out as you'd planned, that's cool. Maybe you're big on serendipity. That can be fun.

But if serendipity is rarely on your side and you have a pile of unworn nonwool things as a result, it's time to embrace the geeky things as part of your knitting process. It's not a hardship. It's a bit of mindless knitting that you can do when you're not sure what you want to knit next. Take a ball of whatever you have a sweater's worth of in your stash and get to know it. Or do the Jillian and buy a single ball of the things you think you'd like to turn into sweaters— you'll be a geeky thing geek in no time.

How to Make the Most of the Geeky Thing

Step 1. Read the ball band. Even if it seems like the yarn companies were on some sort of hallucinogen when they chose the suggested needle sizes for their yarns, they *are* the yarn company. They had a specific look in mind for each yarn. Give them the benefit of the doubt and knit with their suggested needle size for at least a few rows. If they offer a range of needle sizes, use your judgment. Are you a tight, average, or loose knitter? Choose the needle size in the range that suits the way you knit—smaller if you're a loose knitter; larger if you're a tight knitter. Don't forget to write the needle size you picked on the yarn's ball band. I promise you won't remember otherwise.

Step 2. Cast on some stitches. How many? No fixed rules here, but you'll want to make a good-size geeky thing. Maybe it's 6" (15 cm) wide, maybe 10" (25.5 cm). It has to be big enough for you to get to know the fabric you're going to create. It certainly has to be bigger than 4" (10 cm) wide, because while you're getting to know the fabric, you might as well get a decent gauge reading, too. But the main reason to knit these geeky things is not to establish your gauge. This is a meet and greet.

Step 3. Knit for a while. How long? Long enough for you to figure out if you either like or don't like this needle size with this yarn. If you find that the needle size isn't right, knit a row in some sort of contrasting stitch (if you're knitting stockinette, purl a right-side row, for example) to indicate where you changed sizes, and then make the change. Make note of the new needle size on the ball band. Knit for another while. Like this better? Good. Keep going.

Knit enough fabric so that you can lay it on your lap, pet it, stretch it, drape it over your wrist. Again, at least 6" (15 cm) tall, and more is always better. This geeky thing needs to tell you all it can about the yarn, its structure, and what it can and can't do, so Do. Not. Skimp. What's it gonna take you . . . an hour? You can spend an hour making sure the next sixty hours of knitting are going where you want them to.

Step 4. Get to know it. As I mentioned in Step 3, now's the time to play with the geeky thing to see if you like it enough to build a relationship with it. Fondle it. Pet it. Scrunch up the fabric and smooth it out again. Lay it on your skin and see if you like how it feels. Look at it. Did it turn out like you wanted? Yes?* Okay, now take an accurate gauge reading, both in stitches and rows. Write this on the ball band too.

  *If the answer is no, you need to start over with a different yarn. You've gone as far as you can with this one.

Step 5. Do not skip this step. If after all this, you decide you want a whole whatever made out of this stuff at this gauge, there's still one more thing to do. Wash and dry it. For me, living happily with a handknitted thing means I need to be able to care for it easily. I don't much like dry cleaners and I am not fond of handwashing. So I tend to choose yarns that are known to be machine washable. But what about a yarn that you don't know? The yarn's ball band will tell you how the yarn company wants you to care for what you knit out of their yarn. You have a choice: you can follow the ball band care instructions to the letter or you can take my approach: if it's a cotton-based yarn, put it in a lingerie bag and toss it in the washer.

Don't Push Your Luck

Delicate nonwools should never go in the washing machine, no matter how brave you're feeling today. That means laceweight anything (even in a lingerie bag) and anything silk or rayon. For these, handwash and dry as you plan to wash and dry the finished thing.

Learn How to Test Yarn from a Pro

If you are feeling exceptionally frisky, take a look at http://www.knittersreview.com/yarn.asp. The editor of *Knitter's Review*, Clara Parkes, has made a science out of testing yarn for everything from dye fastness to knitability to the dreaded prone-to-pill syndrome. Take a look at her yarn reviews and follow her lead. Her exacting process is especially warranted for really precious yarns. Better to know after experimenting with one ball that a yarn is not right for you than after you've bought enough for an entire afghan. If you discover that it is the best yarn in the world, you can go back and buy every ball the yarn shop has in stock before anyone else gets their mitts on it.

Saturday

Sunday

And then toss it in the dryer until it's barely damp, using the same settings you'd use for the whole garment. Lay it flat and let it air-dry the rest of the way.

Worst thing that could happen: you hate how it looks, or your swatch is kaput and you realize that this stuff isn't machine washable/dryable.**

Best thing: you discover that you like how the fabric looks and feels after this treatment and you can comfortably wash and dry your thing this way over and over again.

If your geeky thing has come through all this and you still like it, measure your final after-wash gauge numbers and record them on the ball band.

You have two choices at this point (again with the choices?). You can stop here, knowing you've done good basic research. Safety pin the ball band to the geeky thing and put your feet up. Or you can go all the way— read on.

Step 6. You now know how this yarn knits, washes, and dries. But what about the sag factor? Clearly you can't wear your geeky thing for a test drive, big as it might be. But you can simulate how it will hang from your shoulders: suspend it and see what its own weight will do to it. Simply pin the top edge of your geeky thing to a bulletin board and measure and write down its length. Then walk away. Leave it for a day. Come back and measure again. (Remember to write the before and after numbers on the ball band.) Has it grown a lot or just a little? You can't necessarily quantify how much a finished sweater will stretch based on this test, but if your swatch barely moves in the 24 hours, you can conclude that the yarn is reasonably stable. If, on the other hand, your geeky thing is an inch or more longer than it was 24 hours ago, red warning lights should be flashing. Back slowly away from the droopy yarn.

Pin that ball band to the thing, and you, my friend, are done. You now know just about everything you possibly can (without having knitted a whole sweater) about this yarn.

**Okay, the worst has happened. What now?

If it looked good before you washed and dried it, you know what to do. Knit another geeky thing and follow the ball band instructions more closely when you launder it. This may involve handwashing it and laying it flat to dry. At least you know now that you can't cut corners with this stuff if you want it to survive. Aren't you glad you learned this lesson on your geeky thing and not your finished but-it-fit-me-so-well sweater?

If the washing and drying didn't ruin it, but you just don't like the look and/or feel of your thing, cut your losses. (See the sidebar at right to learn what I think you should do with the swatch and ball band info rather than tossing it into the trash.) Start over with yarn that might do better, based on what you've learned.

One more thing. Some yarns that show absolutely no hint of stretch while in the ball can knit up into very stretchy fabric. Hemp is one example. The new Natural Silk Aran from Rowan (a viscose, silk, and linen blend) is another. I cannot explain why this happens. But it should serve as the best reason for you to knit geeky things, if you're not already convinced. You can't really know what a yarn can do until you've made it into fabric.

Build Your Own Swatch Journal

I love paper. Blank books are especially irresistible to me. I love them spiral-bound, but I also have a sincere fondness for the traditional Moleskine. You too? Allow me to enable you into a short blank-book-buying binge. Here's what you need to do:

Find a blank book that suits your personal aesthetic and has room for the swatches, because you're going to attach them to the pages. One way to make room is to remove some of the pages. If the book is spiral-bound, this is easy.

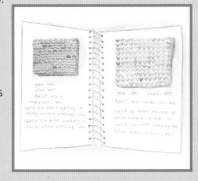

Affix one swatch to a page however you like. Sew it? Sure. Or maybe use some of those butterfly fasteners because you might want to take the swatch out one day. Below it, write the stuff printed on the ball band like the name of the yarn, color name/number, and dyelot. Now add the stuff you wrote on the ball band, like the needle size you used, the gauge measurements before and after washing, how you washed (and dried) it, what you like about it, and what you don't. If you get really reckless, attach the ball band itself. How scrapbooky!

What is the point of this exercise? Well, you've knitted this geeky thing and washed and dried it to learn about this yarn. Writing down what you've learned means you won't have to guess what you already know now the next time you want to find a yarn that does what this stuff does. Or the next time you think you want to buy more of it because you forgot how very much you dislike it.

If you're really organized, you can use something like a binder and group the swatch pages in sections as you learn more about the yarns. Put all the machine washable cottons and blends together. Or put the stuff you love in one section, the stuff that made you cranky in another. Isn't being organized fun?

Bacardi

design by Barbara Gregory

Designer Barbara Gregory is a genius with color. She's taken the mesmerizing yarn shop wall of more than 100 Super 10 Cotton colors (Tahki Cotton Classic in the United States) and distilled it into the most elegant of muted sonatas using simple stripes and occasional rows of two-color short-float stranded knitting. Do not be afraid to knit this sweater. It's much simpler than the finished result might lead you to believe.

Freak out your knitting friends with the last step: when you've finished knitting the body in one piece, pick up the neckband, button-bands and hipband in one continuous round for a seamless finish. Sure, you'll be knitting some very long rounds, but when the mitered corners fall off the needles, your knitting friends will think you're a genius, too.

Stitch Guide

Knit Decrease Row
*Work to 2 sts before marker, ssk (see Glossary, page 154), slip marker (sl m), work to next marker, sl m, k2tog; rep from * once, work to end of row.

Purl Decrease Row
*Work to 2 sts before marker, p2tog, sl m, work to next marker, sl m, ssp (see Glossary, page 154); rep from * once, work to end of row.

Knit Increase Row
*Work to marker, M1L (see Glossary, page 156), sl m, work to next marker, sl m, M1R (see Glossary, page 156); rep from * once, work to end of row.

Purl Increase Row
*Work to marker, M1R pwise (see Glossary, page 156), sl m, work to next marker, sl m, M1L pwise (see Glossary, page 156); rep from * once, work to end of row.

Finished Size

About 34¼ (38½, 43, 47¼, 51¾, 54½)" (87 [98, 109, 120, 131.5, 138.5] cm) chest circumference. Garment shown measures 38½" (98 cm).

Yarn

DK-weight (CYCA #3 Light) yarn.
Shown here: S. R. Kertzer Butterfly Super 10 (100% cotton; 250 yd [229 m]/125 g): #3568 gold (A), 1 (1, 1, 1, 2, 2) skein(s); #3701 granny smith (yellow-green; B), 1 (1, 1, 1, 1, 2) skein(s); #3715 sage green (C), 1 (1, 2, 2, 2, 2) skein(s); #3546 maize (pale yellow; D), 1 (1, 1, 2, 2, 2) skein(s); #3242 flax (light tan; E), 1 (1, 1, 2, 2, 2) skein(s); #3606 peridot (olive; F), 1 (1, 2, 2, 2, 2) skein(s).

Needles

Body and sleeves—size 6 (4 mm): 29" (70 cm) or longer circular (cir). Edging—size 5 (3.75 mm): 29" (70 cm) or longer cir. Adjust needle size if necessary to obtain the correct gauge.

Notions

Markers (m); stitch holders; tapestry needle; 46" (117 cm) ½" (1.3 cm) wide grosgrain ribbon (optional) in matching color (available at fabric stores); sewing thread and needle; six (six, six, seven, seven, seven) ⅝" (1.5 cm) plastic rings for buttons (you may substitute commercial buttons if desired).

Gauge

22 stitches and 29 rows = 4" (10 cm) in stockinette stitch on larger needle.

BACARDI

◿	gold (A)
·	granny smith (B)
□	sage green (C)
−	maize (D)
+	flax (E)
◼	peridot (F)
☐	pattern repeat

Notes

- The pieces are knitted back and forth in rows using a circular needle so that the yarn can be picked up to start a row from either side. Slide the stitches to the opposite end of the needle if necessary to use a yarn that has been left hanging, then knit or purl as appropriate. Carry colors not in use loosely up the sides, and where possible, bring the working yarn under the other yarns at the beginning of a row to keep the edge tidy. Where shaping occurs, yarns may have to be cut and rejoined.
- There will occasionally be rows in which two colors are used, but the yarns are at opposite sides of the piece. In this case you have two options. *Option 1:* Work the row with one of the yarns (if one yarn is the same as the previous row, choose the one that contrasts with the previous row) slipping the stitches that should be in the second color. Then work the row again in the second color, this time slipping the stitches that have just been worked in the first color. This counts as one row in pattern directions. (Stitches should be slipped so that they are ready to work on the following row; for most knitters this means slipping purlwise.) *Option 2:* Cut one of the yarns, join it at the other edge and work across the row carrying both colors.
- If you would like to lengthen or shorten the sleeves, ensure that the sleeve cap shaping begins on the same row as the body underarm bind-off by using the body length as a guide to estimate the chart row on which to begin the sleeve.

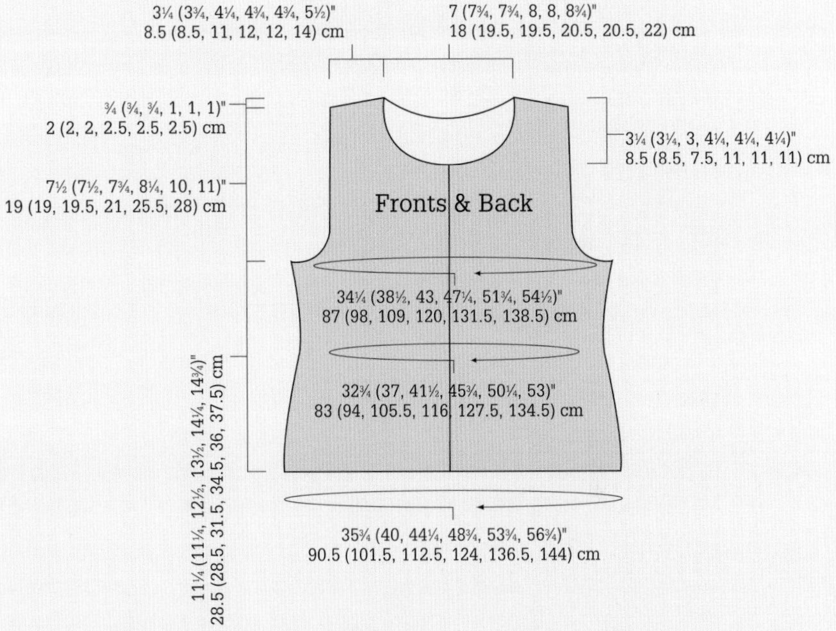
3¼ (3¾, 4¼, 4¾, 4¾, 5½)"
8.5 (8.5, 11, 12, 12, 14) cm
7 (7¾, 7¾, 8, 8, 8¾)"
18 (19.5, 19.5, 20.5, 20.5, 22) cm
¾ (¾, ¾, 1, 1, 1)"
2 (2, 2, 2.5, 2.5, 2.5) cm
3¼ (3¼, 3, 4¼, 4¼, 4¼)"
8.5 (8.5, 7.5, 11, 11, 11) cm
7½ (7½, 7¾, 8¼, 10, 11)"
19 (19, 19.5, 21, 25.5, 28) cm
Fronts & Back
34¼ (38½, 43, 47¼, 51¾, 54½)"
87 (98, 109, 120, 131.5, 138.5) cm
11¼ (11¼, 12½, 13½, 14¼, 14¾)"
28.5 (28.5, 31.5, 34.5, 36, 37.5) cm
32¾ (37, 41½, 45¾, 50¼, 53)"
83 (94, 105.5, 116, 127.5, 134.5) cm
35¾ (40, 44¼, 48¾, 53¾, 56¾)"
90.5 (101.5, 112.5, 124, 136.5, 144) cm

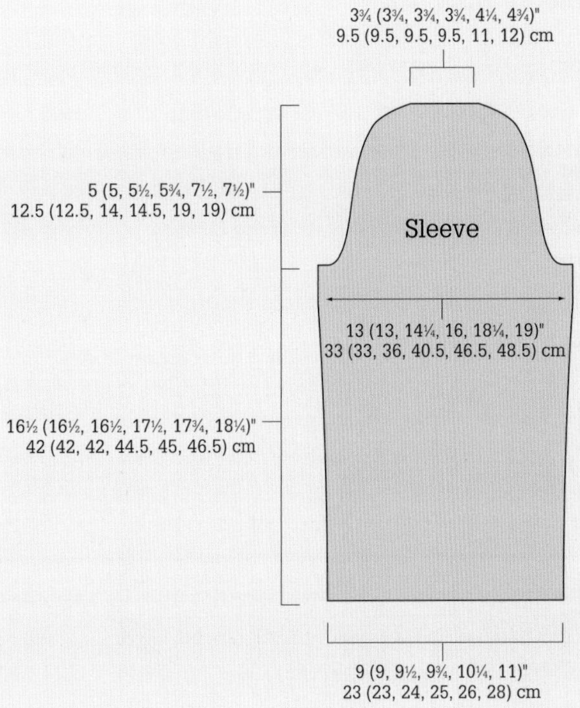
3¾ (3¾, 3¾, 3¾, 4¼, 4¾)"
9.5 (9.5, 9.5, 9.5, 11, 12) cm
5 (5, 5½, 5¾, 7½, 7½)"
12.5 (12.5, 14, 14.5, 19, 19) cm
Sleeve
13 (13, 14¼, 16, 18¼, 19)"
33 (33, 36, 40.5, 46.5, 48.5) cm
16½ (16½, 16½, 17½, 17¾, 18¼)"
42 (42, 42, 44.5, 45, 46.5) cm
9 (9, 9½, 9¾, 10¼, 11)"
23 (23, 24, 25, 26, 28) cm

Body

With E (D, E, D, E, C) and larger needles, CO 196 (220, 244, 268, 296, 312) sts. Working in St st and beg with Row 48 (60, 54, 45, 39, 20) of Bacardi chart, work as foll: Work 42 (48, 54, 60, 67, 71) sts, *place marker (pm), work 12 sts, pm*, work 88 (100, 112, 124, 138, 146) sts; rep from * to * once more, work to end. Work even through Row 62 (70, 64, 53, 45, 40) of chart. *Next row:* (Row 63 [71, 65, 54, 46, 41] of chart) Dec as described in Stitch Guide. Work 7 rows even. Rep the last 8 rows 3 (3, 3, 3, 4, 4) more times—180 (204, 228, 252, 276, 292) sts rem. Work even for 12 (12, 12, 14, 14, 14) rows. *Next row:* Inc as described in Stitch Guide. Work 7 rows even. Rep inc row—188 (212, 236, 260, 284, 300) sts. Work even through Row 129 (141, 144, 141, 141, 126) of chart—piece measures about 11¼ (11¼, 12½, 13½, 14¼, 14¾)" (28.5 [28.5, 31.5, 34.5, 36, 37.5] cm) from CO.

Divide for Fronts and Back

(Row 130 [142, 145, 142, 142, 127] of chart) Work 43 (48, 52, 57, 61, 65) sts and place these sts on a holder for one front, BO the next 6 (8, 12, 14, 18, 18) sts for armhole, work 90 (100, 108, 118, 126, 134) sts and place these sts on another holder for back, BO next 6 (8, 12, 14, 18, 18) sts for other armhole, work to end of row for other front—43 (48, 52, 57, 61, 65) sts rem for each front; 90 (100, 108, 118, 126, 134) sts rem for back. Place left front sts on needle and right front sts on holder.

Left Front

At armhole edge (beg of RS rows; end of WS rows), working dec 1 st in from armhole edge, dec 1 st every row 3 (4, 3, 5, 8, 7) times, then every 2nd row 3 times, then every 4th row 2 (2, 3, 3, 4, 3) times—35 (39, 43, 46, 46, 52) left front sts rem. Work even through Row 166 (178, 184, 179, 191, 184) of chart—armhole measures about 5 (5, 5½, 5¼, 7, 8)" (12.5 [12.5, 14, 13.5, 18, 20.5] cm).

Shape Front Neck and Shoulder

(Row 167 [179, 185, 180, 192, 185] of chart) At neck edge (end of RS rows; beg of WS rows), BO 7 sts—28 (32, 36, 39, 39, 45) sts rem. Dec 1 st at neck edge (working 1 st in from edge as for armhole) every row 8 times, then every 2nd row 2 (4, 4, 5, 5, 7) times—18 (20, 24, 26, 26, 30) sts rem. *At the same time,* beg with chart Row 184 (196, 201, 202, 215, 207), shape shoulder as foll: At armhole edge, BO 6 (6, 8, 6, 6, 7) sts 3 (1, 3, 2, 2, 2) time(s), then BO 0 (7, 0, 7, 7, 8) sts 0 (2, 0, 2, 2, 2) times. *Note:* After working second group of BO sts, do not change color; use the same color for the rest of the shoulder shaping.

Right Front

Place 43 (48, 52, 57, 61, 65) held right front sts on needle and work as for left front, reversing shaping by working armhole shaping at end of RS rows and beg of WS rows, and neck shaping at beg of RS rows and end of WS rows.

Back

Place 90 (100, 108, 118, 126, 134) held back sts on needle and cont as charted and *at the same time* dec 1 st each end of needle (working dec 1 st in from the edge) every row 3 (4, 3, 5, 8, 7) times, then every 2nd row 3 times, then every 4th row 2 (2, 3, 3, 4, 3) times—74 (82, 90, 96, 96, 108) sts rem. Work even through Row 180 (191, 197, 198, 210, 202) of chart—armholes measure about 6½ (7, 7¼, 7¾, 9½, 11¼)" (16.5 [18, 18.5, 19.5, 24, 28.5] cm).

Shape Back Neck and Shoulders

(Row 181 [192, 198, 199, 211, 203] of chart) Work 27 (30, 33, 36, 36, 41) sts and place these sts on a holder for one shoulder, BO 20 (22, 24, 24, 24, 26) sts, work to end—27 (30, 33, 36, 36, 41) sts rem for other shoulder. Work each shoulder separately as foll: Work 1 row even. At neck edge, BO 5 (5, 5, 6, 6, 6) sts—22 (25, 28, 30, 30, 35) sts rem. At neck edge, dec 1 st (working dec 1 st in from the edge) every row 4 (5, 4, 4, 4, 5) times and *at the same time,* beg with chart Row 184 (196, 201, 202, 215, 207), shape shoulder as foll: At armhole edge, BO 6 (6, 8, 6, 6, 7) sts 3 (1, 3, 2, 2, 2) time(s), then BO 0 (7, 0, 7, 7, 8) sts 0 (2, 0, 2, 2, 2) times.

Sleeves

With A and smaller needles, CO 50 (50, 52, 54, 56, 60) sts. Knit 2 rows— 1 garter ridge. Work 1 garter ridge with each of the foll colors: B, C, D, E. Change to larger needles and beg with Row 16 (28, 31, 21, 20, 1) of chart, work in St st and *at the same time* inc 1 st each end of needle every 10 (10, 8, 6, 4, 4)th row 11 (11, 7, 9, 6, 6) times, then every 0 (0, 10, 8, 6, 6)th row 0 (0, 6, 8, 16, 16) times—72 (72, 78, 88, 100, 104) sts. Cont even through Row 129 (141, 144, 141, 141, 126) of chart—piece measures about 16½ (16½, 16½, 17½, 17¾, 18¼)" (42 [42, 42, 44.5, 45, 46.5] cm) from CO.

Shape Cap

BO 3 (4, 6, 7, 9, 9) sts at beg of next 2 rows—66 (64, 66, 74, 82, 86) sts rem. Dec 1 st each end of needle every row 10 (9, 8, 8, 8, 9) times, every 2nd row 4 (4, 4, 13, 4, 4) times, then every 4th row 2 (2, 1, 0, 5, 5) time(s), then every 2nd row 2 (3, 8, 0, 5, 4) times, then every row 5 (4, 2, 6, 7, 8) times—20 (20, 20, 20, 24, 26) sts rem. BO all sts.

Finishing

Seams

With C and RS facing, pick up and knit 1 st in each BO st along right front shoulder. Break yarn. In the same way, pick up and knit the same number of sts along right back shoulder; do not break yarn. Holding pieces with RS together, use the three-needle method (see Glossary, page 153) to BO sts tog. Join left shoulder in the same way. With C threaded on a tapestry needle, sew sleeve caps into armholes and sew sleeve seams.

Front Bands

With F, smaller needle, and beg at left shoulder seam, pick up and knit 1 st for every BO st and 2 sts for every 3 rows around neckline, 2 sts for every 3 rows along left front edge, 1 st for every st along bottom edge, 2 sts for every 3 rows along right front edge, 1 st for every BO st and 2 sts for every 3 rows around rest of neckline—about 420 (454, 494, 528, 580, 622) sts total. Pm and join for working in the round.

Rnd 1: With F, purl, placing marker before each of 4 corner sts (each front lower edge and each front at start of neck shaping).

Rnd 2: With D, *knit to marker, M1L (see Glossary, page 156), sl m, k1 (corner st), M1R (see Glossary, page 156); rep from * 3 more times, knit to end of round—8 sts inc'd.

Rnd 3: With D, purl.

Rnd 4: With C, rep Rnd 2.

Mark placement for 6 (6, 6, 7, 7, 7) buttonholes evenly spaced along right front.

Rnd 5: With C, purl to bottom corner of right front (third marker). Cont to purl and *at the same time* BO 3 sts for each marked buttonhole.

Rnd 6: With E, rep Rnd 2 and *at the same time* use the backward loop method (see Glossary, page 153) to CO 3 sts over each gap to complete the buttonholes.

Rnd 7: With E, purl.

Rnd 8: With B, rep Rnd 2.

With B, BO all sts purlwise.

Weave in loose ends. If desired, use sewing thread and needle to sew ribbon to inside of left front band, turning under about ¼" (6 mm) of ribbon at top and bottom of band. Repeat for buttonhole band, but cut holes in ribbon to correspond to knitted buttonholes. With sewing needle and thread, work buttonhole stitch (see Glossary, page 155) around each buttonhole to secure ribbon to band and to prevent ribbon from raveling.

Make buttons as shown at right.

Buttons

Make 6 (6, 6, 7, 7, 7). With A, C, or F threaded on a tapestry needle, work buttonhole stitch around button ring. Turn ridge of knots to inside of ring *(Figure 1)*. Wrap yarn around ring like spokes of a wheel, so there are five evenly spaced spokes *(Figure 2)*. Bring needle up through spokes close to center where spokes cross, and cross-stitch over center several times to fasten, center, and separate spokes *(Figure 3)*. Tie and cut yarn. With D, backstitch over each spoke—10 stitches *(Figure 4)*. Tie and cut yarn. Neaten back of button by darning over it with sewing needle and thread. Sew buttons to button band.

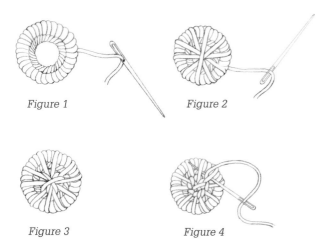

Figure 1   *Figure 2*

Figure 3   *Figure 4*

Why Does Yarn Shrink?

If I say "100% cotton yarn," don't tell me you don't think "that stuff will shrink!" Because whatever you've knitted from pure cotton likely has shrunk when you washed it. But maybe not for the reasons you think.

When yarn is spun from *any* fiber, it's under tension. That tension means the fibers are stretched beyond their natural state. And that goes for all fibers, not just cotton. Bette Hochberg, author of a number of brilliant books on fiber, spinning, and weaving, explains it like this: "shrinkage may be compared to a rubber band that is stretched out and then released. The rubber band does not shrink or become smaller than its original size. It simply returns to normal."

For some yarns, this tension is part of the character of the yarn. Says Kay Gardiner, the passionately nonwool half of the Mason-Dixon knitting team, ". . . denim yarn shrinks 10–15% with the recommended hot wash and drying in the dryer. This freaks a lot of knitters out, but it shouldn't. Denim shrinks only lengthwise, not widthwise, so it's easy to adapt almost any pattern simply by adding a few rows of length. The shrinkage is a one-time thing, and really makes the garment look great."

So what can you do about this? Unless you're going to prewash all your yarn before you knit it, not a darned thing. But doesn't it help to understand why it happens?

Eileen

design by Jillian Moreno

This simple, beautiful shell was inspired by the clean lines of a famous clothing designer named Eileen. I wonder if she knits? Because if she did, she'd certainly want to make one of these for herself: a streamlined linen top with an elegant ballet neck and the sexiest lace back a tank ever had.

Designer Jillian Moreno loves linen because it shows off lace detailing beautifully and only needs blocking for length. This piece is knitted much more tightly than the ball band suggests, and that's on purpose. Otherwise, one's usual feminine frontal undergarments (or lack thereof) would be on display to the whole world. We'd rather show off the linen, not what it's covering.

Finished Size
33½ (37½, 41½, 45½, 49½, 53½)" (85 [95, 105.5, 115.5, 125.5, 136] cm) bust circumference. Sweater shown measures 33½" (85 cm).

Yarn
Worsted-weight (CYCA #4 Medium) yarn.
Shown here: Louet Sales Euroflax Geneva (100% linen; 190 yd [174 m]/ 100 g): eggplant, 3 (4, 4, 5, 6, 6) skeins.

Needles
Body—size 2 (2.75 mm): straight and 16" (40 cm) circular (cir). Hem and edging— size 1 (2.25 mm): straight and 16" (40 cm) cir. Adjust needle size if necessary to obtain the correct gauge.

Notions
Markers (m); stitch holders; tapestry needle.

Gauge
20 stitches and 24 rows = 4" (10 cm) in stockinette stitch on larger needles.

Back

With larger needles, CO 84 (94, 104, 114, 124, 134) sts. *Set-up row:* (WS) P12 (17, 22, 27, 32, 37), place marker (pm), p60, pm, p12 (17, 22, 27, 32, 37). *Next row:* (RS) Knit to first m, slip marker (sl m), work Row 1 of Traveling Vine chart across next 60 sts, sl m, knit to end. Cont in this manner, working the center 60 sts according to Traveling Vine chart and rem sts in St st, until piece measures 11 (11, 11, 11, 14, 14)" (28 [28, 28, 28, 35.5, 35.5] cm) from CO, ending with a WS row.

Shape Armholes

Keeping in patt as established, BO 5 (7, 9, 12, 12, 13) sts at beg of next 2 rows—74 (80, 86, 90, 100, 108) sts rem. Dec 1 st each end of needle every RS row 4 (6, 9, 11, 15, 19) times—66 (68, 68, 68, 70, 70) sts rem. Cont even in patt until armholes measure 7 (7, 8, 8, 9, 9)" (18 [18, 20.5, 20.5, 23, 23] cm), ending with a WS row.

Shape Shoulders

Working all sts in St st, work short-rows (see Glossary, page 157) as foll:
Rows 1 and 2: Work to last 5 (6, 6, 6, 6, 6) sts, wrap next st, turn.
Rows 3 and 4: Work to last 9 (12, 12, 12, 12, 12) sts, wrap next st, turn.
Next row: (RS) Knit, working wrapped sts tog with their wraps.
Next row: (WS) P13 (14, 14, 14, 15, 15), BO 40 sts for back neck, purl to end, working wrapped sts tog with their wraps—13 (14, 14, 14, 15, 15) sts rem each side. Place sts on holders.

☐	**k on RS; p on WS**
b	**knit 1 through back loop (k1tbl)**
o	**yo**
⁄	**k2top on RS; p2tog on WS**
⧵	**ssk**
⧵	**p2tog tbl**
☐	**pattern repeat**

TRAVELING VINE

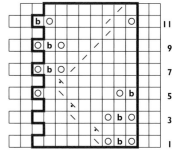

Front

Hem Facing

With smaller needles, CO 84 (94, 104, 114, 124, 134) sts. Work in St st until piece measures 1" (2.5 cm) from CO, ending with a RS row. *Next row:* (WS) Knit all sts to form turning ridge. Change to larger needles and cont even in St st until piece measures 11 (11, 11, 11, 14, 14)" (28 [28, 28, 28, 35.5, 35.5] cm) from turning ridge, ending with a WS row.

Shape Armholes

BO 5 (7, 9, 12, 12, 13) sts at beg of next 2 rows—74 (80, 86, 90, 100, 108) sts rem. Dec 1 st each end of needle every RS row 4 (6, 9, 11, 15, 19) times—66 (68, 68, 68, 70, 70) sts rem. Cont even in St st until armholes measure 5½ (5½, 6½, 6½, 7½, 7½)" (14 [14, 16.5, 16.5, 19, 19] cm), ending with a WS row.

Shape Neck

(RS) K17 (18, 18, 18, 19, 19), join a new ball of yarn and BO center 32 sts, knit to end—17 (18, 18, 18, 19, 19) sts rem each side. Working each side separately, dec 1 st at each neck edge every RS row 4 times—13 (14, 14, 14, 15, 15) sts rem each side. Cont even until armholes measure 7 (7, 8, 8, 9, 9)" (18 [18, 20.5, 20.5, 23, 23] cm), ending with a WS row.

Shape Shoulders

Working each side separately in St st, work short-rows as foll:

Rows 1 and 2: At each armhole edge, work to last 5 (6, 6, 6, 6, 6) sts, wrap next st, turn.

Rows 3 and 4: At each armhole edge, work to last 9 (12, 12, 12, 12, 12) sts, wrap next st, turn.

Work 2 rows even, working wrapped sts tog with their wraps. Do not BO.

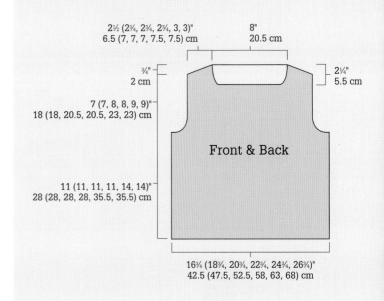

2½ (2¾, 2¾, 2¾, 3, 3)"
6.5 (7, 7, 7, 7.5, 7.5) cm

8"
20.5 cm

¾"
2 cm

2¼"
5.5 cm

7 (7, 8, 8, 9, 9)"
18 (18, 20.5, 20.5, 23, 23) cm

Front & Back

11 (11, 11, 11, 14, 14)"
28 (28, 28, 28, 35.5, 35.5) cm

16¾ (18¾, 20¾, 22¾, 24¾, 26¾)"
42.5 (47.5, 52.5, 58, 63, 68) cm

Finishing

Place held back shoulder sts on spare needles and, with RS tog, use the three-needle method (see Glossary, page 153) to BO shoulder sts tog. With yarn threaded on a tapestry needle, sew side seams. Sew hem facing to WS of front.

Armhole Edging

With smaller cir needle, RS facing, and beg at side seam, pick up and knit 80 (84, 98, 104, 120, 124) sts evenly spaced around armhole edge. Purl 1 rnd. Loosely BO all sts.

Neck Edging

With smaller cir needle, RS facing, and beg at a shoulder seam, pick up and knit 95 sts around neck edge. Purl 1 rnd. Loosely BO all sts.

Weave in loose ends. Block to measurements, pinning out the scalloped lower edge of back.

Network

design by Stephannie Roy

Silk hats might feel great, but silk + hair = static. In winter, we have more than enough of that without external help. And pure silk isn't really suitable for a hat that needs to keep its shape. Designer Stephannie Roy has come up with this clever solution. The outer layer is knitted in shimmery Artyarns silk in a simple lace pattern, for warmth and beauty. The inner layer is all Rowan Calmer, with its amazing stretch and cotton-blend softness. Two balls of very different yarn never worked better together.

Note

■ The end-of-rnd marker changes position on Row 3 and Row 7 of chart; see chart key for marker placement.

Lace Shell

With MC, larger cir needle, and using the provisional method (see Glossary, page 154), CO 84 sts. Place marker (pm) and join for working in the rnd, being careful not to twist sts. [Knit 1 rnd, purl 1 rnd] 2 times, knit 1 rnd—5 rnds total. *Set-up rnd:* *K2, p2; rep from * to end of rnd. Beg with Row 1 and noting special instructions for Rows 3 and 7 (see Note and chart key), rep Rows 1–8 of Lace chart 6 times, then work Rows 1 and 2 once more—piece measures about 5¾" (14.5 cm) from CO.

Finished Size

17" (43 cm) circumference. To fit an adult. *Note:* Hat is designed to fit snuggly; use larger needles and a looser gauge to make a bigger size.

Yarn

Worsted-weight (CYCA #4 Medium) yarn.
Shown here: Lace shell: Artyarns Regal Silk (100% silk; 163 yd [149 m]/50 g): #126 violet (MC), 1 skein.
Warm liner: Rowan Calmer (75% cotton, 25% microfiber; 175 yd [160 m]/50 g): #481 coffee bean (CC), 1 skein.

Needles

Lace shell—size 4 (3.5 mm): 16" (40 cm) circular (cir) and set of 4 or 5 double-pointed (dpn).
Warm liner—size 3 (3.25 mm): 16" (40 cm) cir and set of 4 or 5 dpn. Adjust needle size if necessary to obtain the correct gauge.

Notions

Marker (m); a few yards (meters) of waste yarn for provisional cast-on; tapestry needle.

Gauge

Lace shell: 20 stitches and 36 rounds = 4" (10 cm) in lace pattern worked in the round with MC on larger needles.
Warm liner: 24 stitches and 39 rounds = 4" (10 cm) in stockinette stitch worked in the round with CC on smaller needles.

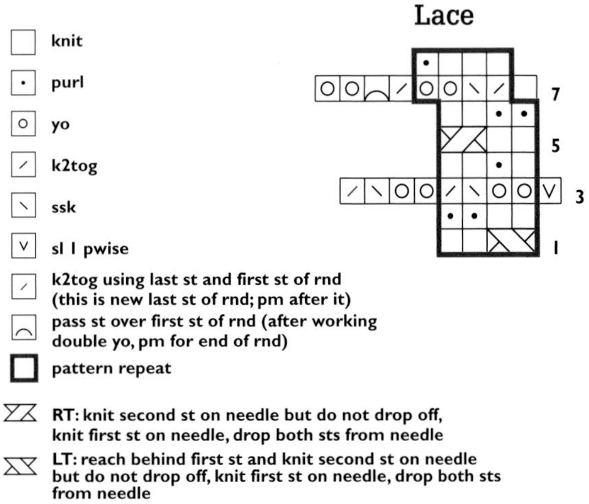

Lace

☐	knit
•	purl
o	yo
╱	k2tog
╲	ssk
v	sl 1 pwise
	k2tog using last st and first st of rnd (this is new last st of rnd; pm after it)
	pass st over first st of rnd (after working double yo, pm for end of rnd)
▣	pattern repeat
RT	RT: knit second st on needle but do not drop off, knit first st on needle, drop both sts from needle
LT	LT: reach behind first st and knit second st on needle but do not drop off, knit first st on needle, drop both sts from needle

(Chart "Lace" with rows numbered 1, 3, 5, 7)

Shape Top

Dec as foll, changing to dpn when necessary:

Rnd 1: Sl 1, *yo 2 times, ssk (see Glossary, page 154), k2tog, yo, ssk, k2tog; rep from * to last 3 sts, yo 2 times, ssk, k2tog using last st and first st of rnd (this creates the last st in the rnd), pm—74 sts rem.

Rnd 2: *K1, p1, k5; rep from * to last 4 sts, k1, p1, k2.

Rnd 3: *K2, RT (see chart key), k1, RT; rep from * to last 4 sts, k2, RT.

Rnd 4: *P2, k2, p1, k2; rep from * to last 4 sts, p2, k2.

Rnd 5: K1, *k2tog, yo, sl 1, k2tog, psso, yo 2 times, ssk; rep from * to last 3 sts, k2tog, yo, pass last st of rnd over first st of rnd (this becomes the new first st of rnd)—63 sts rem.

Rnd 6: *K5, p1; rep from * to last 3 sts, k3.

Rnd 7: *LT (see chart key), k1; rep from * to end of rnd.

Rnd 8: *K2, p1; rep from * to end of rnd.

Rnd 9: Sl 1, *yo, sl 1, k2tog, psso; rep from * to last 2 sts, yo, sl 1, k2tog using last st and first st of rnd, psso (this becomes the last st)—42 sts rem.

Rnds 10, 12, 14, and 16: Knit.

Rnd 11: Sl 1, *yo, k3tog; rep from * to last 2 sts, yo, k3tog using first st of rnd (this becomes the last st)—28 sts rem.

Rnd 13: *Yo, sl 1, k2tog, psso; rep from * to last 4 sts, yo, [sl 1 kwise] 2 times, k2tog, p2sso—18 sts rem.

Rnd 15: *Yo, sl 1, k2tog, psso; rep from * to end—12 sts rem.

Rnd 17: *K2tog; rep from * to end—6 sts rem.

Cut yarn, leaving a 12" (30.5 cm) tail. Thread tail on a tapestry needle, draw through rem sts, pull tight to close hole, and fasten off to WS. Weave in loose ends.

Warm Liner

With CC, smaller cir needle, and using the provisional method, CO 84 sts. Place marker (pm) and join for working in the rnd, being careful not to twist sts. Knit 2 rnds. *Inc rnd:* Knit, inc 12 sts evenly spaced—96 sts. Knit even until piece measures 6½" (16.5 cm) from CO.

Shape Top

Dec as foll, changing to dpn when necessary:

Rnd 1: *K2tog, k6; rep from *—84 sts rem.

Rnd 2: Knit.

Rnd 3: *K2, k2tog; rep from *—63 sts rem.

Rnds 4–6: Knit.

Rnd 7: *K1, k2tog; rep from *—42 sts rem.

Rnds 8–11: Rep Rnds 4–7—28 sts rem after Rnd 11.

Rnds 12 and 14: Knit.

Rnd 13: *K2tog; rep from *—14 sts rem.

Rnd 15: *K2tog; rep from *—7 sts rem.

Cut yarn, leaving a 12" (30.5 cm) tail. Thread tail on a tapestry needle, draw through rem sts, pull tight to close top, and fasten off to WS. Weave in loose ends.

Finishing

Remove waste yarn from provisional CO for both pieces and place live sts on cir needles. Place the warm liner inside the lace hat with RS of warm liner facing WS of lace (purl side of St st will show on inside of hat). With MC threaded on a tapestry needle, use the Kitchener st (see Glossary, page 155) to graft the two sets of sts tog. Weave in loose ends. Block lightly if desired.

How to Wind Slippery Yarn on a Ball Winder

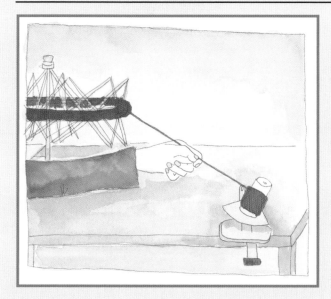

This one is tricky. I give no guarantees, but I will say that it works for me more often than it doesn't.

When winding slippery yarn onto a ball winder, do these two things:

1. **Slip an empty toilet paper tube over the ball winder's center stem.** This gives the yarn more surface area to hang on to, and it's less slippery than the plastic of the ball winder. It can also make for easier removal (and less chance of the ball collapsing into itself) should you successfully wind the ball. Just pull the yarn-wrapped tube off the ball winder and knit with it just like that—the self-supporting core helps keep the ball intact as you work.

2. **Keep the yarn under tension as you wind.** You may think that the built-in tension arm is sufficient to get yarn neatly from the swift onto to the ballwinder, but I'll suggest it's the reason you're having problems (assuming you ARE having problems). The yarn tension needs to be constant as the yarn is fed onto the ball winder or you run the risk of the yarn slipping all over itself and the ball collapsing as it's being wound. That little metal arm is pretty useless at this task.

How do you get adequate tension? Simply run the strand of yarn that's coming off the swift through your hands before it gets to the tension arm. You can control how much tension you give the yarn by pinching the strand with your fingers. The key is to make sure the yarn is always taut as it leads into the ball winder. If you need to stop before the ball is complete, slow down the winding as if you were driving to a stop sign. Then make sure the tension is in place before you start up again. If you make a mess after a good start, no worries. Unwind back to the good part, apply tension, and resume winding.

You'll notice I specifically mention having your yarn on a swift. That's on purpose. You can use someone's hands or the back of a chair if you're winding slippery yarn into a ball by hand, but I wouldn't recommend it if you're using a ball winder. It won't feed consistently enough. A swift is a bit of an investment, but if you find that most of the yarn you use doesn't come in ready-to-knit balls, it's worth the money spent in frustration avoided.

Tuscany

design by Amy R. Singer

This shawl uses the yarn that turned me into an obsessive evangelist for all things sheepless—Handmaiden Silken. It's the yarn that proved to me that knitting without wool is no hardship. It's still my favorite.

This pattern starts at the bottom point of the shawl, and rapidly increases outwards at the edges to give you lots of luscious silk to wrap around yourself. The lace pattern is easily memorized (just think 10, 8, 6, 4) but don't abandon the stitch markers. They're what keep your brain free to enjoy the knitting. And though you may not think it needs it, gently block the shawl when you're done. It will make the leaves sing songs of Brunello and fresh pecorino, budding grapevines, and fragrant wisteria on every balcony. Cheaper than a plane ticket to Tuscany, and almost as delicious.

Finished Size
About 76" (193 cm) wide across the top and 26" (66 cm) long at deepest point.
Yarn
Sportweight (CYCA #2 Fine) yarn.
Shown here: Handmaiden Silken (100% silk; 273 yd [250 m]/100 g): ruby red, 3 skeins.
Needles
Size 6 (4 mm): 40" (100 cm) circular (cir). Adjust needle size if necessary to obtain the correct gauge.
Notions
24 markers (m); tapestry needle; scissors; stainless blocking pins.
Gauge
22 stitches and 30 rows = 4" (10 cm) in stockinette stitch.

Notes

- This pattern has two simple rules to follow. These rules, along with the Tuscany chart, will guarantee a beautiful shawl. *Rule 1:* Always make a yarnover 2 stitches in from each edge on every row (2 stitches increased per row). *Rule 2:* On RS rows, the first stitch after a marker is always purled; on WS rows, the first stitch before a marker is always knitted. (Most of these stitches are included in the chart; you only need to pay attention at the very start and end of each row.) The only time these rules are awkward to follow is on the first wrong-side row of a repeat. The yarn will already be in front of the needle from the previous purl stitch, so to work the yarnover and knit stitch before the first marker, simply bring the yarn over the top of the needle to the back to be in position to knit the stitch before the marker. This will create the yarnover between the purl stitch and the knit stitch. If you fully loop the yarn around the needle, you'll make two stitches instead of one. And yes, you will always purl the stitch after the last marker on the right side, even though you're not knitting the remaining stitches of that row in pattern yet. The pattern loses definition if you don't do this.
- Slip markers as you come to them.
- Add new balls of yarn at a selvedge edge for easier weaving in of ends later.

TUSCANY

knit on **RS**; purl on **WS**	
·	purl on **RS**; knit on **WS**
o	yo
⟋	k3tog
⅄	sl 1 kwise, k2tog, psso
	pattern repeat

Shawl

CO 6 sts very loosely.

Row 1: (WS) P2, yo, p2, yo, p2—8 sts.

Row 2: (RS) K2, yo, k4, yo, k2—10 sts.

Rows 3 and 5: P2, yo, purl to last 2 sts, yo, p2—2 sts inc'd each row.

Rows 4 and 6: K2, yo, knit to last 2 sts, yo, k2—2 sts inc'd each row.

Row 7: Rep Row 3—20 sts.

Row 8: K2, yo, place marker (pm), work Row 1 of Tuscany chart across 16 sts, pm, yo, k2—2 sts inc'd.

Row 9: P2, yo, k1, slip marker (sl m), work Row 2 of chart to next m, sl m, p1, yo, p2—2 sts inc'd.

Cont as established, working center sts according to chart, working inc'd sts and 2 sts at each edge in St st, and remembering to follow Rules 1 and 2 as stated in Notes above, until WS Row 16 of chart has been completed—52 sts; 16 extra sts + 2 edge sts at each side of lace patt. *Next row:* (RS) Incorporate new sts into lace patt as foll: k2, yo, pm, work Row 1 of chart 3 times across next 48 sts, pm, yo, k2—54 sts total; the 16 new sts on each side have been incorporated into the lace patt. Cont in this manner, working inc'd sts in St st until there are 16 new sts on each edge of shawl, then incorporating those new sts into lace patt until the 16-row patt rep has been worked 11 times, ending with a WS row—372 sts total; piece measures about 25" (63.5 cm) from CO.

Finishing

Use the Russian method of binding off as foll (thanks to Galina Khmeleva for this technique): With RS facing, p2tog, *loosen and slip the resulting st back onto the left-hand needle, insert the right-hand needle tip into this st and the next st to the left and gently tighten it, p2tog; rep from * until no sts rem on left needle. Cut yarn, thread tail through rem st on right needle, and pull tight to secure. Weave in loose ends.

Blocking

Smooth the shawl gently outwards on a firm blocking surface to desired width and depth, making sure the two short sides of the triangle are the same length. Place as many pins as necessary to ensure straight edges on all three sides. Spritz generously with water until shawl is completely saturated. Let air-dry completely before removing pins.

Intoxicating

design by Kristi Porter

Designer Kristi Porter is mad for mosaic knitting. And when she combined a coordinating pair of mosaic patterns with lace and pure, shimmery silk, I was Intoxicated. See, pure silk like this can be slippery and hard to manage. Kristi's clever design has built-in control—one color sort of stabilizes the other.

When it comes to the sleeves, the final touch of lusciousness is lace. By the way—did you notice that the front and back are not only knitted in different mosaic patterns, but in different colors? Oh, heavens, I need to sit down and catch my breath. A good silk sweater is a wonderful thing, but this is a *great* silk sweater.

Notes

- In mosaic knitting, each color is worked alone for two rows. On the first row (right side) with color A, knit the stitches that are in color A; slip the stitches that are in color B purlwise with the yarn in back. On the second row (wrong side), purl the stitches that were knitted on the previous row and slip the stitches that were slipped before (slip purlwise with the yarn in front). Each two-row sequence is represented by one row on the charts.

- Change colors every two rows, knitting or purling the stitches of the color being used and slipping the other stitches. On the charts, the color being used for a row is shown to the right of the row number.

- After increasing or decreasing, work the edge stitch with the working yarn, then maintain the pattern across the row. These edge stitches help to stabilize the color-work pattern and will be hidden in the seams.

- When working the left front and right back shoulders, work the specified stitches using the stranded knitting (Fair Isle) technique rather than the mosaic (slip stitch) technique, working the stitches in pattern as follows: When a stitch would have been knitted, knit it as usual; when a stitch would have been slipped, knit it in the color not in use for that row. By doing this, the yarn will be in the correct position to start the next right-side row.

Finished Size

About 34¾ (39, 43¾, 48¼, 50¼, 55)" (88.5 [99, 111, 122.5, 127.5, 139.5] cm) bust circumference. Sweater shown measures 34¾" (88.5 cm).

Yarn

DK-weight (CYCA #3 Light) yarn.
Shown here: Curious Creek Fibers Isalo (100% silk; 262 yd [240 m]/95 g): birches in Norway (green; A), 3 (3, 4, 4, 5, 5) skeins; plum thunder (purple; B) and sunrise on daffodils (orange; C), 1 (1, 2, 2, 2, 2) skein(s) each.

Needles

Body and sleeves—size 7 (4.5 mm): 24" (60 cm) circular (cir). Neck—sizes 5 and 6 (3.75 and 4 mm): 16" or 24" (40 or 60 cm) cir. Adjust needle size if necessary to obtain the correct gauge.

Notions

Stitch holders; marker (m); tapestry needle.

Gauge

24½ stitches and 39 rows = 4" (10 cm) in pinbox or maze mosaic pattern, unblocked; 23 stitches and 35 rows = 4" (10 cm) in pinbox or maze mosaic pattern, blocked, both on largest needles. 20 stitches and 24 rows = 4" (10 cm) in lace pattern, unblocked; 17 stitches and 20 rows = 4" (10 cm) in lace pattern, blocked, both on largest needles.

- Both the mosaic and lace patterns look smaller on the needles than they will be when the top is finished. Mosaics and lace change significantly in size when blocked, so *block your swatch before measuring*. The sweater will stretch slightly with wear for a perfect fit—the fabric you create has marvelous drape and is meant to fit closely like a T-shirt.

Stitch Guide

Pinbox Mosaic

(multiple of 12 sts + 3; from Barbara G. Walker's *A Second Treasury of Knitting Patterns*, 1970)

Note: On all RS rows, slip the slip sts with the yarn in back (i.e., hold yarn on WS when slipping sts).

Row 1: (RS): With A, knit.

Row 2: (WS) With A, purl.

Row 3: With B, k1, *sl 1, k11; rep from * to last 2 sts, sl 1, k1.

Row 4 and all remaining WS rows: Purl all sts that were knitted on previous row with the same color; slip all sts (with yarn in front) that were slipped on previous row.

Row 5: With A, k2, *sl 1, k9, sl 1, k1; rep from * to last st, k1.

Row 7: With B, [k1, sl 1] 2 times, *k7, [sl 1, k1] 2 times, sl 1; rep from * to last 11 sts, k7, [sl 1, k1] 2 times.

Row 9: With A, k2, sl 1, k1, sl 1, *k5, [sl 1, k1] 3 times, sl 1; rep from * to last 10 sts, k5, sl 1, k1, sl 1, k2.

Row 11: With B, [k1, sl 1] 3 times, *k3, [sl 1, k1] 4 times, sl 1; rep from * to last 9 sts, k3, [sl 1, k1] 3 times.

Row 13: With A, k2, *sl 1, k1; rep from * to last st, k1.

Rows 15, 17, 19, 21, 23, and 25: Rep Rows 11, 9, 7, 5, 3, and 1.

Row 27: With B, k7, *sl 1, k11; rep from *, end last rep k7.

Row 29: With A, k6, *sl 1, k1, sl 1, k9; rep from *, end last rep k6.

Row 31: With B, k5, *[sl 1, k1] 2 times, sl 1, k7; rep from *, end last rep k5.

Row 33: With A, k4, *[sl 1, k1] 3 times, sl 1, k5; rep from *, end last rep k4.

Row 35: With B, k3, *[sl 1, k1] 4 times, sl 1, k3; rep from *.

Row 37: With A, rep Row 13.

Rows 39, 41, 43, 45, and 47: Rep Rows 35, 33, 31, 29, and 27.

PINBOX MOSAIC

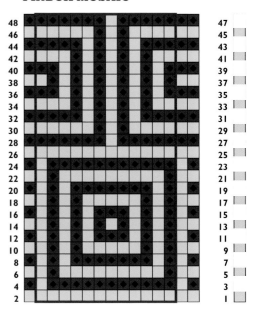

MAZE MOSAIC

green (A)

purple (B)

orange (C)

pattern repeat

Row 48: Purl all sts that were knitted on previous row with the same color; slip all sts (with yarn in front) that were slipped on previous row.

Repeat Rows 1–48 for pattern.

Maze Mosaic

(multiple of 14 sts + 2; from Barbara G. Walker's *A Second Treasury of Knitting Patterns*, 1970)

Note: On all RS rows, slip the slip sts with the yarn in back (i.e., hold yarn on WS when slipping sts).

Row 1: (RS) With C, k1, *k7, [sl 1, k1] 3 times, sl 1; rep from * to last st, k1.

Row 2 and all wrong-side rows: Purl all sts that were knitted on previous row with the same color; slip all sts (with yarn in front) that were slipped on previous row.

Row 3: With A, k1, *sl 1, k7, [sl 1, k1] 3 times; rep from * to last st, k1.

Row 5: With C, k2, *sl 1, k7, [sl 1, k1] 3 times, rep from *.

Row 7: With A, *[k1, sl 1] 2 times, k7, sl 1, k1, sl 1; rep from * to last 2 sts, k2.

Row 9: With C, k2, *sl 1, k1, sl 1, k7, [sl 1, k1] 2 times; rep from *.

Row 11: With A, *[k1, sl 1] 3 times, k7, sl 1; rep from * to last 2 sts, k2.

Row 13: With C, k1, *[k1, sl 1] 3 times, k7, sl 1; rep from * to last st, k1.

Row 15: With A, k1, *[sl 1, k1] 3 times, sl 1, k7; rep from * to last st, k1.

Row 17: With C, rep Row 1.

Row 19: With A, *k7, [sl 1, k1] 3 times, sl 1; rep from * to last 2 sts, k2.

Row 21: With C, k6, *[sl 1, k1] 3 times, sl 1, k7; rep from *, end last rep k3.

Row 23: With A, k5, *[sl 1, k1] 3 times, sl 1, k7; rep from *, end last rep k4.

Row 25: With C, k4, *[sl 1, k1] 3 times, sl 1, k7; rep from *, end last rep k5.

Row 27: With A, k3, *[sl 1, k1] 3 times, sl 1, k7; rep from *, end last rep k6.

Row 29: With C, k2, *[sl 1, k1] 3 times, sl 1, k7; rep from *.

Row 31: With A, rep Row 15.

Row 32: Purl all sts that were knitted on previous row with the same color; slip all sts (with yarn in front) that were slipped on previous row.

Repeat Rows 1–32 for pattern.

4¼ (4¾, 5¼, 5½, 5½, 5½)"
11 (12, 13.5, 14, 14, 14) cm

6¾ (6¾, 7¼, 7¼, 8¼, 8½)"
17 (17, 18.5, 18.5, 21, 21.5) cm

¾"
2 cm

5½"
14 cm

7½ (7½, 8¼, 8¼, 9¼, 10)"
19 (19, 21, 21, 23.5, 25.5) cm

14 (14, 15¼, 15¼, 16, 16)"
35.5 (35.5, 38.5, 38.5, 40.5, 40.5) cm

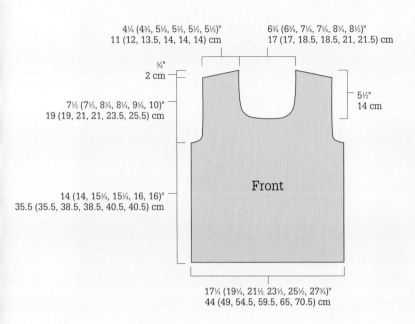

Front

17¼ (19¼, 21½, 23½, 25½, 27¾)"
44 (49, 54.5, 59.5, 65, 70.5) cm

4 (4, 5, 5, 5, 5)"
10 (10, 12.5, 12.5, 12.5, 12.5) cm

14 (14¼, 15¼, 16¾, 17¼, 18)"
35.5 (36, 38.5, 42.5, 44, 45.5) cm

7¼ (7¼, 6½, 6½, 6¾, 7½)"
18.5 (18.5, 16.5, 16.5, 17, 19) cm

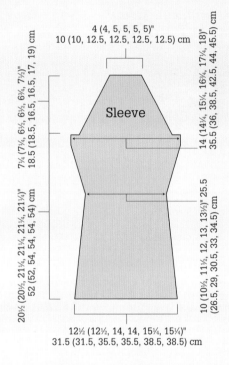

Sleeve

14
35.5

10 (10½, 11½, 12, 13, 13½)"
(26.5, 29, 30.5, 33, 34.5) cm

25.5

20½ (20½, 21¼, 21¼, 21¼, 21¼)"
52 (52, 54, 54, 54, 54) cm

12½ (12½, 14, 14, 15¼, 15¼)"
31.5 (31.5, 35.5, 35.5, 38.5, 38.5) cm

4¼ (4¾, 5¼, 5½, 5½, 5½)"
11 (12, 13.5, 14, 14, 14) cm

7 (7¼, 8, 8¼, 7¼, 8)"
18 (18.5, 20.5, 21, 18.5, 20.5) cm

¾"
2 cm

7½ (7½, 8¼, 8¼, 9¼, 10)"
19 (19, 21, 21, 23.5, 25.5) cm

14 (14, 15¼, 15¼, 16, 16)"
35.5 (35.5, 38.5, 38.5, 40.5, 40.5) cm

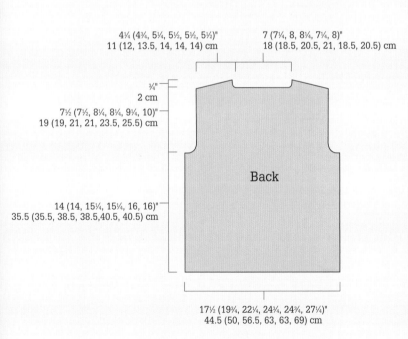

Back

17½ (19¾, 22¼, 24¾, 24¾, 27¼)"
44.5 (50, 56.5, 63, 63, 69) cm

All measurements shown after blocking.

Front

With A and largest needle, CO 99 (111, 123, 135, 147, 159) sts. Knit 1 row. Do not cut yarn. Join B and knit 2 rows. Do not cut yarn. Knit 2 rows with A—piece should measure about ½" (1.3 cm) from CO. Work Rows 3–48 of Pinbox Mosaic patt (see Stitch Guide or chart), then work Rows 1–48 once, then work Rows 1–24 (24, 36, 36, 42, 42)—piece measures about 12½ (12½, 13¾, 13¾, 14½, 14½)" (31.5 [31.5, 35, 35, 37, 37] cm) from CO; piece will block to measure about 14 (14, 15¼, 15¼, 16, 16)" (35.5 [35.5, 38.5, 38.5, 40.5, 40.5] cm).

Shape Armholes

(Row 25 [25, 37, 37, 43, 43] of patt) Keeping in pinbox patt as established, BO 4 (5, 7, 10, 10, 10) sts at beg of next 2 rows—91 (101, 109, 115, 127, 139) sts rem. Dec 1 st each end of needle every RS row 2 (3, 4, 5, 8, 13) times—87 (95, 101, 105, 111, 113) sts rem. Work even through WS Row 48 (48, 18, 18, 34, 40) of patt—armholes measure about 2½ (2½, 3, 3, 4, 4¾)" (6.5 [6.5, 7.5, 7.5, 10, 12] cm), unblocked.

Shape Neck

(RS Row 1 [1, 19, 19, 35, 41] of patt) Keeping in patt, work 25 (29, 31, 33, 33, 33) sts for left side of neck, join new yarn and BO center 37 (37, 39, 39, 45, 47) sts, work to end for right side of neck—25 (29, 31, 33, 33, 33) sts rem each side.

Right Neck

Work 25 (29, 31, 33, 33, 33) right neck sts in patt as foll:
Next row: Dec 1 st at neck edge—24 (28, 30, 32, 32, 32) sts rem. Cont even in patt for 40 more rows, ending with WS Row 42 (42, 12, 12, 28, 34) of patt—armhole measures about 6¾ (6¾, 7½, 7½, 8½, 9)" (17 [17, 19, 19, 21.5, 23] cm), unblocked; armhole will block to measure about 7½ (7½, 8¼, 8¼, 9¼, 10)" (19 [19, 21, 21, 23.5, 25.5] cm).

Right Shoulder

Keeping in patt, work short-rows (see Glossary, page 157) as foll:
Row 1: (RS) Beg at neck edge, work 18 (21, 22, 24, 24, 24) sts, wrap next st, turn work.
Rows 2 and 4: (WS) Purl.
Row 3: Work 12 (14, 14, 16, 16, 16) sts, wrap next st, turn.
Row 5: Work 6 (7, 7, 8, 8, 8) sts, wrap next st, turn.
Row 6: Purl.
Next row: With A, knit all sts, working wrapped sts tog with their wraps. Place sts on holder.

Left Neck

With WS facing, join yarn at left neck edge. Dec 1 st at neck edge, work to end of row in patt—24 (28, 30, 32, 32, 32) sts rem. Cont even in patt for 40 more rows, ending with WS Row 42 (42, 12, 12, 28, 34) of patt—armhole measures about 6¾ (6¾, 7½, 7½, 8½, 9)" (17 [17, 19, 19, 21.5, 23] cm), unblocked; armhole will block to measure about 7½ (7½, 8¼, 8¼, 9¼, 10)" (19 [19, 21, 21, 23.5, 25.5] cm).

Left Shoulder

Keeping in patt, work short-rows as foll:
Row 1: (RS) Work first 6 (7, 8, 8, 8, 8) sts using the stranded knitting technique (see Notes), knit to end in mosaic patt as established.
Row 2: P18 (21, 22, 24, 24, 24), wrap next st, turn work.
Row 3: K6 (7, 8, 8, 8, 8) in stranded knitting as before, knit to end in mosaic patt.
Row 4: P12 (14, 14, 16, 16, 16) sts in patt, wrap next st, turn.
Row 5: K6 (7, 7, 8, 8, 8) in stranded knitting, knit to end in mosaic patt.
Row 6: P6 (7, 7, 8, 8, 8) sts in patt, wrap next st, turn.
Row 7: K6 (7, 7, 8, 8, 8) in stranded knitting.
Next row: With A, purl all sts, working wrapped sts tog with their wraps. Place sts on holder.

Back

With A and smaller needles, CO 100 (114, 128, 142, 142, 156) sts. Knit 1 row. Do not cut yarn. Join C and knit 2 rows. Do not cut yarn. With A, knit 2 rows—piece measures about ½" (1.3 cm) from CO. Work Rows 3–32 of maze mosaic patt (see Stitch Guide or chart), then work Rows 1–32 two (two, three, three, three, three) times, then work Rows 1–24 (24, 4, 4, 10, 10)—piece measures same as front to armholes.

Shape Armholes

(Row 25 [25, 5, 5, 11, 11] of maze patt) BO 4 (5, 7, 10, 10, 10) sts at beg of next 2 rows—92 (104, 114, 122, 122, 136) sts rem. Dec 1 st each end of needle every RS row 2 (3, 4, 5, 8, 13) times—88 (98, 106, 112, 106, 110) sts rem. Work even in patt until armholes measure 6¾ (6¾, 7½, 7½, 8½, 9)" (17 [17, 19, 19, 21.5, 23] cm), or same as front to shoulder shaping, ending with a WS row.

Shape Shoulders

(RS) Keeping in patt, k27 (31, 33, 35, 35, 35), BO center 34 (36, 40, 42, 36, 40) sts, knit to end—27 (31, 33, 35, 35, 35) sts rem each side. Keeping in patt, work each side separately in short-rows as foll.

Left Shoulder

Row 1: (WS) Purl.

Row 2: (RS) Rejoin second color, k1, ssk (see Glossary, page 154), work in patt to last 6 (7, 8, 8, 8, 8) sts, wrap next st, turn work—1 st dec'd at neck edge.

Row 3: Purl to end.

Row 4: K1, ssk, work in patt to last 12 (14, 16, 16, 16, 16) sts, wrap next st, turn—1 st dec'd at neck edge.

Row 5: Purl to end.

Row 6: K1, ssk, work 4 (5, 5, 6, 6, 6) sts, wrap next st, turn—1 st dec'd at neck edge.

Row 7: Purl to end.

Row 8: With A, knit to end, working wrapped sts tog with their wraps. Place rem 24 (28, 30, 32, 32, 32) sts on holder.

Right Shoulder

Row 1: (WS) Rejoin yarn at neck edge, purl to end.

Row 2: (RS) Knit first 6 (7, 8, 8, 8, 8) sts using the stranded knitting technique (see Notes), work in mosaic patt as established to last 3 sts, k2tog, k1—1 st dec'd at neck edge.

Row 3: Keeping in patt, p20 (23, 24, 26, 26, 26), wrap next st, turn.

Row 4: K6 (7, 8, 8, 8, 8) in stranded knitting as before, work in patt to last 3 sts, k2tog, k1—1 st dec'd at neck edge.

Row 5: P13 (15, 15, 17, 17, 17), wrap next st, turn.

Row 6: K6 (7, 7, 8, 8, 8) in stranded knitting as before, work in patt to last 3 sts, k2tog, k1—1 st dec'd at neck edge.

Row 7: P6 (7, 7, 8, 8, 8), wrap next st, turn.

Row 8: Knit to end in stranded knitting.

Row 9: With A, purl to end, working wrapped sts tog with their wraps. Place rem 24 (28, 30, 32, 32, 32) sts on holder.

Sleeves

With A and largest needles, CO 53 (53, 59, 59, 65, 65) sts. Knit 5 rows, ending with a WS row—piece measures about ½" (1.3 cm) from CO. Work lace patt as foll, slipping all slip sts kwise.

Row 1: (RS) K2, ssk, *[k1, yo] 2 times, k1, sl 1, k2tog, psso; rep from * to last 7 sts, [k1, yo] 2 times, k1, k2tog, k2.

Row 2: Purl.

Rows 3–6: Rep Rows 1 and 2 two more times.

Dec 1 st each end of needle every 6th row 5 (4, 5, 4, 5, 4) times by working (sl 1, k2tog, psso) in place of ssk at beg of row and in place of k2tog at end of row as foll:

Row 7: (RS) K7, sl 1, k2tog, psso, *[k1, yo] 2 times, k1, sl 1, k2tog, psso; rep from * to last 13 sts, [k1, yo] 2 times, k1, sl 1, k2tog, psso, k7—2 sts dec'd.

Row 8 and all WS rows: Purl.

Rows 9 and 11: K7, ssk, *[k1, yo] 2 times, k1, sl 1, k2tog, psso; rep from * to last 12 sts, [k1, yo] 2 times, k1, k2tog, k7.

Row 13: K6, sl 1, k2tog, psso, *[k1, yo] 2 times, k1, sl 1, k2tog, psso; rep from * to last 12 sts, [k1, yo] 2 times, k1, sl 1, k2tog, psso, k6—2 sts dec'd.

Rows 15 and 17: K6, ssk, *[k1, yo] 2 times, k1, sl 1, k2tog, psso; rep from * to last 11 sts, [k1, yo] 2 times, k1, k2tog, k6.

Row 19: K5, sl 1, k2tog, psso, *[k1, yo] 2 times, k1, sl 1, k2tog, psso; rep from * to last 11 sts, [k1, yo] 2 times, k1, sl 1, k2tog, psso, k5—2 sts dec'd.

Rows 21 and 23: K5, ssk, *[k1, yo] 2 times, k1, sl 1, k2tog, psso; rep from * to last 10 sts, [k1, yo] 2 times, k1, k2tog, k5.

Row 25: K4, sl 1, k2tog, psso, *[k1, yo] 2 times, k1, sl 1, k2tog, psso; rep from * to last 10 sts, [k1, yo] 2 times, k1, sl 1, k2tog, psso, k4—2 sts dec'd.

Rows 27 and 29: K4, ssk, *[k1, yo] 2 times, k1, sl 1, k2tog, psso; rep from * to last 9 sts, [k1, yo] 2 times, k1, k2tog, k4.

Sizes 34¾", 43¾", and 50¼" only:

Row 31: K3, sl 1, k2tog, psso, *[k1, yo] 2 times, k1, sl 1, k2tog, psso; rep from * to last 9 sts, [k1, yo] 2 times, k1, sl 1, k2tog, psso, k3—2 sts dec'd.

All sizes: There will be 43 (45, 49, 51, 55, 57) sts. *Next row:* (RS) K3 (4, 3, 4, 3, 4), ssk, *[k1, yo] 2 times, k1, sl 1, k2tog, psso; rep from * to last 8 (9, 8, 9, 8, 9) sts, [k1, yo] 2 times, k1, k2tog, k3 (4, 3, 4, 3, 4). *Next row:* (WS) Purl. Rep the last 2 rows until a total of 62 lace rows have been completed—piece measures about 10¾" (27.5 cm) from CO, unblocked; piece will block to measure about 13" (33 cm). Inc 1 st each end of needle every 4th row 8

(8, 8, 10, 9, 10) times by working k2 in place of the dec at the beg and end of the rows—59 (61, 65, 71, 73, 77) sts. *Note:* When there are 8 sts available before the first patt rep, add another patt rep of the lace at each end of needle by working next inc row as foll: K2, *[k1, yo] 2 times, k1, sl 1, k2tog, psso; rep from * to last 5 sts, [k1, yo] 2 times, k3—2 sts inc'd. Work even until 100 (100, 104, 104, 104, 104) lace rows have been completed, ending with a WS row—piece measures about 17¼ (17¼, 17¾, 17¾, 17¾, 17¾)" (44 [44, 45, 45, 45, 45] cm) from CO, unblocked; piece will block to measure about 20½ (20½, 21¼, 21¼, 21¼, 21¼)" (52 [52, 54, 54, 54, 54] cm).

Shape Cap

Keeping in patt as established, BO 4 (5, 7, 10, 10, 10) sts at beg of the next 2 rows—51 (51, 51, 51, 53, 57) sts rem. *Dec row:* (RS) Work in St st to 3 sts before first (k1, yo) sequence, work first dec as sl 1, k2tog, psso; work in patt to end of last (k1, yo) sequence, work last dec as sl 1, k2tog, psso; work in St st to end of row—2 sts dec'd. Dec 1 st each end of needle in this manner every RS row 16 (16, 14, 14, 15, 17) more times—17 (17, 21, 21, 21, 21) sts rem. *Note:* When there are not enough sts before first (k1, yo) sequence to work dec, work the first and last patt reps in St st as foll: work in St st to 3 sts before second patt rep, sl 1, k2tog, psso, cont in patt to last patt rep, work in St st to end of row—2 sts dec'd. Loosely BO all sts (use the larger needle if necessary) so that top of cap can stretch to accommodate openwork of sleeve.

Finishing

Place held shoulder sts on spare needles and, with RS tog, use the three-needle method (see Glossary, page 153) to BO shoulder sts tog. Block pieces thoroughly, stretching sleeve cap to fit into armhole. With yarn threaded on a tapestry needle, sew sleeve caps into armholes. Sew sleeve and side seams.

Neckband

With A, middle-size cir needle, RS facing, and beg at a shoulder seam, pick up and knit 108 (110, 114, 116, 116, 120) sts around neck opening. Place marker (pm) and join for working in the rnd. Purl 1 rnd. Join C and knit 1 rnd then purl 1 rnd. Cut off C. Return to A and, with smallest cir needle, knit 1 rnd, then purl 1 rnd. Loosely BO all sts.
Weave in loose ends.

Are You Really Allergic to Wool?

Although I understand it's not commonly done now, when I was a little kid, I had the allergy patch test and was diagnosed "allergic to wool." By a real doctor, even. Since then, I've had a heck of a time trying to convince people that my symptoms aren't just in my head.

But they're not. Lots of knitters feel like I do . . . or worse. What complicates this situation is that many knitters are sensitive to the ingredients in wool-based yarn, which can include the wool itself, as well as anything the wool came in contact with—dyes, finishes, soaps, or the animal's natural oils. Anything.

I spoke with Dr. Sandra Gawchik, board-certified allergist, and asked her about what fiber allergies and sensitivities mean for knitters. (Not only is she an expert in her field, but her sister can't tolerate wool and her mom was a knitter.) It seems we're all correct, the yarn stores, our doctors, and our own itchy selves.

There are three basic things going on when you react to wool:

- You're reacting to the microscopically barbed shape of the wool fibers. It's those wee barbs that give wool the properties knitters so deeply adore, and it's those same barbs that make some of us call wool "itchy." If you have the same reaction to other scratchy fibers like coarse linen, this likely applies to you.

- You're reacting to something *in* the wool itself (sort of like when a person is allergic to cats). If you only react to wool (or other animal fibers), this likely applies to you.

- You're reacting to something on the wool, which might be a natural substance (like lanolin) or something the wool has come in contact with (like soaps, finishing treatments, or dyes—natural or not. Who ever said natural = nonirritating? It's not true).

The kinds of reactions differ, too. An irritant reaction happens when the irritating substance comes in contact with the skin. The longer the contact, the worse the reaction.

An allergic reaction happens when a person's immune system overreacts to the presence of a substance. You could touch the substance; you could breathe it in. The more you are exposed to this substance, the worse the allergic reaction will become over time. This reaction can affect your whole body, because your immune system has become involved.

You can experience none of these problems, some of them, or all of them. It's a very complex situation. Dr. Gawchik says there are more than 3,000 different coloring agents used on fiber, and any one of them might be the cause of a person's response. Or several. Or none. It could be what the fiber was processed with (soaps, chemical finishes) or it could be a naturally occurring substance in the fiber (like lanolin for wool).

So, what can you do? I believe the joke goes like this:
    Patient: Doctor, it hurts when I do this.
    Doctor: So don't do that.

Ha ha. But Dr. Gawchik makes it quite clear: our bodies are stubborn and if something irritates it, it irritates it. If it makes our immune system go into overdrive, such is life. You'll just have to avoid it.

She suggests a few basic remedies, if avoidance isn't possible. If you find that touching something causes the reaction, washing your hands as soon as you can is helpful (washing away the irritant, basically). Or try to prevent the irritant from coming in contact with your skin by using cotton gloves or a protective-barrier hand cream.

You could also try a little pseudo-scientific experiment to see if it's just the dyes and/or finishes that are irritating you. All caveats about common sense and consulting your doctor before you do anything that might affect your health apply here. Dr. Gawchik suggests that finding pure, untreated, unwashed, undyed wool yarn would be the first step. If you can knit comfortably with that and wear it, it's possible that your itchies are caused by the dyes or finishes on the wool, rather than the wool itself. If this turns out to be the case, pre-washing some wool yarns with soap that doesn't irritate your skin might help you.

Still, for some of us, no matter what we try, no wool is knittable. Fine by me. I'll stick with silk.

Twist

design by Jillian Moreno

Designer Jillian Moreno says Rowan Summer Tweed is an unpredictable yarn unless you knit it tighter than ball-band gauge. But she loves it for its nubby texture and this tweedy ribbed baby is the result. Follow her pattern and you'll get a rustic silk vest, perfect for any sweater guy (or girl). The silk content makes it a warm layer when the weather turns cool.

A tip: when seaming, you might want to use a color-matched smooth cotton yarn. Summer Tweed can break easily when used for sewing.

Notes

- This pattern is worked with twisted knit stitches on a reverse stockinette stitch background.
- Twisted stitches are worked through their back loops every row (either k1tbl or p1tbl).

Stitch Guide

Seed Stitch

Row 1: *K1, p1; rep from * to end of row, end k1 for odd number of sts.
Row 2: Purl the knits and knit the purls.
Repeat Row 2 for pattern.

Finished Size

About 33½ (37½, 40½, 44, 48, 52½)" (85 [95, 103, 112, 122, 133.5] cm) chest circumference. Vest shown measures 37½" (95 cm).

Yarn

Worsted-weight (CYCA #4 Medium) yarn.
Shown here: Rowan Summer Tweed (70% silk, 30% cotton; 118 yd [108 m]/50 g): #514 reed (light brown tweed), 6 (6, 7, 8, 9, 10) skeins.

Needles

Body—size 6 (4 mm): straight. Edging—size 5 (3.75 mm): straight and 16" (40 cm) circular (cir). Adjust needle size if necessary to obtain the correct gauge.

Notions

Markers (m); stitch holders; tapestry needle.

Gauge

18 stitches and 24 rows = 4" (10 cm) in stockinette stitch on larger needles.

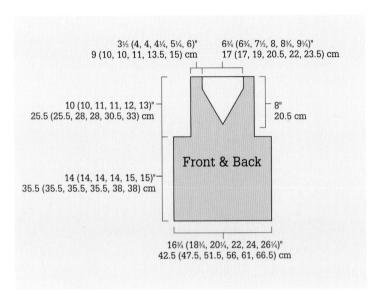

3½ (4, 4, 4¼, 5¼, 6)"
9 (10, 10, 11, 13.5, 15) cm

6¾ (6¾, 7½, 8, 8¾, 9¼)"
17 (17, 19, 20.5, 22, 23.5) cm

10 (10, 11, 11, 12, 13)"
25.5 (25.5, 28, 28, 30.5, 33) cm

8"
20.5 cm

Front & Back

14 (14, 14, 14, 15, 15)"
35.5 (35.5, 35.5, 35.5, 38, 38) cm

16¾ (18¾, 20¼, 22, 24, 26¼)"
42.5 (47.5, 51.5, 56, 61, 66.5) cm

Back

With smaller needles, CO 70 (80, 89, 95, 106, 116) sts. Work in seed st (see Stitch Guide) until piece measures 2" (5 cm) from CO, ending with a RS row. *Inc row:* (WS) Knit, inc 11 (11, 10, 12, 11, 11) sts evenly spaced—81 (91, 99, 107, 117, 127) sts. Change to larger needles. *Set-up row:* (RS) P13 (17, 18, 19, 22, 24), [k1 through back loop (k1tbl), p1] 2 times, k1tbl, p11 (12, 15, 18, 20, 23), k1tbl, p6, [k1tbl, p1] 4 times, k1tbl, p6, k1tbl, p11 (12, 15, 18, 20, 23), [k1tbl, p1] 2 times, k1tbl, purl to end. *Next row:* Work sts as they appear (knit the knits and purl the purls) and *at the same time* work the sts that were k1tbl on previous row as p1tbl. Rep these 2 rows until piece measures 14 (14, 14, 14, 15, 15)" (35.5 [35.5, 35.5, 35.5, 38, 38] cm) from CO, ending with a WS row.

Shape Armholes

BO 7 (10, 12, 13, 12, 12) sts at beg of the next 2 rows—67 (71, 75, 81, 93, 103) sts rem. Cont even in patt as established until armholes measure 10 (10, 11, 11, 12, 13)" (25.5 [25.5, 28, 28, 30.5, 33] cm), ending with a WS row.

Shape Shoulders

Keeping in patt, work 17 (19, 19, 21, 25, 29) sts for right shoulder, join new yarn and BO center 33 (33, 37, 39, 43, 45) sts for back neck, work to end for left shoulder—17 (19, 19, 21, 25, 29) sts each side. Place sts on holders.

Front

CO and work as for back until armholes measure 2 (2, 3, 3, 4, 5)" (5 [5, 7.5, 7.5, 10, 12.5] cm), ending with a WS row—67 (71, 75, 81, 93, 103) sts.

Shape Neck

Keeping in patt, work to center st, place center st on a holder or safety pin, join another ball of yarn and work to end of row—33 (35, 37, 40, 46, 51) sts each side. Working each side separately and maintaining patt as established, dec 1 st at each neck edge every RS row 12 (12, 16, 18, 21, 22) times, then every 4th row 4 (4, 2, 1, 0, 0) time(s)—17 (19, 19, 21, 25, 29) sts rem. Cont even in patt until piece measures same as back to shoulders. Do not BO sts.

Finishing

Place held back shoulder sts on spare needles and, with RS tog, use the three-needle method (see Glossary, page 153) to BO the shoulder sts tog. With yarn threaded on a tapestry needle, sew side seams.

Armhole Edging

With smaller cir needle, RS facing, and beg at side seam, pick up and knit 94 (100, 112, 114, 120, 130) sts around armhole edge. Place marker (pm) and join for working in the rnd. Work in seed st for ½" (1.3 cm). Loosely BO all sts in patt.

Neck Edging

With smaller cir needle, RS facing, and beg at right shoulder seam, pick up and knit 30 (30, 34, 36, 40, 42) sts along back neck, 34 sts along left front neck edge, k1 held center st (leave marker on this st), pick up and knit 34 sts along right front neck edge—99 (99, 103, 105, 109, 111) sts total. Pm and join for working in the rnd. *Next rnd:* Work in seed st to 1 st before marked center st, k3tog or p3tog as needed to maintain patt, work to end of rnd in seed st—2 sts dec'd. Rep this rnd 2 more times—93 (93, 97, 99, 103, 105) sts rem. Loosely BO all sts in patt.

Weave in loose ends. Pin vest to measurements and spritz with water. Allow to air-dry completely before removing pins.

The Myth of the Center-Pull Ball

It sounds so tantalizing, doesn't it? A tidy cake of yarn with a single neat strand waving up at you from its enticing middle. "Pull me," it seems to say. And, I mean, we've named the thing a "center-pull ball." Shouldn't we be pulling the yarn from the center?

No. With few exceptions, a nonwool center-pull ball where you actually pull the yarn from the center is the first step to your own canvas jacket with sleeves that buckle in the back. Don't do it.

What makes a center-pull ball work is the natural attraction of each strand of yarn to any other strand it touches. The fibers want to stick together, so even as the hole in the center of the ball gets bigger and bigger, the outer core keeps its shape until the very end. That makes for an enjoyable center-pull ball experience. This works brilliantly with wool and other animal fibers—and some nonwools like crunchy silk.

But for most nonwools, this rarely happens. The first few inches . . . maybe even yards . . . will pull out of the center, lulling you into believing you're smarter than the rest of us and ha-ha-ha! But trust me . . . there's just not enough tooth for the outer part of the ball to hold together, and what you will soon run into, especially with something as slippery as rayon or shimmery silk, is a collapsed mess that not only tangles on itself but gets maddeningly knotted as well.

Don't risk it, unless you love untangling knots. Pull nonwool yarns from the outside of the ball. I promise it will be better for your mental health.

Bespoke

design by Libby Baker

Designer Libby Baker loves the texture, flow, and crisp feel of linen. For her tailored, classic coat, she chose an affordable cotton/linen blend that gives heft, drape, and crispness without pomposity. Added bonus: the blend is a little easier on the hands than pure linen, which helps when you're knitting this much fabric. Libby recommends a gentle, cold machine wash to even out the stitches, stop the edges from curling, and maximize drape. For stubborn curly spots, try a little steam.

Notes

- Work all decreases in this pattern as follows:
  When working a decrease at the beginning of a row: if the first stitch in pattern would have been a knit, then work the decrease as follows: Sl 2 sts to right needle, lift second st up and over first st and off the needle, bring yarn from back of work around selvedge and across front of decreased st (decreased st will be wrapped by working yarn). Otherwise, work k2tog as written.
  When working a decrease at the end of a row: if the second-to-last st in pattern would have been a slipped st, then work the decrease as follows: Bring yarn to front, sl last st up and over second-to-last st and off the needle, sl last st to right needle, bring yarn across front of decreased st and around selvedge to back. Otherwise, work ssk (see Glossary, page 154) as written.

Finished Size
36 (40, 44, 48, 52, 56)" (91.5 [101.5, 112, 122, 132, 142] cm) bust circumference, buttoned. Coat shown measures 36" (91.5 cm).

Yarn
Worsted-weight (CYCA #4 Medium) yarn.
Shown here: GGH Linova (74% cotton, 26% linen; 109 yd [100 m]/50 g): #16 charcoal, 26 (29, 31, 34, 39, 43) skeins. Yarn is used double throughout.

Needles
Size 7 (4.5 mm): 32" (80 cm) circular (cir). Adjust needle size if necessary to obtain the correct gauge.

Notions
Stitch holder; tapestry needle; three 1" (2.5 cm) buttons.

Gauge
16 stitches and 33 rows = 4" (10 cm) in half linen stitch with yarn held double.

Stitch Guide

Half Linen Stitch (multiple of 2 stitches)

Row 1: (WS) Purl.

Row 2: *K1, sl 1 purlwise with yarn in front (pwise wyf); rep from * to end of row.

Row 3: Purl.

Row 4: *Sl 1 pwise wyf, k1; rep from * to end of row.

Repeat Rows 1–4 for pattern.

Back

Right Tail

With 2 strands of yarn held tog, CO 42 (46, 50, 54, 58, 62) sts. Beg with WS Row 1, work half linen stitch (see Stitch Guide) until piece measures 3½" (9 cm) from CO, ending with a WS row. *Dec row:* (RS) K2tog, work to end of row in patt—1 st dec'd. Work 29 rows even in patt. Rep the last 30 rows 2 more times, then work dec row once more. *At the same time*, when piece measures 6" (15 cm) from CO, ending with a RS row, place sts on holder (shaping will cont after tails are joined).

Left Tail

CO and work as for right tail until piece measures 3½" (9 cm) from CO, ending with a WS row. *Dec row:* (RS) Work in patt as established to last 2 sts, ssk (see Glossary, page 154)—1 st dec'd. Work 29 rows even in patt. Rep the last 30 rows 2 more times, then work dec row once more. *At the same time*, when piece measures 6" (15 cm) from CO, ending with a RS row, join tails as foll.

Join Tails

Place right tail sts on spare needle. With WS facing, purl to last 4 sts of left tail, place needle holding right tail sts in front of and parallel to needle holding left tail sts, [purl the next left tail st tog with the next right tail st] 4 times, purl to end of right tail sts—78 (86, 94, 102, 110, 118) sts. Cont in patt until all shaping is complete—72 (80, 88, 96, 104, 112) sts rem. Cont even in patt until piece measures 19½ (19½, 19½, 19½, 21, 21)" (49.5 [49.5, 49.5, 49.5, 53.5, 53.5] cm) from CO, ending with a WS row.

Shape Armholes

Cont in patt, BO 2 (3, 4, 6, 6, 7) sts at beg of next 2 rows—68 (74, 80, 84, 92, 98) sts rem. *Next row:* (RS)

K2tog, work in patt to last 2 sts, ssk—2 sts dec'd. Work 1 WS row even. Rep the last 2 rows 2 (2, 4, 6, 7, 8) more times—62 (68, 70, 70, 76, 80) sts rem. Cont even in patt until armholes measure 9½ (9½, 9½, 10, 10½, 11)" (24 [24, 24, 25.5, 26.5, 28] cm), ending with a WS row.

Shape Shoulders

Cont in patt, BO 10 sts at beg of next 2 rows, then BO 9 (11, 12, 12, 13, 14) sts at beg of foll 2 rows— 24 (26, 26, 26, 30, 32) sts rem. BO all sts.

Right Front

With 2 strands of yarn held tog, CO 44 (48, 52, 56, 60, 64) sts. Beg with WS Row 1, work half linen st until piece measures 3½" (9 cm) from CO, ending with a WS row. *Dec row:* (RS) Work in patt to last 2 sts, ssk—1 st

dec'd. Work 29 rows even in patt. Rep the last 30 rows 2 more times, then work dec row once more—40 (44, 48, 52, 56, 60) sts rem. *At the same time*, when piece measures 8½ (8, 8, 8, 9, 9)" (21.5 [20.5, 20.5, 20.5, 23, 23] cm) from CO, ending with a WS row, work buttonholes as foll. *Buttonhole row:* (RS) Work 3 sts in patt, BO 2 sts, work in patt to end of row. *Next row:* (WS) Purl to gap made by BO sts on previous row, use the backward loop method (see Glossary, page 153) to CO 2 sts over gap to complete buttonhole, purl to end. Cont even in patt until piece measures 5 (5, 5, 5, 5½, 5½)" (12.5 [12.5, 12.5, 12.5, 14, 14] cm) from buttonhole. Make another buttonhole, then work 5 (5, 5, 5, 5½, 5½)" (12.5 [12.5, 12.5, 12.5, 14, 14] cm) even, ending with a WS row—2 buttonholes; piece measures about 18½ (18, 18, 18, 20, 20)" (47 [45.5, 45.5, 45.5, 51, 51] cm) from CO.

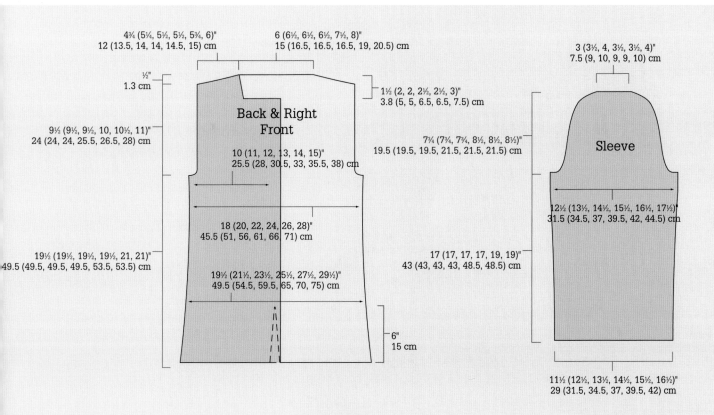

Shape Lapel

Note: The lapel and armhole shaping are worked at the same time; read through the following sections before proceeding. (RS) P2, k1, work buttonhole as before, work to end of row in patt. *Next row:* (WS) Cont in patt, work to gap formed on previous row, CO 2 sts as before, p1, work rem 2 sts as for RS Row 2 of half linen st—2 sts in half linen st for lapel. *Next row:* (RS) P2, work in patt to end of row. *Next row:* (WS) Purl to last 2 sts, work 2 sts as for next RS row of half linen st. Keeping in patt, rep these 2 rows once more. *Next row:* (RS) P3, work to end in patt as established. *Next row:* (WS) Purl to last 3 sts, work 3 sts as for next RS row of half linen st—3 sts in half linen st for lapel. Cont in this manner, adding 1 st to half linen st patt at lapel every 6th row 11 more times, ending with a WS row—14 sts in half linen st for lapel. Work 4 rows even in patt, ending with a WS row—6 rows total with 14 lapel sts.

Shape Armhole

At the same time, when piece measures about 19½ (19½, 19½, 19½, 21, 21)" (49.5 [49.5, 49.5, 49.5, 53.5, 53.5] cm) from CO, shape armhole as foll: With WS facing, BO 2 (3, 4, 6, 6, 7) sts, work to end—38 (41, 44, 46, 50, 53) sts rem. *Next row:* (RS) Cont in patt to last 2 sts, ssk—1 st dec'd. Work 1 WS row even. Rep the last 2 rows 2 (2, 4, 6, 7, 8) more times—35 (38, 39, 39, 42, 44) sts rem. Cont even in patt until lapel shaping is complete.

Shape Neck

With RS facing and cont in patt, BO 15 sts, work to end of row—20 (23, 24, 24, 27, 29) sts rem. Work 5 (5, 5, 5, 3, 3) rows even in patt. *Next row:* (RS) K2tog, work in patt to end of row—1 st dec'd. Rep the last 6 (6, 6, 6, 4, 4) rows 0 (1, 1, 1, 3, 4) more time(s)—19 (21, 22, 22, 23, 24) sts rem. Work even in patt until armhole measures 9½ (9½, 9½, 10, 10½, 11)" (24 [24, 24, 25.5, 26.5, 28] cm), ending with a RS row.

Shape Shoulder

Cont in patt, at armhole edge (beg of WS rows), BO 10 sts once, then BO rem 9 (11, 12, 12, 13, 14) sts.

Left Front

With 2 strands of yarn held tog, CO 44 (48, 52, 56, 60, 64) sts. Work as for right front until piece measures 3½" (9 cm) from CO, ending with a WS row. *Dec row:* (RS) K2tog, work to end of row in patt—1 st dec'd. Work 29 rows even in patt. Rep the last 30 rows 2 more times, then work dec row once more—40 (44, 48, 52, 56, 60) sts rem. Work even in patt until piece measures 8½ (8, 8, 8, 9, 9)" (21.5 [20.5, 20.5, 20.5, 23, 23] cm) from CO, ending with a WS row. Mark button placement as foll: work in patt to last 4 sts, mark edge with safety pin or waste yarn, work to end. Repeat button marking every 5 (5, 5, 5, 5½, 5½)" (12.5 [12.5, 12.5, 12.5, 14, 14] cm) 2 more times, and *at the same time,* on the last button marking row, shape lapel as foll:

Shape Lapel

Note: The lapel and armhole shaping are worked at the same time; read through the following sections before proceeding. With RS facing, work to last 4 sts, mark button placement, work to last 2 sts, p2. *Next row:* (WS) Work 2 sts as for RS Row 2 of half linen st, purl to end of row—2 sts in half linen st for lapel. *Next row:* (RS) Work in patt to last 2 sts, p2. *Next row:* (WS) Work 2 sts as for next RS row of half linen st, purl to end of row. Rep the last 2 rows once more. *Next row:* (RS) Work in patt to last 3 sts, p3. *Next row:* (WS) Work 3 sts as for next RS row of half linen st, purl to end—3 sts in half linen st for lapel. Cont in this manner, adding 1 st to half linen st patt at lapel every 6th row 11 more times, ending with a WS row—14 sts in half linen st for lapel. Work 3 rows even in patt, ending with a RS row—5 rows total with 14 lapel sts.

Shape Armhole

At the same time, when piece measures about 19½ (19½, 19½, 19½, 21, 21)" (49.5 [49.5, 49.5, 49.5, 53.5, 53.5] cm) from CO, shape armhole as foll: With RS facing, BO 2 (3, 4, 6, 6, 7) sts, work to end—38 (41, 44, 46, 50, 53) sts rem. Work 1 WS row even. *Next row:* (RS) K2tog, work in patt to end of row—1 st dec'd. Work 1 WS row even. Rep the last 2 rows 2 (2, 4, 6, 7, 8) more times—35 (38, 39, 39, 42, 44) sts rem. Cont even in patt until lapel shaping is complete.

Shape Neck

With WS facing and cont in patt, BO 15 sts, work to end of row—20 (23, 24, 24, 27, 29) sts rem. Work 6 (6, 6, 6, 4, 4) rows even in patt. *Next row:* (RS) Work in patt to last 2 sts, ssk—1 st dec'd. Rep the last 6 (6, 6, 6, 4, 4) rows 0 (1, 1, 1, 3, 4) more time(s)—19 (21, 22, 22, 23, 24) sts rem. Work even in patt until armhole measures 9½ (9½, 9½, 10, 10½, 11)" (24 [24, 24, 25.5, 26.5, 28] cm), ending with a WS row.

Shape Shoulder

Cont in patt, at armhole edge (beg of RS rows), BO 10 sts once, then BO rem 9 (11, 12, 12, 13, 14) sts.

Sleeves

With 2 strands of yarn held tog, CO 46 (50, 54, 58, 62, 66) sts. Beg with WS Row 1, work half linen st until piece measures 7" (18 cm) from CO, ending with a WS row. *Inc row:* (RS) K1f&b, work in patt to last st, k1f&b—2 sts inc'd. Work even in patt until piece measures 5" (12.5 cm) from Inc row. Rep Inc row—50 (54, 58, 62, 66, 70) sts. Cont even in patt until piece measures 17 (17, 17, 17, 19, 19)" (43 [43, 43, 43, 48.5, 48.5] cm) from CO, ending with a WS row.

Shape Cap

BO 2 (3, 4, 6, 6, 7) sts at beg of next 2 rows—46 (48, 50, 50, 54, 56) sts rem. Dec 1 st each end of needle every RS row 5 times, then every 8th row 5 (5, 5, 6, 6, 6) times—26 (28, 30, 28, 32, 34) sts rem. Work 5 rows even. Dec 1 st each end of needle—24 (26, 28, 26, 30, 32) sts rem. Work 1 WS row even. BO 3 (3, 3, 3, 4, 4) sts at beg of next 4 rows—12 (14, 16, 14, 14, 16) sts rem. BO rem sts.

Finishing

With single strand of yarn threaded on a tapestry needle, sew shoulder seams.

Collar

With 2 strands of yarn held tog, RS facing, and beg at top of lapel on right front neck, pick up and knit 46 (48, 50, 52, 56, 58) sts evenly spaced along front neck edge, across back neck, and down opposite front edge to top of lapel. Beg with RS row of half linen st (WS of coat is RS of collar), work as foll: K1f&b, work in patt to last st, k1f&b—2 sts inc'd. Purl 1 row. Rep the last 2 rows 4 more times—56 (58, 60, 62, 66, 68) sts. Cont even in patt until collar measures 3½" (9 cm) from pick-up at back neck, ending with a WS row. With RS facing, loosely BO all sts in patt.

Pockets (optional)

With single strand of yarn, sew side seams from bottom edge for 6 (6, 6, 6, 7, 7)" (15 [15, 15, 15, 18, 18] cm) to bottom of pocket opening. With RS facing and 2 strands of yarn held tog, pick up and knit 24 sts along the back side edge of coat, beg at top of side seam. Purl 1 WS row. *Next row:* (RS) K1f&b, work in half linen st to last st, k1f&b—26 sts. Cont even in patt until pocket measures 5" (12.5 cm) from pick-up row. BO all sts.
With single strand of yarn, sew sleeve caps into armholes. Sew angled edge of collar to top (BO edge) of lapel. Sew side seam from pockets to armholes. Sew sleeve seams. Sew pockets to front inside of coat. Sew buttons at markers opposite buttonholes.

The Needle Fuss Factor

I've heard more than one knitter say they hate a specific type of needle. For every one of those people, there's someone else who loves that particular needle. There is no right or wrong here. Needle preference is as personal a thing as you can get, right up there with boxers or briefs, cotton or Lycra. There's no way I'm gonna tell you what you should use. But I do have a few pointy tips to share if things aren't going as well as you'd hoped.

All needles are not created equal. That includes all needles made of the same material. You will find brand-loyal knitters who have tried every type of bamboo straight they can get their hands on, but will only use Acme brand, because they like it best.

Nonwool yarns are not all the same either, even if made of the same fiber or blend. There are slippery nonwools and there are sticky ones. There are two different kinds of silk, for example. Your nonwool knitting experience will be very different depending on what your chosen yarn is made of, how it's spun, and what you're knitting it on.

Straights or circulars? It's up to you. But when it comes to circulars, you can't just consider the material the tips are made out of; the cables can be sticky or slippery, flexible or rigid, and you'll need to experiment to figure which ones make you happiest. And if the transition from needle tip to cable isn't a smooth one, even the best tip won't save a circular.

Yes, needles are a fussy business.

My Rule of Thumb for Needles

Contrast. I find the most enjoyable knitting experience comes when I pair a slippery yarn with needles that have some traction like bamboo, casein, resin, or wood. For sticky yarns, there are a variety of types and brands of metal needles, each having its own charms. Get to know them all.
Sticky yarn: use slippery needles.
Slippery yarn: use needles with traction.

But what if you've tried every possible needle material short of pulling out your own femur and whittling it down to a point at one end, and still you can't knit a specific yarn comfortably? Get this: Try a longer needle. Whether you knit on straights or circulars, having too many stitches on your needle can make it seem like the stitches are sticking when they're really just overcrowded. Really, this works. Try it.

River Rock Scarf

design by Sivia Harding

Inspired by water flowing around pebbles in a bubbling creek, the River Rock Scarf does not pretend to be an exact imitation of nature, although the sumptuous silk yarn does indeed flow like water around the beaded rocks.

Designer Sivia Harding loves beads and knitting them with slippery Silken presented a challenge . . . the beads wouldn't stay where she put them. She added twisted knit stitches and voilà, stationary rocks, just like in nature.

Stitch Guide

Place Bead (PB)
Slide the specified number of beads next to the last stitch worked, then continue knitting as usual, leaving the beads resting between the knitted stitches.

Beaded River Rock Pattern (worked over 2 sts)
Row 1: (RS) K1 through back loop (k1tbl), PB1, k1tbl.
Row 2: (WS) P1, PB2, p1.
Row 3: K1tbl, PB4, k1tbl.
Row 4: P1, PB4, p1.
Row 5: K1tbl, PB2, k1tbl.
Row 6: P1, PB1, p1.
Work Rows 1–6 for each "rock."

Finished Size
About 8" (20.5 cm) wide and 60" (152.5 cm) long.

Yarn
Sportweight (CYCA #2 Fine) yarn.
Shown here: Handmaiden Silken (100% silk; 273 yd [250 m]/100 g): glacier (aqua), 2 skeins.

Needles
Size 7 (4.5 mm). Adjust needle size if necessary to obtain the correct gauge.

Notions
1,534 [(89 rocks × 14 beads/rock) + 144 beads for each end] size 6/0 berry-lined light topaz seed beads (available at earthfaire.com); Big-Eye beading needle (available at bead and craft stores) or dental floss threader (available at drug stores); markers (m); tapestry needle.

Gauge
26½ stitches and 24 rows = 4" (10 cm) in k2, p2 rib, unblocked and slightly stretched.

Notes

- For stringing beads, use a Big-Eye beading needle or a dental floss threader (used to thread floss around braces and bridges). To use a dental floss threader, pass the knitting yarn through the loop of the threader, then pick up beads with the opposite end of the threader and slide the beads over the loop and onto the yarn.

- Because each skein of handpainted yarn is different, alternate between two balls every two rows to minimize color differences. To keep the openwork side sections free, change yarns just inside the second side marker, making sure not to pull too tightly on the yarn, and twisting the two yarns around each other on the wrong side to prevent holes from forming at the yarn changes.

- The beading technique used for the "rocks" is an easy variation of the beaded rib used at the ends of the scarf. Simply increase, then decrease the number of beads placed in the center of a rib, twisting the knit stitches on the right side of the work to keep the beads in place. Each rock requires 14 beads. Because each "rock" is formed on a single rib, you can easily create several in the same row, as there are 12 ribs in which to place "rocks." Use the placement provided in the chart or make up your own arrangement, but adjust the number of beads accordingly if you make changes.

- On the chart, one row represents six rows of knitting, and one pink line represents two rows of knitting (see chart key).

RIVER ROCK

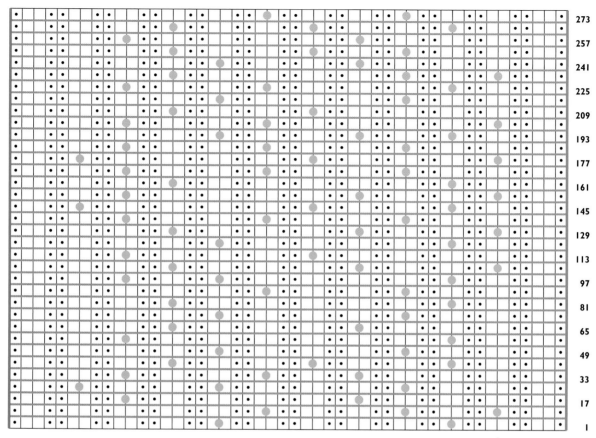

273
257
241
225
209
193
177
161
145
129
113
97
81
65
49
33
17
1

☐	knit on RS; purl on WS
⊡	purl on RS; knit on WS
◉	beaded river rock patt (worked over 6 rows, see Stitch Guide)
—	2 rows in rib
❘	marker position

Scarf

Thread 767 seed beads onto each ball of yarn. With one of the balls, CO 56 sts. Alternating 2 rows each of 2 balls of yarn (See Notes), work beaded rib patt as foll:

Row 1: (RS) K2, yo, k2tog, place marker (pm), p1, *k1, PB1, k1, p2; rep from * to last 7 sts, k1, PB1, k1, p1, change to other ball of yarn, pm, k2, yo, k2tog.

Row 2: (WS) K2, yo, k2tog, slip marker (sl m), k1, *p1, PB1, p1, k2; rep from * to last 7 sts, p1, PB1, p1, k1, sl m, k2, yo, k2tog. Rep Rows 1 and 2 five more times (12 rows total). Cont in rib patt as established (without placing beads) for 6 more rows—

when viewed from the RS, there will be 12 beaded ribs. Work Rows 1—278 of River Rock chart, working the beaded patt (see Stitch Guide) over the 2 sts of each "rock" rib for 6 rows, and working all other sts in rib as established for those 6 rows. Work 2 rows of plain rib between each section of "rocks," shown on the chart as pink lines. After chart is complete, work 6 rows of plain rib (without placing beads). Work 12 rows of beaded rib as for beg of scarf. Loosely BO all sts.

Finishing

Weave in loose ends.

Manly Maze

design by Celeste Culpepper

Men are hard to knit for. (The male knitters and sweater-wearers I know agree.) But what guy wouldn't be intrigued by a sweater made from hemp? When they put this one on, they may not want to take it off. But when they do, the best news is that they can toss it in the washer and then in the dryer, and it just gets softer and softer.

Notes

- This sweater is knitted from the top down in the round.
- Hemp, like linen, has very little elasticity. When washed and blocked, hemp will "relax" and once stretched to size will remain at this size. A washed and blocked sample swatch is a must to make sure that you obtain gauge.
- In order to create the neck shaping, the sweater is knitted back and forth for the first several inches. The neckband is worked last.
- Directions are given for a straight body and a tapered body.

Finished Size

About 36¼ (38, 42, 46, 50, 54)" (92 [96.5, 106.5, 117, 127, 137] cm) chest measurement. Sweater shown measures 38" (96.5 cm).

Yarn

DK-weight (CYCA #3 Light) yarn. *Shown here:* Hemp for Knitting Allhemp6 (100% hemp; 150 yd [137 m]/92 g): marble (dark teal; MC), 7 (7, 8, 9, 10, 11) skeins; sprout (lime green; CC), 1 skein (all sizes). *Note:* For a nontapered body, you'll need 7 (8, 9, 9, 11, 12) skeins of MC.

Needles

Body—sizes 3, 4, and 5 (3.25, 3.5, and 3.75 mm): 24" (60 cm) circular (cir). Sleeves—size 5 (3.75): set of 5 double-pointed (dpn) for all sizes; size 4 (3.5 mm): set of 5 dpn for sizes 36¼ (38, 46)" only. Neckband—size 3 (3.25 mm): 16" (40 cm) cir. Adjust needle size if necessary to obtain the correct. gauge.

Notions

Markers (m), one of which is a unique color; stitch holders or waste yarn; tapestry needle.

Gauge

21 stitches and 26 rounds = 4" (10 cm) in stockinette stitch on largest needle after washing and blocking.

MAZE

V	•	V	•	V	•	V	•	•	•	•	•	•	•	
+	V	+	V	+	V	+	V	+	+	+	+	+	+	15
•	•	V	•	V	•	V	•	V	•	•	•	•	•	
+	+	V	+	V	+	V	+	V	+	+	+	+	+	13
•	•	•	•	V	•	V	•	V	•	V	•	•	•	
+	+	+	+	+	V	+	V	+	V	+	V	+	+	11
•	•	•	•	•	•	V	•	V	•	V	•	V	•	
+	+	+	+	+	+	+	V	+	V	+	V	+	V	9
V	•	V	•	V	•	V	•	•	•	•	•	•	V	
+	V	+	V	+	V	+	+	+	+	+	+	+	V	7
•	•	V	•	V	•	V	•	•	•	•	•	•	V	
+	V	+	V	+	+	+	+	+	+	+	+	+	V	5
V	•	V	•	•	•	V	•	V	•	V	•	•	•	
+	V	+	+	+	+	+	+	+	V	+	V	+	V	3
V	•	•	•	•	•	V	•	V	•	V	•	•	•	
+	+	+	+	+	+	+	V	+	V	+	V	+	V	1

V	sl 1 pwise with yarn in back (wyb)
•	k using MC
+	k using CC
☐	pattern repeat

Upper Body

With middle-size cir needle and using the long-tail method (see Glossary, page 153), CO 71 (72, 74, 76, 78, 80) sts, placing markers (pm) as foll: CO 2 sts for right front, pm, CO 16 sts for right sleeve, pm, CO 35 (36, 38, 40, 42, 44) sts for back, pm (use a unique color for this marker), CO 16 sts for left sleeve, pm, CO 2 sts for left front. Do not join. Work back and forth in rows as foll:

Row 1: (RS) K1f&b (see Glossary, page 156), *knit to
    next m, use the backward loop method (see Glossary,
    page 153) to CO 1 st, slip marker (sl m), k1, CO 1 st;
    rep from * to last st, k1f&b—10 sts inc'd.
Row 2: Purl.

Rep these 2 rows 3 (4, 5, 6, 6, 7) more times—111 (122, 134, 146, 148, 160) sts. *Next row:* Rep Row 1 and at the

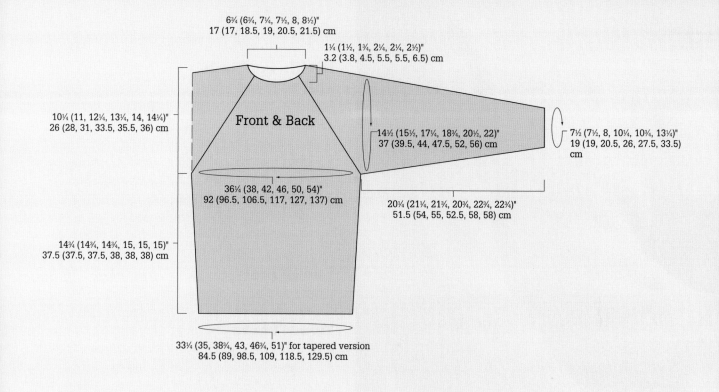

6¾ (6¾, 7¼, 7½, 8, 8½)"
17 (17, 18.5, 19, 20.5, 21.5) cm

1¼ (1½, 1¾, 2¼, 2¼, 2½)"
3.2 (3.8, 4.5, 5.5, 5.5, 6.5) cm

10¼ (11, 12¼, 13¼, 14, 14¼)"
26 (28, 31, 33.5, 35.5, 36) cm

Front & Back

14½ (15½, 17¼, 18¾, 20½, 22)"
37 (39.5, 44, 47.5, 52, 56) cm

7½ (7½, 8, 10¼, 10¾, 13¼)"
19 (19, 20.5, 26, 27.5, 33.5) cm

36¼ (38, 42, 46, 50, 54)"
92 (96.5, 106.5, 117, 127, 137) cm

20¼ (21¼, 21¾, 20¾, 22¾, 22¾)"
51.5 (54, 55, 52.5, 58, 58) cm

14¾ (14¾, 14¾, 15, 15, 15)"
37.5 (37.5, 37.5, 38, 38, 38) cm

33¼ (35, 38¾, 43, 46¾, 51)" for tapered version
84.5 (89, 98.5, 109, 118.5, 129.5) cm

end of this row, use the backward loop method to CO 21 (20, 20, 20, 22, 22) sts—142 (152, 164, 176, 180, 192) sts total; 45 (48, 52, 56, 58, 62) sts each for back and front, 26 (28, 30, 32, 32, 34) sts for each sleeve. Cut yarn. With RS facing, slip sts to unique-colored m, which denotes new beg of rnd (at the left back shoulder). Change to largest 24" (60 cm) cir needle and join for working in the rnd, being careful not to twist, as foll: Rejoin yarn at unique-color m and knit 1 rnd even, ending at the same m. Cont in rnds, inc 1 st each side of each m as foll:

Rnd 1: *K1, CO 1 st, knit to next m, CO 1 st, sl m; rep from * to end of rnd—8 sts inc'd.

Rnd 2: Knit.

Rep these 2 rnds 18 (18, 20, 22, 25, 27) more times—294 (304, 332, 360, 388, 416) sts total; 83 (86, 94, 102, 110, 118) sts for back. Work the foll 2 rnds a total of 0 (1, 1, 1, 1, 1) time for sleeve increases:

Rnd 3: *Knit to next m, sl m, k1, CO 1 st, knit to next marker, CO 1 st, sl m; rep from * to end of rnd—4 sts inc'd.

Rnd 4: Knit.

There will be 294 (308, 336, 364, 392, 420) sts total; 83 (86, 94, 102, 110, 118) sts each for back and front, 64 (68, 74, 80, 86, 92) sts for each sleeve. Join CC and work Rnds 1–16 of Maze chart once, pm after each 14-st rep. Note that the slip-stitch patt will pull in, but will stretch back out after washing and blocking. With MC, knit 3 (3, 5, 6, 5, 1) rnd(s) (work more or fewer rnds here to lengthen or shorten the upper body as desired), and on the last rnd remove all but the unique-color m.

Divide For Body and Sleeves

Remove m, *k83 (86, 94, 102, 110, 118) sts for back, place next 64 (68, 74, 80, 86, 92) sts for sleeve on a holder or waste yarn, use the provisional method (see Glossary, page 154) to CO 6 (7, 8, 10, 11, 12) sts for underarm, pm, CO 6 (7, 8, 9, 10, 12) more sts for same underarm; rep from * once more—190 (200, 220, 242, 262, 284) sts total; markers denote side seams; last m placed denotes beg of rnd.

Lower Body

Choose a tapered or straight body.

Tapered Version

Knit 19 rnds even (work more or fewer rnds here to make the sweater longer or shorter). *Dec rnd:* *K1, k2tog, knit to 2 sts before next m, ssk (see Glossary, page 154), sl m; rep from * once—4 sts dec'd. Rep the last 20 rnds 3 more times—174 (184, 204, 226, 246, 268) sts rem. *Next rnd:* Dec 2 (0, 0, 2, 2, 0) sts evenly spaced—172 (184, 204, 224, 244, 268) sts rem; piece measures about 12½" (31.5 cm) from armhole.

Straight Version

Knit every rnd until piece measures 12¼" (31 cm) from armhole. *Next rnd:* Dec 10 (8, 8, 10, 10, 8) sts evenly spaced—180 (192, 212, 232, 252, 276) sts rem.

Ribbing

Change to smallest 24" (60 cm) cir needle. *K3, p1; rep from * to end of rnd. Rep this rnd for 2¼ (2¼, 2¼, 2½, 2½, 2½") (5.5 [5.5, 5.5, 6.5, 6.5, 6.5] cm). BO all sts purlwise. Cut yarn, leaving a 12" (30.5 cm) tail. Thread tail on a tapestry needle and use it to neaten the join between beg and end of rnd.

Sleeves

Carefully remove waste yarn from provisional CO and evenly distribute 12 (14, 16, 19, 21, 24) underarm sts and 64 (68, 74, 80, 86, 92) held sleeve sts on 4 largest-size dpn—76 (82, 90, 99, 107, 116) sts total. Arrange sts so that there is a break between needles at the center of the underarm sts. Rnd begins at center of underarm. Join MC. Dec 1 st at beg and end of rnd every 6th rnd 17 (8, 7, 0, 8, 0) times, then every 5th rnd 0 (12, 14, 21, 14, 23) times, as foll: K1, k2tog, knit to last 2 sts, ssk—42 (42, 48, 57, 63, 70) sts rem. *Next rnd:* Dec 0 (0, 6, 1, 7, 0) st(s) evenly spaced, and *at the same time* pm after every 14 sts—42 (42, 42, 56, 56, 70) sts rem. Work even until piece measures 17½ (18½, 19, 18, 20, 20)" (44.5 [47, 48.5, 45.5, 51, 51] cm) from armhole.

For sizes 36¼, 38, and 46 only: Change to middle-size needles.

For all sizes: Cont as foll: Join CC and work Rnds 1–16 of Maze chart.

For sizes 36¼, 38, and 46 only: Change to largest needles.

For all sizes: With MC, knit 2 rnds, removing all but beg m—piece measures about 20¼ (21¼, 21¾, 20¾, 22¾, 22¾)" (51.5 [54, 55, 52.5, 58, 58] cm) from armhole. Do not cut yarn. Use the I-cord method to BO all sts as foll: With RS facing and using the knitted method (see Glossary, page 153), CO 3 sts onto left needle. K2, ssk. *Do not turn work, sl 3 sts from right needle to left needle, carry working yarn tightly across back of work, k2, ssk; rep from * until no sleeve sts rem. Do not turn work, carry yarn across back of work, k1, k2tog—2 sts rem. Do not turn work, carry yarn across back of work, k2tog—1 st rem. Cut yarn, leaving a 12" (30.5 cm)

tail. Thread tail on a tapestry needle, bring it through last st, and use it to join the ends of the I-cord band.

Finishing

Neckband

With MC, smallest 16" (40 cm) cir needle, RS facing, and beg at left back shoulder, pick up and knit 16 sts across left shoulder, 12 (14, 15, 16, 16, 17) sts along left front, 21 (20, 20, 20, 22, 22) sts across center front, 12 (14, 15, 16, 16, 17) sts along right front, 16 sts across right shoulder, and 35 (36, 38, 40, 42, 44) sts across back—112 (116, 120, 124, 128, 132) sts total. Pm and join for working in the rnd. *K3, p1; rep from * to end of rnd. Rep this rnd until neckband measures 1 (1, 1¼, 1¼, 1½, 1½)" (2.5 [2.5, 3.2, 3.2, 3.8, 3.8] cm). BO all sts in patt. Cut yarn, leaving a 12" (30.5 cm) tail. Thread tail on a tapestry needle and use it to neaten up join between beg and end of rnd.

Note: The neckband may roll outward, but will lie flat after being washed and blocked.

Weave in loose ends. Block to measurements.

Sweet Indulgence

design by Deb White

This exquisite-but-simple silk robe is knitted in the most intriguing of silk yarns—a bulky-weight shimmery silk from Classic Elite. Softer than belief and possibly the knitted definition of extravagance, it's styled timelessly so that it will last as long as you do, and may be the first thing your heirs fight over when it's time to split up your stuff.

    This robe takes full advantage of the indulgent silk yarn, and doesn't trick you into knitting a useless belt . . . how would it stay tied? Instead, it's fastened with a single button.

Notes

- Silk yarn will catch on every rough surface—apply hand cream often and be sure to use smooth stitch markers (plastic markers are recommended).
- The yarn is very slippery and will collapse on itself if wound on a ball winder. Wind the yarn by hand and use a yarn bra to prevent tangles.
- Change balls of yarn at the transition from ribbing to stockinette stitch (not at the end and not in the middle of a row). This makes it easier to disguise the thick spot where the tails are woven in.
- Use a sharp tapestry needle when sewing in loose ends and skim the needle through the purl bumps along the back of the fabric. For extra security, sew back through the yarn end a few times.

Finished Size

About 39½ (42¾, 47½, 53¼, 58¼, 64)" (100.5 [108.5, 120.5, 135, 148, 162.5] cm) circumference around chest/bust, from right front overlap to left front overlap. Back measures about 15½ (17¼, 19½, 21¾, 24, 26¼)" (39.5 [44, 49.5, 55, 61, 66.5] cm) wide at underarm. Robe shown measures 42¾" (108.5 cm).

Yarn

Chunky weight (CYCA #5 Bulky) yarn. *Shown here:* Classic Elite Temptation (100% silk; 110 yd [101 m]/100 g): #17 green, 10 (11, 13, 14, 16, 18) skeins.

Needles

Size 9 (5.5 mm): 16" and 32" (40 and 80 cm) circular (cir). Adjust needle size if necessary to obtain the correct gauge.

Notions

Stitch holders; markers (m); tapestry needle; one 1½" (3.8 cm) or larger button; one ¾" (2 cm) facing button; sewing needle and thread.

Gauge

14 stitches and 20 rows = 4" (10 cm) in stockinette stitch, blocked; 16 stitches and 18 rows = 4" (10 cm) in stockinette stitch, unblocked.

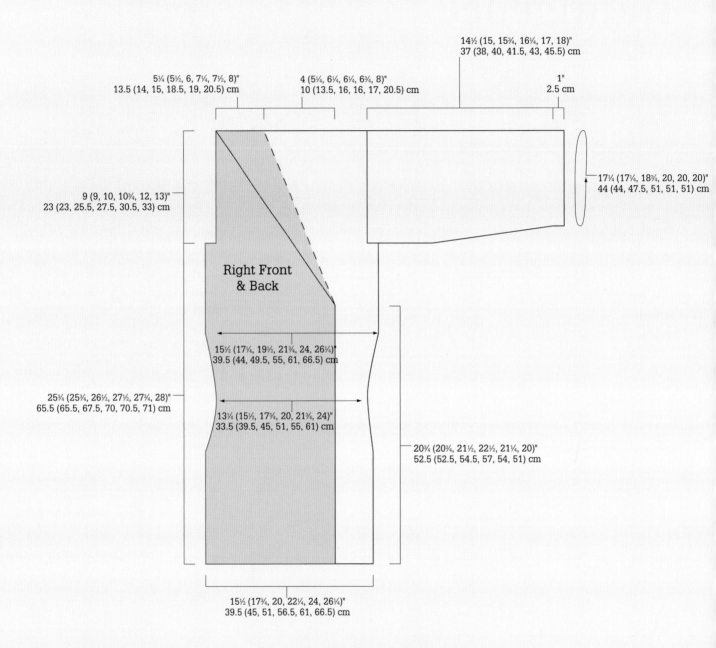

5¼ (5½, 6, 7¼, 7½, 8)"
13.5 (14, 15, 18.5, 19, 20.5) cm

4 (5¼, 6¼, 6¼, 6¾, 8)"
10 (13.5, 16, 16, 17, 20.5) cm

14½ (15, 15¾, 16¼, 17, 18)"
37 (38, 40, 41.5, 43, 45.5) cm

1"
2.5 cm

9 (9, 10, 10¾, 12, 13)"
23 (23, 25.5, 27.5, 30.5, 33) cm

17¼ (17¼, 18¾, 20, 20, 20)"
44 (44, 47.5, 51, 51, 51) cm

Right Front
& Back

15½ (17¼, 19½, 21¾, 24, 26¼)"
39.5 (44, 49.5, 55, 61, 66.5) cm

25¾ (25¾, 26½, 27½, 27¾, 28)"
65.5 (65.5, 67.5, 70, 70.5, 71) cm

13¼ (15½, 17¾, 20, 21¾, 24)"
33.5 (39.5, 45, 51, 55, 61) cm

20¾ (20¾, 21½, 22½, 21¼, 20)"
52.5 (52.5, 54.5, 57, 54, 51) cm

15½ (17¾, 20, 22¼, 24, 26¼)"
39.5 (45, 51, 56.5, 61, 66.5) cm

All measurements shown after blocking.

Body

With longer needle and holding 2 strands of yarn tog, CO 139 (155, 171, 191, 205, 225) sts. Work 2 rows with 2 strands of yarn as foll:

Row 1: (RS) *K1, p1; rep from * to last st, k1.

Row 2: (WS) *P1, k1; rep from * to last st, p1.

Cut off 1 strand of yarn, leaving a 6" (15 cm) tail to weave in later. Cont with 1 strand of yarn. *Next row:* (RS) [K1, p1] 2 times (edge sts), knit to last 4 sts, working k2tog once along the way, [p1, k1] 2 times (edge sts)—138 (154, 170, 190, 204, 224) sts rem. Cont as established, working edge sts in k1, p1 rib as established and center 130 (146, 162, 182, 196, 216) sts in St st, until piece measures 10 (10, 11, 12, 12½, 13)" (25.5 [25.5, 28, 30.5, 31.5, 33] cm) from CO, unblocked, ending with a WS row. Piece will block to measure about 9 (9, 10, 10¾, 11¼, 11¾)" (23 [23, 25.5, 27.5, 28.5, 30] cm).

Shape Waist

(RS) Work 42 (46, 50, 56, 60, 66) sts as established for right front, place marker (pm), k54 (62, 70, 78, 84, 92) for back, pm, work to end as established for left front. Work 1 WS row even as established. *Dec row:* (RS) *Work to 3 sts before m, k2tog, k1, slip marker (sl m), k1, ssk (see Glossary, page 154); rep from * once, work to end of row—4 sts dec'd. Work 3 rows even. Rep the last 4 rows 3 more times—122 (138, 154, 174, 188, 208) sts rem. Cont even, maintaining border sts, until piece measures about 16 (16, 17, 18, 18½, 19)" (40.5 [40.5, 43, 45.5, 47, 48.5] cm) from CO, unblocked, ending with a WS row. Piece will block to measure about 14½ (14½, 15¼, 16¼, 16¾, 17)" (37 [37, 38.5, 41.5, 42.5, 43] cm). *Inc row:* (RS) *Work to 2 sts before m, k1f&b (see Glossary, page 156), k1, sl m, k1, k1f&b; rep from * once, work to end of row—4 sts inc'd. Work 3 rows even. Rep the last 4 rows 3 (2, 2, 2, 3, 3) more times—138 (150, 166, 186, 204, 224) sts. Keeping markers in place, cont even as established until piece measures 23 (23, 24, 25, 23½, 22¼)" (58.5 [58.5, 61, 63.5, 59.5, 56.5] cm) from CO, unblocked, ending with a WS row. Piece will block to measure about 20¾ (20¾, 21½, 22½, 21¼, 20)" (52.5 [52.5, 54.5, 57, 54, 51] cm).

Nasty, Stinky Ends

Ends aren't much of a problem for people who knit with wool. I'm forced to mention this again (my apologies): woolly fibers have a natural sticking-togetherness that nonwool fibers don't. So when you weave in an end of wool yarn, it wants to stay where you put it. When it comes to nonwools, we're often talking about slippery stuff.

*Pierce

Here are my best tips for weaving in ends without the benefit of tooth:

- Start new balls of yarn at the edge of a piece, so you can weave the ends into the seams of the garment. It's a little wasteful of yarn sometimes, but when you're dealing with the thick, the slippery, the bulky, and the awkward, it might be your best option.

- Be sure the piece is really finished before you try this next technique. For slippery silk yarns, especially when knitted in a lace pattern, use a sharp-pointed yarn needle and split-backstitch the ends in place. Sew the first few stitches the same as you'd normally do when weaving in ends; tuck them somewhere secure with several stitches. Then, pierce each previous finishing stitch with the needle and complete a new stitch. You're locking the yarn into itself. Do this several times, then snip the end closely.

- When using a thick tape yarn like Colinette Wigwam, you may be forced to tie square knots. If the fabric you've knit is solid, and you make the knot tiny and unobtrusive, it really shouldn't show on the right side.

- For a more sophisticated approach, overlap the ends of ribbon or tape yarns and secure with tiny stitches in a color-matched strong sewing thread. Laborious? No kidding. But it won't come undone.

Shape Lapels

With RS facing, work 4 border sts, k1, p1, knit to last 6 sts, p1, k1, work 4 border sts—there are now 6 border sts at each edge. Add 2 sts to border sts on each edge in this manner every 6th row 8 (9, 10, 11, 12, 14) more times—22 (24, 26, 28, 30, 34) border sts each edge. *At the same time*, when piece measures 28½ (28½, 29½, 30½, 30¾, 31)" (72.5 [72.5, 75, 77.5, 78, 78.5] cm) from CO, unblocked, ending with a WS row, work next RS row as foll: *work to 2 (2, 2, 2, 4, 4) sts before m, BO 2 (2, 2, 2, 4, 4) sts, remove m, BO 2 (2, 2, 2, 4, 4) sts; rep from * once, work to end of row—130 (142, 158, 178, 188, 208) sts rem; 40 (43, 47, 53, 56, 62) sts for each front, 50 (56, 64, 72, 76, 84) sts for back. Do not cut yarn; this ball will be used to work the left front later.

Back

With WS facing, join new ball of yarn and work 50 (56, 64, 72, 76, 84) back sts until piece measures 10 (10, 11, 12, 13¼, 14½)" (25.5 [25.5, 28, 30.5, 33.5, 37] cm) from dividing row, unblocked. Piece will block to measure about 9 (9, 10, 10¾, 12, 13)" (23 [23, 25.5, 27.5, 30.5, 33] cm). Place sts on holder or waste yarn. Cut yarn.

Left Front

With WS facing and beg with yarn already attached to left front, cont to inc border sts until there are 22 (24, 26, 28, 30, 34) border sts—18 (19, 21, 25, 26, 28) sts rem in St st. *At the same time,* when armhole measures 7¼ (7¼, 8, 8¼, 9¼, 10½)" (18.5 [18.5, 20.5, 21, 23.5, 26.5] cm), unblocked, ending with a WS row, work short-rows (see Glossary, page 157) to shape lapel as foll:

Row 1: (RS) Work 26 (27, 29, 33, 34, 36) sts, wrap next st, turn work.

Rows 2, 4, 6, 8, and 10: (WS) Work to end of row.

Row 3: Work 24 (25, 27, 31, 32, 34) sts, wrap next st, turn.

Row 5: Work 22 (23, 25, 29, 30, 32) sts, wrap next st, turn.

Row 7: Work 20 (21, 23, 27, 28, 30) sts, wrap next st, turn.

Row 9: Work 18 (19, 21, 25, 26, 28) sts, wrap next st, turn.

Row 11: Work to end of row, working wrapped sts tog with their wraps.

Cont even until armhole measures same as back. Place 22 (24, 26, 28, 30, 34) border sts on a holder—18 (19, 21, 25, 26, 28) sts rem for shoulder. With RS tog and using the three-needle method (see Glossary, page 153), BO the front and back shoulder sts tog.

Right Front

With WS facing, join yarn to right front. Work as for left front, reversing shaping (i.e., beg short-rows on WS rows).

Collar

With RS facing and longer needle, work across 22 (24, 26, 28, 30, 34) held right front sts in k1, p1 rib as established, pick up and knit (see Glossary, page 157) 2 sts at top of shoulder, *k1, p1; rep from * across 14 (18, 22, 22, 24, 28) back sts and *at the same time* dec 1 st by substituting k2tog for a k1, pick up and knit 2 sts at other shoulder seam, work rem 22 (24, 26, 28, 30, 34) front sts in k1, p1 rib as established—61 (69, 77, 81, 87, 99) sts total. Work even in rib as established until collar measures 10" (25.5 cm) from pick-up row. BO all sts loosely in patt.

Sleeves

With shorter needle, RS facing, and beg at base of armhole, pick up and knit 68 (68, 74, 78, 90, 98) sts around armhole as foll: pick up and knit 2 (2, 2, 2, 4, 4) sts along BO edge, then pick up about 2 sts for every 3 rows to 2 rows before top of shoulder, pick up and knit 1 st in each row for 4 rows, then pick up and knit 2 sts for every 3 rows to armhole, and 2 (2, 2, 2, 4, 4) sts along armhole BO. Pm and join for working in the rnd. Cont in St st until piece measures 6" (15 cm) from pick-up rnd, unblocked; piece will block to measure about 5½" (14 cm). *Dec rnd:* K1, ssk, knit to last 3 sts, k2tog, k1—2 sts dec'd. Work 6 (6, 6, 6, 4, 3) rnds even. Rep the last 7 (7, 7, 7, 5, 4) rnds 3 (3, 3, 3, 9, 13) more times—60 (60, 66, 70, 70, 70) sts rem. Cont even until piece measures about 16 (16¾, 17½, 18, 19, 20)" (40.5 [42.5, 44.5, 45.5, 48.5, 51] cm), unblocked. Piece will block to measure about 14½ (15, 15¾, 16¼, 17, 18)" (37 [38, 40, 41.5, 43, 45.5] cm). Join a second strand of yarn and work in k1, p1 rib for 2 rnds. BO all sts in patt.

Finishing

Sew in loose ends (see Notes). Lay garment on thick towels and wet-block by spritzing heavily with cool water, patting into shape, then allowing to air-dry. Try on the garment. Mark desired placement of button loop with a safety pin. With a tapestry needle threaded with 2 strands of yarn, make a 2½" (6.5 cm) loop on the right edge of the front at button loop marker, taking care to attach the loop firmly to the robe. With a single strand of yarn, work a series of buttonhole sts (see Glossary, page 155) around the yarn loop. Try on the garment again and mark the desired button placement on the left front (adjust as necessary to achieve the best overlap). Place the small button on the WS of the left front and the large decorative button on the RS, and with matching sewing thread and needle, sew the two together through the left front.

The Bag

design by Wendy Wonnacott

Designer Wendy Wonnacott is well known on the Web for her beautiful knitted bag patterns. She pays attention to detail unlike anyone else, and now she's turned her cotton-loving design eye to hemp. For The Bag, the zing comes from a simple mirror-image slip-stitch pattern knitted in cinnamon and pumpkin hemp. The fabric, though lightweight, has a solid feel to it, like something that will last for ages (with the right care, of course)—especially if you don't skip the finishing touches like lining the bag. When you've knitted something this good looking, those last steps are not optional.

Notes

- The handle is 7½" (19 cm) long when relaxed but will stretch comfortably to about 12" (30.5 cm) when worn over the shoulder.
- All stitches are slipped as if to purl with the yarn held in back of the work.

Bag

With waste yarn, MC, cir needle, and using the provisional method (see Glossary, page 154), CO 165 sts. Place marker (pm) and join for working in the rnd, being careful not to twist sts.

Facing

Cont with MC, knit 12 rnds. *Inc rnd:* K1, [M1, k7] 11 times, k2, [M1, k7] 12 times, k1—188 sts.

Handle Slits

P12, *p2tog, yo 2 times, p2tog, p39, p2tog, yo 2 times, p2tog, p29*, p18, rep from * to * once, p6.

Finished Size
About 11½" (29 cm) wide, 9" (23 cm) tall (excluding handle), and 3" (7.5 cm) deep.

Yarn
DK-weight (CYCA #3 Light) yarn.
Shown here: Hemp for Knitting Allhemp6 (100% hemp; 150 yd [137 m]/92 g): cinnamon (brown; MC) and pumpkin (orange; CC), 2 skeins each.

Needles
Size 4 (3.5 mm): 24" (60 cm) circular (cir) plus 1 spare needle of similar size. Adjust needle size if necessary to obtain the correct gauge.

Notions
Marker (m); a few yards (meters) of waste yarn for CO; tapestry needle; sharp-point sewing needle and matching thread; lining fabric measuring 30 × 12" (76 × 30.5 cm); fabric to cover bottom support measuring 12 × 7" (30.5 × 18 cm); fusible interfacing measuring 30 × 12" (76 × 30.5 cm); cardboard or stiff canvas for bottom support measuring 11 × 3" (28 × 7.5 cm).

Gauge
22 stitches and 28 rounds = 4" (10 cm) in stockinette stitch worked in the round; 26 stitches and 57 rounds = 4" (10 cm) in slip-stitch pattern worked in the round.

Upper Pattern

Note: On the first rep of Rnd 1, work the double yo of the previous rnd as k1, p1tbl. Join CC. Work slip st patt as foll:

Rnd 1: (CC) [K1, sl 1, k1] 10 times, *[k1, sl 1] 2 times, k3, [sl 1, k1] 2 times, [k1, sl 1, k1] 12 times; rep from * 2 more times, [k1, sl 1] 2 times, k3, [sl 1, k1] 2 times, [k1, sl 1, k1] 2 times.

Rnd 2: [P1, sl 1, p1] 10 times, *[p1, sl 1] 2 times, p3, [sl 1, p1] 2 times, [p1, sl 1, p1] 12 times; rep from * 2 more times, [p1, sl 1] 2 times, p3, [sl 1, p1] 2 times, [p1, sl 1, p1] 2 times.

Rnd 3: (MC) [Sl 1, k2] 10 times, sl 1, k3, sl 1, k1, sl 1, k3, sl 1, *[k2, sl 1] 12 times, sl 1, k3, sl 1, k1, sl 1, k3, sl 1*, [sl 1, k2] 12 times, sl 1, k3, sl 1, k1, sl 1, k3, sl 1, rep from * to * once, [sl 1, k2] 2 times.

Rnd 4: [Sl 1, p2] 10 times, sl 1, p3, sl 1, p1, sl 1, p3, sl 1, *[p2, sl 1] 12 times, sl 1, p3, sl 1, p1, sl 1, p3, sl 1*, [sl 1, p2] 12 times, sl 1, p3, sl 1, p1, sl 1, p3, sl 1, rep from * to * once, [sl 1, p2] 2 times.

Rnd 5 (CC): [K2, sl 1] 13 times, k2, *[sl 1, k2] 12 times, [k2, sl 1] 3 times, k2*, [k2, sl 1] 15 times, k2, rep from * to * once, [k2, sl 1] 2 times.

Rnd 6: [P2, sl 1] 13 times, p2, *[sl 1, p2] 12 times, [p2, sl 1] 3 times, p2*, [p2, sl 1] 15 times, p2, rep from * to * once, [p2, sl 1] 2 times.

Rnd 7: With MC, rep Rnd 1.

Rnd 8: With MC, rep Rnd 2.

Rnd 9: With CC, rep Rnd 3.

Rnd 10: With CC, rep Rnd 4.

Rnd 11: With MC, rep Rnd 5.

Rnd 12: With MC, rep Rnd 6.

Rep Rnds 1–12 five more times, changing colors as specified—piece measures about 5" (12.5 cm) from beg of patt.

Lower Pattern

Cont as foll:

Rnd 1: (CC) [Sl 1, k2] 10 times, sl 1, k3, sl 1, k1, sl 1, k3, sl 1, *[k2, sl 1] 12 times, sl 1, k3, sl 1, k1, sl 1, k3, sl 1*, [sl 1, k2] 12 times, sl 1, k3, sl 1, k1, sl 1, k3, sl 1, rep from * to * once, [sl 1, k2] 2 times.

Rnd 2: [S1, p2] 10 times, sl 1, p3, sl 1, p1, sl 1, p3, sl 1, *[p2, sl 1] 12 times, sl 1, p3, sl 1, p1, sl 1, p3, sl 1*, [sl 1, p2] 12 times, sl 1, p3, sl 1, p1, sl 1, p3, sl 1, rep from * to * once, [sl 1, p2] 2 times.

Rnd 3: (MC) [K1, sl 1, k1] 10 times, *[k1, sl 1] 2 times, k3, [sl 1, k1] 2 times, [k1, sl 1, k1] 12 times; rep from * 2 more times, [k1, sl 1] 2 times, k3, [sl 1, k1] 2 times, [k1, sl 1, k1] 2 times.

Rnd 4: [P1, sl 1, p1] 10 times, *[p1, sl 1] 2 times, p3, [sl 1, p1] 2 times, [p1, sl 1, p1] 12 times; rep from * 2 more times, [p1, sl 1] 2 times, p3, [sl 1, p1] 2 times, [p1, sl 1, p1] 2 times.

Rnd 5: (CC) [K2, sl 1] 13 times, k2, *[sl 1, k2] 12 times, [k2, sl 1] 3 times, k2*, [k2, sl 1] 15 times, k2, rep from * to * once, [k2, sl 1] 2 times.

Rnd 6: [P2, sl 1] 13 times, p2, *[sl 1, p2] 12 times, [p2, sl 1] 3 times, p2*, [p2, sl 1] 15 times, p2, rep from * to * once, [p2, sl 1] 2 times.

Rnds 7 and 8: With MC, rep Rnds 1 and 2.

Rnds 9 and 10: With CC, rep Rnds 3 and 4.

Rnds 11 and 12: With MC, rep Rnds 5 and 6.

Rep Rnds 1–12 six more times, changing colors as specified—piece measures about 11" (28 cm) from beg of upper patt. Cut yarns. Slip 11 sts from right-hand needle tip to left-hand needle tip. Turn work inside out so that RS of bag face tog and needle tips are parallel to each other. With MC, use the three-needle method (see Glossary, page 153) to BO sts.

Finishing

Handles (make 2)

With CC, CO 6 sts. Work in garter st (knit every row) until piece measures 11" (28 cm) from CO. *Next row:* [K2tog] 3 times—3 sts rem. Wrap working yarn counterclockwise around these 3 sts 4 times. [K1f&b (see Glossary, page 156)] 3 times—6 sts.* Cont in garter st until piece measures 19" (48.5 cm) from wraps. Rep from * to * once. Cont in garter st until piece measures 11" (28 cm) from second set of wraps. BO all sts.

Weave in loose ends. Wash bag by machine to loft fibers, and allow to air-dry completely. Lay bag flat, fold facing to inside of bag, and measure length and width. Record these numbers for use in cutting the lining fabric. Remove waste yarn from provisional CO and carefully place live sts on cir needle. With MC, BO these sts, keeping even tension to avoid puckering.

Sew Gussets

Turn bag WS out. Open bottom of bag flat and position so that bottom seam meets bag side edge, forming a triangle at lower corner of bag. Measure 3" (7.5 cm) from corner along bottom seam. With MC threaded on a tapestry needle, sew a straight seam from fold to fold, crossing the 3" (7.5 cm) mark on bottom seam as shown above. Tack gusset point to bottom seam. Repeat for second gusset.

Attach Handles

Insert handles by rolling the bottom edges of handles, then pulling the rolled ends through the handle slots to the inside of the bag, aligning the wraps with the handle slots and making sure not to twist the handles. With CC threaded on a tapestry needle, sew handles to bag body on inside of bag.

Bottom Support

Use scissors to round the corners on the cardboard or

Gussets

Open bottom of bag flat and position so that bottom seam meets bag side edge, forming a triangle at lower corner of bag. Measure 3" (7.5 cm) from corner along bottom seam. With MC threaded on a tapestry needle, sew a straight seam from fold to fold, crossing the 3" (7.5 cm) mark on bottom seam.

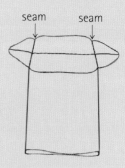

canvas bottom support. Fold the smaller piece of lining fabric in half lengthwise, insert the support between the layers, then sew lining fabric together.

Lining

For best results consult the bag's flat measurements before sewing lining. Apply interfacing to WS of lining fabric. To allow for ½" (1.3 cm) seam allowance, cut lining fabric to twice width of bag plus 1" (2.5 cm), and height of bag plus 1" (2.5 cm). (For example, if bag measures 14½" [37 cm] wide by 9" [23 cm] tall, cut lining fabric to 30" [76 cm] wide by 10" [25.5 cm] tall.) Fold lining fabric in half with RS tog. Sew a ½" (1.3 cm) seam allowance along the side and bottom edges, leaving top edge open. Trim excess fabric from seam allowances. Sew 3" (7.5 cm) gussets as for bag. Tack gusset points to bottom seam. Insert bottom support into bag, then insert lining into bag so that WS of lining faces WS of bag. Fold down ½" (1.3 cm) seam allowance at top of bag so that seam allowance falls between bag and lining. Fold down bag facing to cover top of lining. Pin into place. With sewing thread and sharp-point sewing needle, sew lining in place through all layers along bottom of facing.

He and She Ganseys

design by Jeannine Sims

Ganseys are the coolest things. Texture without fuss, and so comfy, who could refuse? Designer Jeannine Sims made one for him and one for her. The He Gansey is quite clever . . . cotton mixed with super-stretchy poly makes this sweater hold its shape sheeplessly. It's a woolless classic! For the women who like the look, a hint: this yarn comes in a ton of great colors.

The She Gansey is slimmer fitting and incorporates waist shaping, a more body-conscious fit, and a slightly cropped length. The yarn is just a little nuts, in a good way. It's a cotton/elastic blend that's full of texture, spring, and hints of subtle color. It looks almost wispy in the ball, but knits into a firm, stretchy, comfy fabric. Because this yarn is so full of texture, the patterning in the She Gansey is much more subtle, made with more openwork than textured stitches. Me, I want one of each.

Stitch Guide

Selvedge Stitches
When noted, work selvedge st as foll:
RS Rows: Sl 1 knitwise, work in patt to last st, p1.
WS Rows: Sl 1 knitwise, work to end of row in patt.

Double Moss Stitch (multiple of 4 sts)
Rows 1 and 2: *K2, p2; rep from * to end of row.
Rows 3 and 4: *P2, k2; rep from * to end of row.
Repeat Rows 1–4 for pattern.

Finished Size
38 (41½, 45¼, 49, 52¾, 58¼)" (96.5 [105.5, 115, 124.5, 134, 148] cm) chest circumference. Sweater shown measures 41½" (105.5 cm).
She Gansey: 33¾ (35¾, 41¼, 44¾, 49¼, 54¾)" (85.5 [90.5, 105, 113.5, 125, 139] cm) bust circumference. Sweater shown measures 35¾" (90.5 cm).

Yarn
Worsted-weight (CYCA #4 Medium) yarn.
Shown here: Schulana Supercotton (70% cotton, 30% polyester; 98 yd [90 m]/50 g): #22 taupe, 15 (16, 19, 22, 24, 26) skeins.
She Gansey: Artful Yarns Candy (64% cotton, 32% acrylic, 3% nylon, 1% elastic; 119 yd [109 m]/50 g): #9351 toffee, 13 (15, 17, 19, 23, 26) skeins (used double).

Needles
He Gansey: Size 10 (6 mm): 16" and 24" (40 and 60 cm) circular (cir) and set of 4 or 5 double-pointed (dpn).
She Gansey: Size 8 (5 mm): 16" and 24" (40 and 60 cm) circular (cir) and set of 4 or 5 double-pointed (dpn). Adjust needle size if necessary to obtain the correct gauge.

Notions
Markers (m); stitch holders or waste yarn; tapestry needle.

Gauge
He Gansey: 17 stitches and 24 rounds = 4" (10 cm) in stockinette stitch, worked in the round.
She Gansey: 17½ stitches and 27 rounds = 4" (10 cm) in stockinette stitch, worked in the round, with 2 strands of yarn held together.

Notes

- The garter stitch welts for the front and back of the He Gansey are worked flat, then joined together.
- For both versions, the body is worked in the round to the armholes, with gusset stitches added at the underarms. The front and back are then worked separately to the shoulders, which are joined with a three-needle bind-off. Stitches for the sleeves are picked up around the armholes and worked downward to the cuffs.

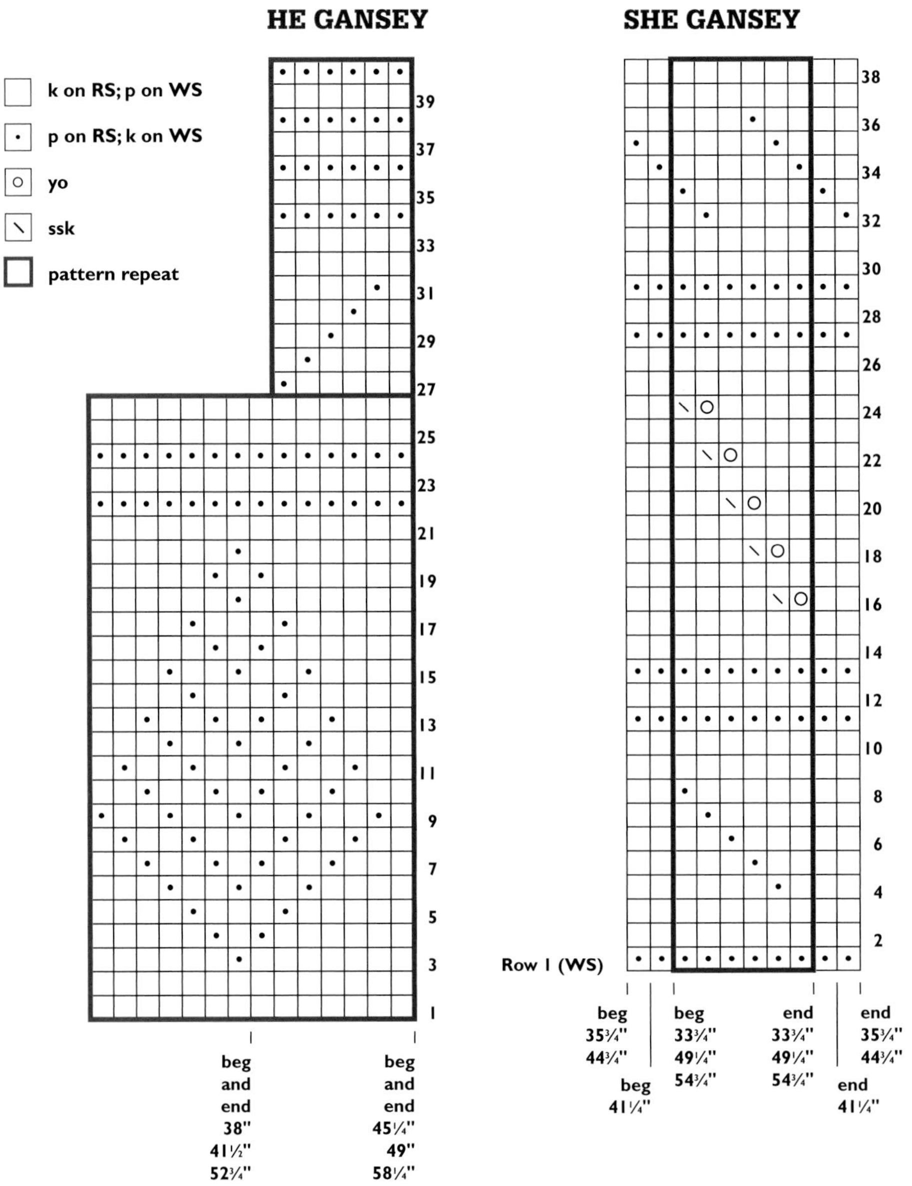

HE GANSEY
SHE GANSEY
k on RS; p on WS
p on RS; k on WS
yo
ssk
pattern repeat
Row 1 (WS)
beg and end 38" 41½" 52¾"
beg and end 45¼" 49" 58¼"
beg 35¾" 44¾"
beg 41¼"
beg 33¾" 49¼" 54¾"
end 33¾" 49¼" 54¾"
end 35¾" 44¾"
end 41¼"

He Gansey
Body
Welts

With longer cir needle, CO 75 (82, 89, 96, 104, 116) sts.
Working back and forth in rows, knit 18 rows (9 garter
ridges). Place sts on holder; this will be the back welt.
Make another welt to match but leave sts on needle; this
will be the front welt.

Join for Body

Knit to last st of front welt, place back welt sts on a
spare needle and hold it behind the front welt, place
marker (pm) to denote side "seam," k2tog (1 st from front
welt tog with 1 st from back welt), pm, work to last st
of back welt, pm to denote side "seam," place first st of
front welt in front of last st of back welt and k2tog, pm to
denote end of rnd—148 (162, 176, 190, 206, 230) sts total.
Next rnd: Knit to first m and *at the same time* inc 7 (7,
8, 9, 9, 9) sts evenly spaced, slip marker (sl m), p1, sl m,
knit to next marker and *at the same time* inc 7 (7, 8, 9, 9,
9) sts evenly spaced, sl m, p1, sl m—162 (176, 192, 208,
224, 248) sts total. The individual sts between markers
are seam sts; work them in seed st (alternate rows of
knitting and purling them). Cont even as established
until piece measures 12 (11½, 12, 13, 13, 13)" (30.5 [29,
30.5, 33, 33, 33] cm) from CO.

Shape Gussets

*Knit to side seam m, sl m, M1R (see Glossary, page
156), k1, M1L (see Glossary, page 156), sl m; rep from *
once more—3 sts bet markers at each side "seam."
Next rnd: *Knit to m, sl m, p1, k1, p1; rep from * once
more. *Next rnd:* *Knit to m, sl m, k3, sl m; rep from * once
more. *Inc rnd:* *Knit to m, sl m, work 1 st in seed st, M1R,
knit to 1 st before next m, M1L, work 1 st in seed st,
sl m; rep from * once more—2 sts inc'd bet markers each
side. Work 2 rnds even. Rep the last 3 rnds 4 (5, 6, 6, 6, 6)
more times—13 (15, 17, 17, 17, 17) sts bet markers; piece
measures about 15 (15, 16, 17, 17, 17)" (38 [38, 40.5, 43,
43, 43] cm) from CO.

Back

Working the back sts back and forth in rows and working the first and last st as selvedge sts (see Stitch Guide), purl 1 row and *at the same time* inc 2 (inc 3, inc 3, dec 1, inc 3, inc 3) st(s) evenly spaced—82 (90, 98, 102, 114, 126) sts. Knit 5 rows, purl 1 (WS) row, then knit 4 rows. Work in double moss st (see Stitch Guide), maintaining selvedge sts, until armholes measure 9 (9, 10¾, 11¾, 12¼, 12½)" (23 [23, 27.5, 30, 31, 31.5] cm), ending with a WS row. Knit 6 rows—3 garter ridges. Place sts on holder.

Front

With WS facing, join yarn at right underarm. Working back and forth in rows and working the first and last st as selvedge sts, purl 1 row and *at the same time* inc 2 (inc 3, inc 3, dec 1, inc 3, inc 3) st(s) evenly spaced—82 (90, 98, 102, 114, 126) sts. Knit 5 rows, purl 1 (WS) row, then knit 4 rows. Work in double moss st, maintaining selvedge sts, until armholes measure 4 (4, 5¾, 6¾, 7¼, 7½)" (10 [10, 14.5, 17, 18.5, 19] cm), ending with a WS row. Knit 4 rows, inc 4 (dec 4, inc 2, dec 2, inc 0, inc 2) sts evenly spaced on first row—86 (86, 100, 100, 114, 128) sts. Working first and last st as selvedge sts and beg and ending as indicated for your size, work center 84 (84, 98, 98, 112, 126) sts according to Rows 1–26 of He Gansey chart—armholes measure about 7¾ (7¾, 9½, 10½, 11, 11¼)" (19.5 [19.5, 24, 26.5, 28, 28.5] cm).

Shape Neck

Mark center 14 (16, 18, 18, 26, 28) sts for front neck. With RS facing and cont with Row 27 of chart, work to 3 sts before marked center sts, k2tog, k1, place center 14 (16, 18, 18, 26, 28) sts on holder, join new ball of yarn and k1, ssk, work in patt to end—35 (34, 40, 40, 43, 49) sts rem each side. Working each side separately and cont to work chart, dec 1 st at neck edge as before every RS row 6 more

Divide for Front and Back

K80 (87, 95, 103, 111, 123) front sts, place 13 (15, 17, 17, 17, 17) gusset sts on a holder, join new ball of yarn and k80 (87, 95, 103, 111, 123) back sts, place rem 13 (15, 17, 17, 17, 17) gusset sts on another holder.

times—29 (28, 34, 34, 37, 43) sts rem each side. Work last row of chart.

Join Shoulders

Place 29 (28, 34, 34, 37, 43) left back shoulder sts on a spare needle, and with WS tog, use the three-needle method (see Glossary, page 153) to BO the left front and back shoulder sts tog. Rep for right shoulder. Place rem 24 (34, 30, 34, 40, 40) sts on a holder for back neck.

Sleeves

With shorter cir needle, RS facing, and beg at base of armhole, pick up and knit 80 (88, 96, 104, 114, 120) sts evenly spaced around armhole opening, pm to denote beg of rnd, then work 13 (15, 17, 17, 17, 17) held gusset sts as foll: work 1 st in seed st for seam st, k11 (13, 15, 15, 15, 15), work 1 st in seed st, pm, purl to end of rnd—93 (103, 113, 121, 131, 137) sts total. Sl markers every rnd. Work gusset sts in St st, seam sts in seed st, and rem sts in double moss st. *Dec rnd:* Work 1 st in seed st, ssk, knit to last 3 sts of gusset, k2tog, work 1 st in seed st, ssk, work in patt to last 2 sts, k2tog—4 sts dec'd. Work 2 rnds even in patt. Rep the last 3 rnds 4 (5, 6, 6, 6, 6) more times— 3 gusset sts rem. *Next rnd:* Sl 1, k2tog, psso, remove m, ssk, work in patt to last 2 sts, k2tog—1 gusset st and 68 (74, 80, 88, 98, 104) double moss sts rem. Discontinue seed st; work all sts in double moss st. *Next rnd:* Ssk, work to last 2 sts, k2tog—2 sts dec'd. Work 3 rnds even. Rep the last 4 rnds 14 (16, 17, 19, 23, 25) more times—39 (41, 45, 49, 51, 53) sts rem. Work even until sleeve measures 15½ (16½, 17½, 18, 20, 20)" (39.5 [42, 44.5, 45.5, 51, 51] cm) from pick-up rnd. *Next rnd:* Knit, dec 5 (5, 5, 7, 7, 7) sts evenly spaced— 34 (36, 40, 42, 44, 46) sts rem. Work in garter st (alternate purl 1 rnd, knit 1 rnd) for 8 rnds—4 garter ridges. Loosely BO all sts purlwise.

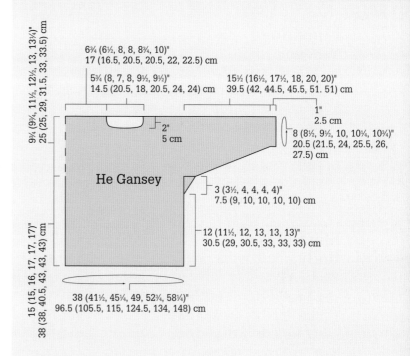

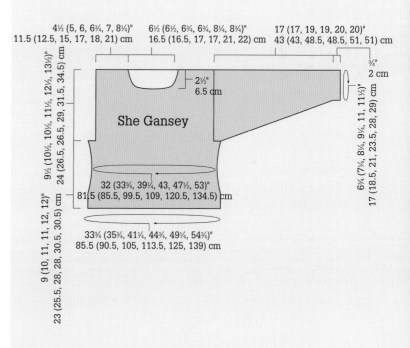

101

Finishing
Neckband
Place 24 (34, 30, 34, 40, 40) held back sts onto shorter cir needle. With RS facing and beg at left shoulder, pick up and knit 14 sts to held front neck sts, k14 (16, 18, 18, 26, 28) held front neck sts, pick up and knit 14 sts to right shoulder—66 (78, 76, 80, 94, 96) sts total. Work in k1, p1 rib for 4 rnds. Change to St st and work even until neckband measures 2" (5 cm) from pick-up rnd. Loosely BO all sts. Weave in loose ends. Block lightly to measurements.

She Gansey
Body
Welt
With longer cir needle and holding 2 strands tog, CO 132 (140, 162, 176, 196, 220) sts. Place marker (pm) and join for working in the rnd, being careful not to twist sts. [Knit 1 rnd, purl 1 rnd] 3 times—3 garter ridges.

Lower Body
Knit 1 rnd, inc 16 (16, 18, 20, 20, 20) sts evenly spaced—148 (156, 180, 196, 216, 240) sts. *Next rnd:* Yo, ssk, work 72 (76, 88, 96, 106, 118) sts for front, pm for side seam, yo, ssk, work to end for back—74 (78, 90, 98, 108, 120) sts each for front and back. Slip markers every rnd. Knit 1 rnd even. *Next rnd:* *Yo, ssk, knit to marker; rep from *. Rep these 2 rnds to armhole and *at the same time,* when piece measures 2" (5 cm) from CO, shape waist as foll:

Shape Waist
Dec 1 st before and after each side seam openwork detail by working ssk after each side seam and k2tog before each side seam every 12th rnd 2 times—140 (148, 172, 188, 208, 232) sts rem. Inc 1 st before and after each side seam openwork detail by working a lifted increase (see Glossary, page 156) every 12th rnd 2 times—148 (156, 180, 196, 216, 240) sts. Cont even, working side seam sts as established, until piece measures 9 (10, 11, 11, 12, 12)" (23 [25.5, 28, 28, 30.5, 30.5] cm) from CO or desired length to armholes.

Divide for Front and Back
Work to 2 (2, 3, 3, 4, 4) sts before first m, place next 6 (6, 8, 8, 10, 10) sts on holder (centering the yo, ssk openwork detail), join a new ball of yarn, knit to 2 (2, 3, 3, 4, 4) sts before next marker, place next 6 (6, 8, 8, 10, 10) sts on holder (centering the yo, ssk openwork detail)—68 (72, 82, 90, 98, 110) sts rem each for front and back.

Back
Work the 68 (72, 82, 90, 98, 110) back sts back and forth in rows, working the first and last st as selvedge sts (see Stitch Guide), and cont even until armholes measure 9 (10, 10, 11, 12, 13)" (23 [25.5, 25.5, 28, 30.5, 33] cm), ending with a WS row. Knit 4 rows, ending with a WS row—2 garter ridges. Place sts on holder.

Front
Rejoin yarn to 68 (72, 82, 90, 98, 110) front sts and cont back and forth in rows, working the first and last st as selvedge sts and center 66 (70, 80, 88, 96, 108) sts in St st until armholes measure 2 (3, 3, 4, 5, 6)" (5 [7.5, 7.5, 10, 12.5, 15] cm), ending with a RS row. Maintaining selvedge sts and beg and ending as indicated for your size, work center 66 (70, 80, 88, 96, 108) sts according to Rows 1–38 of She Gansey chart, ending with a RS row—armholes measure about 7 (8, 8, 9, 10, 11)" (18 [20.5, 20.5, 23, 25.5, 28] cm) when chart is completed.

Shape Neck
Mark center 14 (14, 16, 16, 22, 24) sts for front neck. With WS facing, knit to marked center sts, p14 (14, 16, 16, 22, 24), knit to end of row. *Next row:* (RS) Knit to 3 sts before

Join Shoulders

Place 20 (22, 26, 30, 31, 36) left back shoulder sts on a spare needle, and with WS tog, use the three-needle method (see Glossary, page 153) to BO the left front and back shoulder sts tog. Rep for right shoulder. Place rem 28 (28, 30, 30, 36, 38) sts on a holder for back neck.

Sleeves

Place 6 (6, 8, 8, 10, 10) held underarm sts on shorter cir needle. Join yarn. With RS facing, pick up and knit 72 (76, 80, 92, 100, 108) sts evenly spaced around armhole—78 (82, 88, 100, 110, 118) sts total. Join for working in the rnd, work 2 (2, 3, 3, 4, 4) underarm sts, then pm for beg of rnd (before seam sts). Cont openwork patt along "seam" as foll: Yo, ssk, knit to end of rnd. Work 6 rnds even, maintaining openwork patt along seam. *Dec rnd:* Keeping in patt as established, dec 1 st each side of marker as foll: Yo, ssk, ssk, work to last 2 sts, k2tog—2 sts dec'd. Work 3 rnds even. Rep the last 4 rnds 21 (22, 23, 27, 28, 31) more times, changing to dpn when necessary—34 (36, 40, 44, 52, 54) sts rem. Cont even until sleeve measures 17 (17, 19, 19, 20, 20)" (43 [43, 48.5, 48.5, 51, 51] cm), or desired length to wrist. *Next rnd:* Knit, dec 4 sts evenly spaced—30 (32, 36, 40, 48, 50) sts rem. [Purl 1 rnd, knit 1 rnd] 2 times, then purl 1 rnd. Loosely BO all sts.

Finishing
Neckband

Place 28 (28, 30, 30, 36, 38) held back sts onto shorter cir needle. With RS facing and beg at left shoulder, pick up and knit 15 sts along left front neck, k14 (14, 16, 16, 22, 24) held front neck sts, pick up and knit 15 sts along right front neck—72 (72, 76, 76, 88, 92) sts total. Purl 1 rnd. Loosely BO all sts kwise.

Weave in loose ends. Block lightly to measurements.

marked sts, k2tog, k1, place center 14 (14, 16, 16, 22, 24) sts on holder, join new ball of yarn, k1, ssk, work to end of row—26 (28, 32, 36, 37, 42) sts rem each side. Working each side separately, dec 1 st at neck edge as before every RS row 6 more times—20 (22, 26, 30, 31, 36) sts rem each side. Cont even in St st if necessary until piece measures ½" (1.3 cm) less than finished back length, ending with a RS row. Knit 4 rows even, ending with a RS row—2 garter ridges.

Berthe Collar

design by Karin Maag-Tanchak

I would be quite surprised if you didn't have a few one-skein delights in your stash . . . single skeins of something dramatically delicious that you couldn't put down in the yarn shop, but had no idea what to do with when you got them home.

This collar is what those skeins were meant for. It almost defies physics: it curves and lies flat all at the same time. Which way do you like it? You can knit it looser than ball-band gauge and let the front flow into ruffles. Or knit it at ball-band gauge or snugger and go for the sleek-and-tailored look. Whatever you do, secure it in place with the simplest of pins. Designer Karin Maag-Tanchak first showed it to me with a simple wooden double-pointed needle holding it closed. Gorgeous.

Note

- This scarf is shown in two versions that use different yarns and different gauges. The instructions are written for the green version followed by the blue version in parentheses, i.e., green version (blue version).

Scarf

Using the long-tail method (see Glossary, page 153), CO 81 (101) sts. Knit 1 row. Cont in patt as foll:

Row 1: (RS) *K19, k1f&b; rep from * to last 19 or fewer sts, knit to end of row.
Row 2: (WS) Knit.
Rep Rows 1 and 2 until scarf measures about 4½" (11.5 cm) from CO, or desired shoulder width, ending with a WS row. With RS facing, BO all sts knitwise.

Finishing

Weave in loose ends. Block lightly if desired.

Finished Size

About 4½" (11.5 cm) wide and 17 (20¼)" (43 [51.5] cm) long along CO edge.

Yarn

Green version: Worsted-weight (CYCA #4 Medium) yarn. *Blue version:* Sportweight (CYCA #2 Fine) yarn.

Shown here: Green version: Blue Heron Yarns Cotton/Rayon Seed (32% cotton, 68% rayon; 475 yd [434 m]/8 oz): Leaf, 1 skein. *Blue version:* Alchemy Yarns Bamboo (100% bamboo; 138 yd [126 m]/50 g): #40C Madre Deus, 2 skeins.

Needles

Green version: Size 5 (3.75 mm). *Blue version:* Size 4 (3.5 mm). Adjust needle size if necessary to obtain the correct gauge.

Notions

Tapestry needle.

Gauge

Green version: 19 stitches and 40 rows = 4" (10 cm) in garter stitch. *Blue version:* 20 stitches and 45 rows = 4" (10 cm) in garter stitch.

Cables and Os

design by Brooke Snow

This luscious, sexy cardigan is knitted in kissable pink from a linen-rich cotton blend yarn. Yummy. You've got your drape (thanks, linen), you've got your stitch definition (thanks, cotton), and you've got a pattern that holds your interest to the last stitch. The twisted rib is designer Brooke Snow's trick to help the ribbing keep its shape.

Body

With smaller needle, CO 224 (256, 288, 320, 352, 384) sts. Do not join. Work twisted rib back and forth in rows as foll:

Row 1: (RS) *K1 through back loop (k1tbl), p1; rep from * to end of row.

Row 2: *K1, p1 through back loop (p1tbl); rep from * to end of row.

Rep Rows 1 and 2 until piece measures 1¼" (3.2 cm) from CO, ending with a WS row, and placing markers (pm) to denote side "seams" on last row as foll: work 56 (64, 72, 80, 88, 96) sts for left front, pm, work 112 (128, 144, 160, 176, 192) sts for back, pm, work rem 56 (64, 72, 80, 88, 96) sts for right front. Change to larger needle. Work Rows 1 and 2 of Cables and Os chart once, then rep Rows 3–10 of chart until piece measures 14 (14, 14½, 15½, 16½, 16¾)" (35.5 [35.5, 37, 39.5, 42, 42.5] cm) from CO, ending with a WS row.

Divide for Fronts and Back

Work to 4 (5, 7, 8, 8, 9) sts before first m, BO 4 (5, 7, 8, 8, 9) sts, remove m, BO 4 (5, 7, 8, 8, 9) sts, work to 4 (5, 7, 8, 8, 9) sts before second m, BO 4 (5, 7, 8, 8, 9) sts, remove m, BO 4 (5, 7, 8, 8, 9) sts, work to end—52 (59, 65, 72, 80, 87) sts rem for each front; 104 (118, 130, 144, 160, 174) sts rem for back.

Left Front

Cont on 52 (59, 65, 72, 80, 87) left front sts only, work 1 WS row even. At armhole edge (beg of RS rows), dec 1 st every RS row 6 (9, 9, 9, 14, 17) times—46 (50, 56, 63, 66, 70) sts rem. Cont even in patt until armhole measures 6 (6½, 7½, 7¾, 8¼, 8¾)" (15 [16.5, 19, 19.5, 21, 22] cm), ending with a RS row.

Finished Size

31½ (36, 40½, 45, 49½, 54)" (80 [91.5, 103, 114.5, 125.5, 137] cm) bust circumference. Garment shown measures 31½" (80 cm).

Yarn

DK-weight (CYCA #3 Light) yarn.
Shown here: Queensland Collection Cotolino (60% cotton, 40% linen; 115 yd [105 m]/50 g): #17 pink, 9 (11, 13, 15, 16, 18) skeins.

Needles

Body and sleeves—size 4 (3.5 mm): 24" (60 cm) circular (cir). Ribbing—size 2 (2.75 mm): 24" (60 cm) cir. Adjust needle size if necessary to obtain the correct gauge.

Notions

Markers (m); cable needle (cn); tapestry needle; ten ³⁄₈" (1 cm) buttons; sewing needle and matching thread for attaching buttons.

Gauge

28½ stitches and 32 rows = 4" (10 cm) in cable rib pattern. One 16-stitch pattern repeat = 2¼" (5.5 cm).

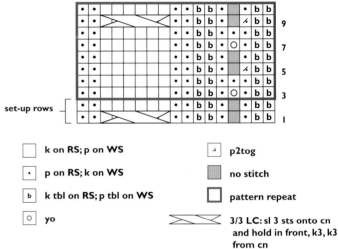

CABLES AND Os

set-up rows

	k on RS; p on WS		p2tog
•	p on RS; k on WS		no stitch
b	k tbl on RS; p tbl on WS		pattern repeat
○	yo		3/3 LC: sl 3 sts onto cn and hold in front, k3, k3 from cn

Shape Shoulder and Neck

At neck edge (beg of RS rows), BO 10 (10, 11, 11, 11, 12) sts 2 times—26 (30, 34, 41, 44, 46) sts rem. Dec 1 st at neck edge every RS row 6 (6, 6, 7, 8, 8) times—20 (24, 28, 34, 36, 38) sts rem. Cont even in patt until armhole measures 8 (8½, 9½, 10, 10¾, 11¼)" (20.5 [21.5, 24, 25.5, 27.5, 28.5] cm), ending with a RS row. At armhole edge (beg of WS rows) BO 7 (8, 10, 12, 12, 13) sts once, then BO 7 (8, 9, 11, 12, 13) sts once—6 (8, 9, 11, 12, 12) sts rem. BO all sts.

Back

With WS facing, join yarn to armhole edge of 104 (118, 130, 144, 160, 174) back sts and work 1 WS row. Dec 1 st at each end of needle every RS row 6 (9, 9, 9, 14, 17) times—92 (100, 112, 126, 132, 140) sts rem. Cont even until armholes measure 6½ (7, 7¾, 8¼, 9, 9½)" (16.5 [18, 19.5, 21, 23, 24] cm), ending with a RS row.

Shape Shoulders and Neck

With WS facing, work 1 row even, marking center 34 (34, 36, 38, 40, 42) sts for back neck. *Next row:* (RS) Work to marked center sts, join new yarn and BO marked 34 (34,

Shape Shoulder and Neck

At neck edge (beg of WS rows), BO 10 (10, 11, 11, 11, 12) sts 2 times—26 (30, 34, 41, 44, 46) sts rem. Dec 1 st at neck edge every RS row 6 (6, 6, 7, 8, 8) times—20 (24, 28, 34, 36, 38) sts rem. Work even in patt until armhole measures 8 (8½, 9½, 10, 10¾, 11¼)" (20.5 [21.5, 24, 25.5, 27.5, 28.5] cm), ending with a WS row. At armhole edge (beg of RS rows) BO 7 (8, 10, 12, 12, 13) sts once, then BO 7 (8, 9, 11, 12, 13) sts once—6 (8, 9, 11, 12, 12) sts rem. BO all sts.

Right Front

With WS facing, join yarn to armhole edge of 52 (59, 65, 72, 80, 87) right front sts and work 1 WS row. At armhole edge (end of RS rows), dec 1 st every RS row 6 (9, 9, 9, 14, 17) times—46 (50, 56, 63, 66, 70) sts rem. Cont even in patt until armhole measures 6 (6½, 7½, 7¾, 8¼, 8¾)" (15 [16.5, 19, 19.5, 21, 22] cm), ending with a WS row.

108

36, 38, 40, 42) sts, work to end—29 (33, 38, 44, 46, 49) sts rem each side. Working each side separately, dec 1 st at each neck edge every row 9 (9, 10, 10, 10, 11) times—20 (24, 28, 34, 36, 38) sts rem each side. Work even until armholes measure 8 (8½, 9½, 10, 10¾, 11¼)" (20.5 [21.5, 24, 25.5, 27.5, 28.5] cm), ending with a WS row. BO 7 (8, 10, 12, 12, 13) at each armhole edge, then BO 7 (8, 9, 11, 12, 13) sts at beg of foll armhole edge—6 (8, 9, 11, 12, 12) sts rem each side. BO all sts.

Sleeves

With smaller needle, CO 64 (80, 80, 96, 96, 96) sts. Work in twisted rib until piece measures 3" (7.5 cm) from CO, ending with a WS row. Change to larger needle. Work Rows 1 and 2 of Cables and Os chart once, then rep Rows 3–10 of chart, and *at the same time* inc 1 st each end of needle every 6 (6, 6, 8, 8, 8)th row 9 (6, 10, 5, 6, 7) times, working new sts into patt—82 (92, 100, 106, 108, 110) sts. Cont even until piece measures 12½ (12¾, 12¾, 13, 13, 13½)" (31.5 [32.5, 32.5, 33, 33, 34.5] cm) from CO, ending with a WS row.

Shape Cap

BO 4 (5, 7, 8, 8, 9) sts at beg of next 2 rows—74 (82, 86, 90, 92, 92) sts rem. Dec 1 st each end of needle every RS row 14 (16, 18, 24, 26, 29) times, then every row 11 (12, 12, 6, 4, 0) times—24 (26, 26, 30, 32, 34) sts rem. BO 3 st at beg of next 4 rows—12 (14, 14, 18, 20, 22) sts rem. BO rem sts.

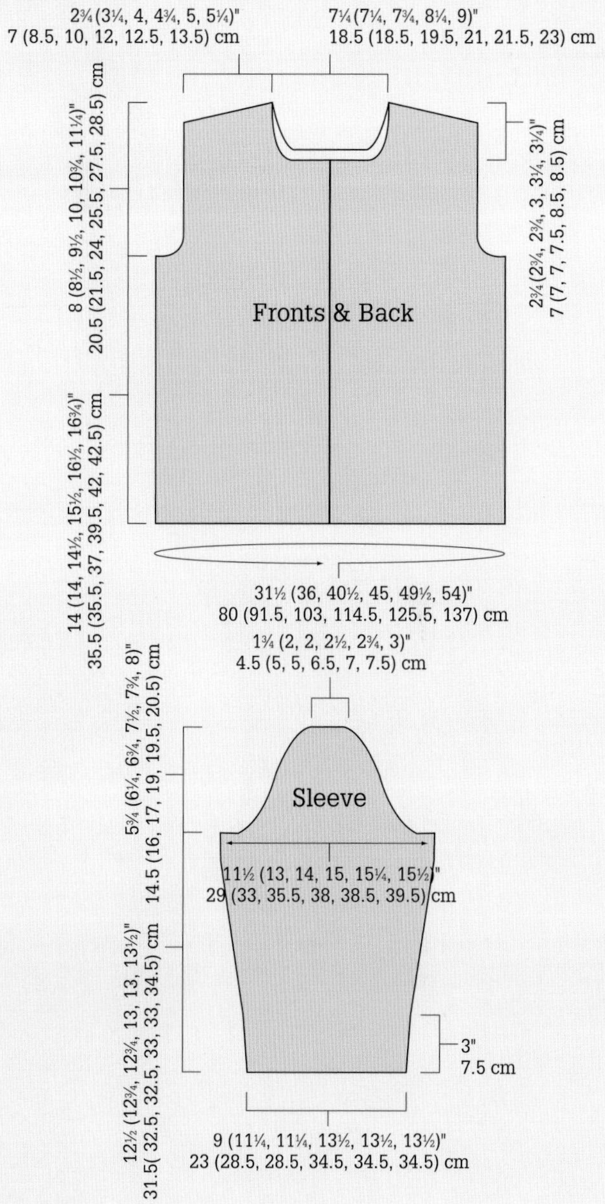

2¾ (3¼, 4, 4¾, 5, 5¼)"
7 (8.5, 10, 12, 12.5, 13.5) cm
7¼ (7¼, 7¾, 8¼, 9)"
18.5 (18.5, 19.5, 21, 21.5, 23) cm
8 (8½, 9½, 10, 10¾, 11¼)"
20.5 (21.5, 24, 25.5, 27.5, 28.5) cm
2¾ (2¾, 2¾, 3, 3¼, 3¼)"
7 (7, 7, 7.5, 8.5, 8.5) cm
Fronts & Back
14 (14, 14½, 15½, 16½, 16¾)"
35.5 (35.5, 37, 39.5, 42, 42.5) cm
31½ (36, 40½, 45, 49½, 54)"
80 (91.5, 103, 114.5, 125.5, 137) cm
1¾ (2, 2, 2½, 2¾, 3)"
4.5 (5, 5, 6.5, 7, 7.5) cm
5¾ (6¼, 6¾, 7½, 7¾, 8)"
14.5 (16, 17, 19, 19.5, 20.5) cm
Sleeve
11½ (13, 14, 15, 15¼, 15½)"
29 (33, 35.5, 38, 38.5, 39.5) cm
12½ (12¾, 12¾, 13, 13, 13½)"
31.5 (32.5, 32.5, 33, 33, 34.5) cm
3"
7.5 cm
9 (11¼, 11¼, 13½, 13½, 13½)"
23 (28.5, 28.5, 34.5, 34.5, 34.5) cm

Finishing

With yarn threaded on a tapestry needle, sew shoulder seams. Sew sleeve caps into armholes. Sew sleeve seams.

Neckband

With smaller needle and RS facing, pick up and knit 103 (103, 111, 119, 125, 133) sts. Beg and end with p1tbl, work in twisted rib for 4 rows. With WS facing, loosely BO all sts kwise.

Buttonband

With smaller needle and RS facing, pick up and knit 143 (143, 153, 157, 165, 173) sts along left front edge. Beg and end with p1tbl, work in twisted rib for 4 rows. With WS facing, loosely BO all sts kwise.

Weave in loose ends. Sew buttons to left front evenly spaced along band, aligning each button with an eyelet on right front. Use the corresponding eyelet as a buttonhole.

Midwest-Style Thrummed Mitts

design by Amy Swenson

These ultra-warm mittens are a take-off on the traditional Maritime design. Originally, thrummed mitts were knitted from leftover bits of raw wool fleece and sturdy lanolin-rich yarn. While the cotton won't be as waterproof as wool, the raw layers of unspun silk will keep your fingers and palms toasty warm.

Designer Amy Swenson picked a sticky cotton for maximum friction with the thrums. Silk thrums. Silk fiber is longer and thinner than the wool that's usually used, so to compensate, just fold the fiber more times than you would with wool. This will help take advantage of silk's longer fiber length and also help better secure the thrums.

Stitch Guide

Thrum 1

Insert needle into next st as if to knit, fold thrum in half and position it over the right needle with thrum ends pointing downward (if you hold the working yarn in your left hand as for the Continental method of knitting, make sure that the working yarn is above the thrum and that no part of the thrum is yet covering the working yarn), then complete the knit stitch by pulling both the working yarn and the thrum through the stitch. After pulling the stitch off the left needle, use the left needle tip to pull the thrum over and off the new stitch, as if to bind off. Don't worry if your thrums look uneven at this point; you can manually adjust them before finishing the mittens.

Thrum Pattern

Rnds 1–3: Knit.

Rnd 4: *K3, thrum 1; rep from * to end of rnd.

Rnds 5–7: Knit.

Rnd 8: K1, *thrum 1, k3; rep from * to last 3 sts, thrum 1, k2.

Repeat Rnds 1–8 for pattern.

Finished Size

About 8½" (21.5 cm) hand circumference and 10½" (26.5 cm) long. To fit an adult.

Yarn

Worsted-weight (CYCA #4 Medium) yarn.

Shown here: Blue Sky Alpacas Dyed Cotton (100% cotton; 150 yd [137 m]/100 g): #621 expresso (MC), 2 skeins. Furryarns Tussah Silk Roving (100% silk; 2 oz/bundle): waterfall (CC), 2 bundles (4 oz).

Needles

Size 5 (3.75 mm): set of 4 or 5 double-pointed (dpn). Adjust needle size if necessary to obtain the correct gauge.

Notions

Markers (m); stitch holder or waste yarn; tapestry needle.

Gauge

20 stitches and 28 rounds = 4" (10 cm) in stockinette stitch worked in the round.

Note

■ When knitting in the thrums, add a little twist into the fiber in order to help it stay in one piece. Remember, the fuzzier the thrums look while working, the fuzzier they will get over time. Starting out with smooth thrums means that the fiber is well compacted.

Thrum Preparation

Before beginning to knit, prepare the silk thrums. Because silk has a relatively long fiber length, the instructions are different than if working with wool. With your hands about 8" (20.5 cm) apart, gently tug on the roving until it separates into a 7–9" (18–23 cm) clump. Separate this clump into several strands, each about ¼" (6 mm) thick, so that if twisted, the strand would be as thick as worsted-weight yarn. Fold each strand in half, then in half again so that it is quadruple thickness and about 2½" (6.5 cm) long. Prepare 10 to 20 thrums at a time so that they'll be available as you knit. It's not a good idea to prepare all of the thrums at once because they may tangle before you're ready to use them.

Mitten

The mittens can be worn on either hand with equal comfort.

Cuff

With MC, CO 40 sts. Arrange sts as evenly as possible on 3 or 4 dpn, place marker (pm), and join for working in the rnd, being careful not to twist sts. Work in k1, p1 rib until piece measures about 1¾" (4.5 cm) from CO, or desired cuff length.

Lower Hand

Work Rnds 1–8 of thrum patt (see Stitch Guide) once, then work Rnds 1–7 once more.

Shape Thumb Gusset

(Rnd 8 of patt) Keeping in patt, work 19 sts, pm, k2, pm, work to end of rnd—2 gusset sts between markers. Cont to rep Rnds 1–8 of patt and *at the same time* inc 1 st each side of gusset every other rnd 8 times, working gusset sts in St st without thrums as foll: Work to first m, slip marker (sl m), knit into the front and back of the next st (k1f&b), knit to 1 st before next m, k1f&b, sl m, work to end of rnd—2 gusset sts inc'd; 18 gusset sts after all inc rnds have been worked. *Next rnd:* Work in patt to first m, remove m and place 18 gusset sts on a holder or piece of waste yarn, remove second m, use the backward loop method (see Glossary, page 153) to tightly CO 1 st, pm to denote side "seam" of mitten, tightly CO 1 st more, work to end of rnd in patt—40 sts.

Upper Hand

Cont in patt as established until piece measures 3" (7.5 cm) from end of gusset, or about 1¼" (3.2 cm) less than desired total length.

Shape Top

Cont in patt as established, but omit working thrums on dec sts. *Dec rnd:* *K1, ssk, work in patt to 3 sts before m, k2tog, k1, sl m; rep from * once—4 sts dec'd. Work 1 rnd even in patt. Rep the last 2 rnds 2 more times—28 sts rem. Work Dec rnd every rnd 3 times—16 sts rem. Cut yarn, leaving a 12" (30.5 cm) tail.

Finishing

Divide the rem sts on 2 dpn so that 8 palm sts are on one needle and 8 back-of-hand sts are on the other. Use the three-needle method (see Glossary, page 153) to BO the sts tog. (Alternatively, use the Kitchener st [see Glossary, page 155] to graft the live sts tog.)

Thumb

Place 18 held gusset sts on 3 dpn. With MC, pick up and knit 4 sts along CO at base of thumb—22 sts total. Work thumb without thrums as foll: K20, pm. Rnd begins at center of picked-up sts. *Next rnd:* K1, k2tog, k16, ssk, k1—20 sts rem. *Next rnd:* K1, k2tog, k14, ssk, k1—18 sts rem. Cont even until thumb measures 2" (5 cm) from pick-up rnd, or to desired total length. *Next rnd:* *K2tog; rep from *—9 sts rem. Cut yarn, draw tail through rem sts, pull tight, and secure to WS.

Weave in loose ends. Using your fingers or the point of a dpn, adjust the thrums as necessary so that they are as uniform as possible when viewed from the RS of the mitt. To set the fibers in place, turn the mitts inside out, cover with a tea towel, and gently steam-block the mitts without pressing or tugging on the fabric. Don't worry if your thrums are loose at first—with a little wear, the raw silk will mesh together to form a felt-like layer on the inside.

Drunken Argyle

design by Holli Yeoh

When designer Holli Yeoh came up with the first Drunken Argyle (see Knitty: knitty.com/issuesummer05/PATTdrunkenargyle.html), a man's crazy argyle vest knitted in fine-gauge wool, I was in love. Thankfully Holli was glad to oblige the other half of the population, and take on the sheepless challenge at the same time.

This sweater takes everything in the original design, twists it up, and tops it off with pink ribbon, metaphorically speaking. The yarn is a soft, stretchy handpainted cotton/elite blend. (Have any left after this sweater's done? Knit yourself some killer socks.) Holli's given us girls a little shimmer with our argyle, too. Rock.

Notes

- This fabric will shrink just over 10% in length when washed.
- At times the waist, armhole, and neck shaping will break up the diagonal argyle lines on the chart. Don't worry about following the chart exactly; simply join up with the charted lines within a couple of rows of working the shaping sts. The meandering, uneven nature of the design will hide these discrepancies.
- When working short-rows at hem and shoulders, work the first and last stitches of diagonal argyle lines using the main color, then work duplicate stitch using yarn tails when finishing.
- The short-rows at hem involve regular yarnovers and backward yarnovers; both are illustrated in the Glossary (page 157).

Finished Size
35 (39, 43, 46½, 50, 54)" (89 [99, 109, 118, 127, 137] cm) bust circumference. Sweater shown measures 35" (89 cm).

Yarn
Fingering weight (CYCA #1 Super Fine) yarn.
Shown here: Blue Moon Fiber Arts Sock Candy (96% cotton, 4% elite; 200 yd [183 m]/2 oz): buttercream (off-white; MC), 7 (8, 9, 10, 11, 12) skeins; spring fling (multicolored pink; A), 3 (3, 4, 4, 4, 5) skeins. Lang Yarns Opal (58% polyamide, 42% viscose; 170 yd [155 m]/50 g): #48 pink (B), 1 (1, 1, 2, 2, 2) ball(s).

Needles
Body and sleeves—size 2 (2.75 mm): straight. Sleeve and neck edging—size 1 (2.25 mm): 16" (40 cm) circular (cir). Adjust needle size if necessary to obtain the correct gauge.

Notions
Stitch holders; small stitch holder or coiless safety pin; markers (m); tapestry needle; sewing needle and thread; Fray Stop (optional).

Gauge
29 stitches and 41 rows = 4" (10 cm) in intarsia stockinette-stitch pattern on larger needles *before* washing; 29 stitches and 46 rows = 4" (10 cm) in pattern on larger needles *after* washing. *Note:* This knitted fabric will shrink just over 10% in length when washed.

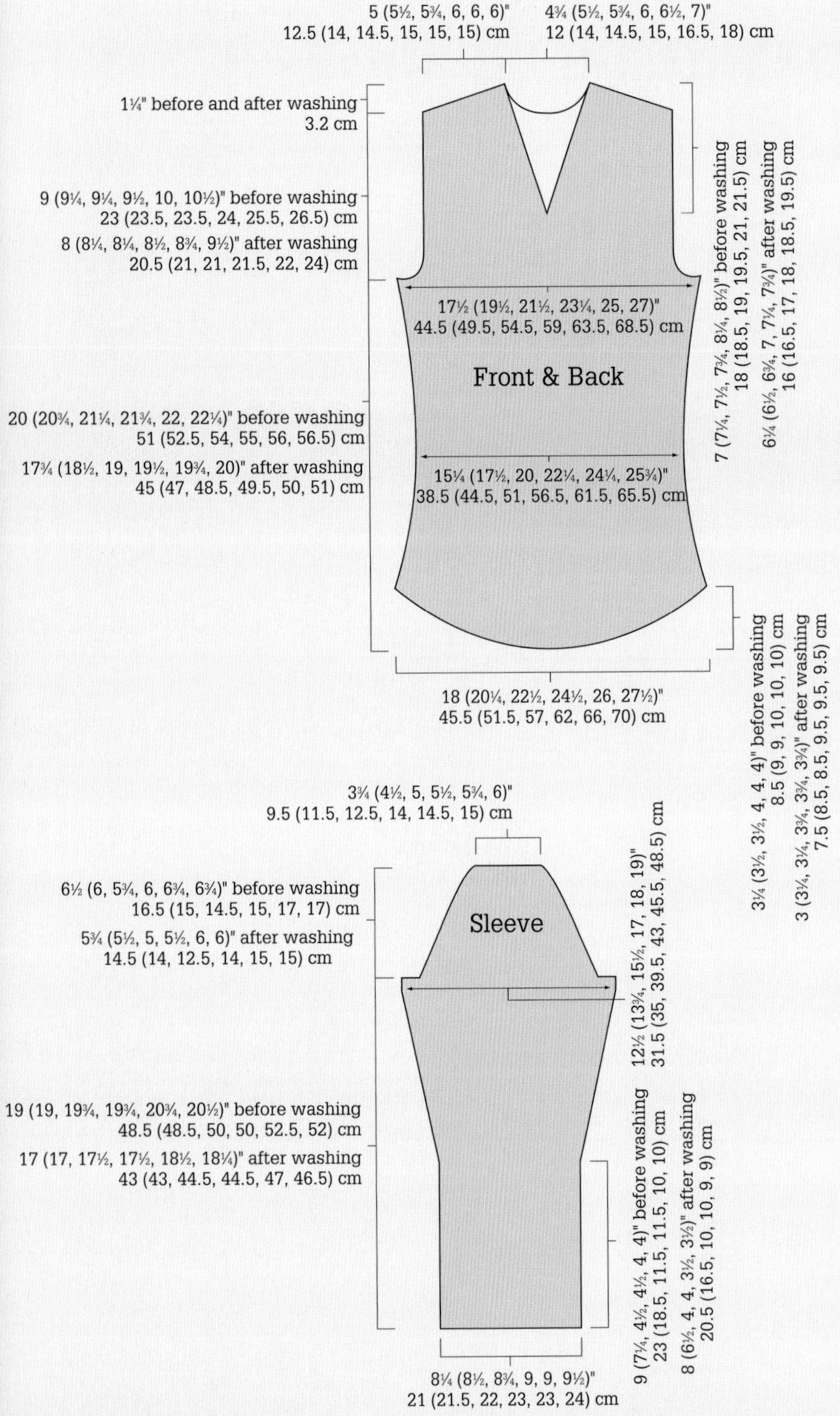
5 (5½, 5¾, 6, 6, 6)"
12.5 (14, 14.5, 15, 15, 15) cm
4¾ (5½, 5¾, 6, 6½, 7)"
12 (14, 14.5, 15, 16.5, 18) cm
1¼" before and after washing
3.2 cm
9 (9¼, 9¼, 9½, 10, 10½)" before washing
23 (23.5, 23.5, 24, 25.5, 26.5) cm
8 (8¼, 8¼, 8½, 8¾, 9½)" after washing
20.5 (21, 21, 21.5, 22, 24) cm
17½ (19½, 21½, 23¼, 25, 27)"
44.5 (49.5, 54.5, 59, 63.5, 68.5) cm
Front & Back
20 (20¾, 21¼, 21¾, 22, 22¼)" before washing
51 (52.5, 54, 55, 56, 56.5) cm
17¾ (18½, 19, 19½, 19¾, 20)" after washing
45 (47, 48.5, 49.5, 50, 51) cm
15¼ (17½, 20, 22¼, 24¼, 25¾)"
38.5 (44.5, 51, 56.5, 61.5, 65.5) cm
7 (7¼, 7½, 7¾, 8¼, 8½)" before washing
18 (18.5, 19, 19.5, 21, 21.5) cm
6¼ (6½, 6¾, 7, 7¼, 7¾)" after washing
16 (16.5, 17, 18, 18.5, 19.5) cm
18 (20¼, 22½, 24½, 26, 27½)"
45.5 (51.5, 57, 62, 66, 70) cm
3¼ (3½, 3½, 4, 4, 4)" before washing
8.5 (9, 9, 10, 10, 10) cm
3 (3¼, 3¼, 3¾, 3¾, 3¾)" after washing
7.5 (8.5, 8.5, 9.5, 9.5, 9.5) cm
3¾ (4½, 5, 5½, 5¾, 6)"
9.5 (11.5, 12.5, 14, 14.5, 15) cm
6½ (6, 5¾, 6, 6¾, 6¾)" before washing
16.5 (15, 14.5, 15, 17, 17) cm
5¾ (5½, 5, 5½, 6, 6)" after washing
14.5 (14, 12.5, 14, 15, 15) cm
Sleeve
12½ (13¾, 15½, 17, 18, 19)"
31.5 (35, 39.5, 43, 45.5, 48.5) cm
19 (19, 19¾, 19¾, 20¾, 20½)" before washing
48.5 (48.5, 50, 50, 52.5, 52) cm
17 (17, 17½, 17½, 18½, 18¼)" after washing
43 (43, 44.5, 44.5, 47, 46.5) cm
9 (7¼, 4½, 4½, 4, 4)" before washing
23 (18.5, 11.5, 11.5, 10, 10) cm
8 (6½, 4, 4, 3½, 3½)" after washing
20.5 (16.5, 10, 10, 9, 9) cm
8¼ (8½, 8¾, 9, 9, 9½)"
21 (21.5, 22, 23, 23, 24) cm

Notes

- When working the decreases at the armholes and V-neck, if a cross-hatching line (B) crosses over the decreases, make sure to work a decrease that leaves the B stitch lying on top. For example, if the pattern calls for k2tog, but that places the B st underneath, then work ssk instead and vice versa.
- Use a separate ball or bobbin of yarn for each intarsia diamond motif. Do not carry unused colors across the back. When changing colors, twist the two yarns around each other to avoid forming holes.
- If necessary, the chart may be enlarged using a photocopier.
- Lang Yarns Opal is very slippery, so keep your tension tight and give the yarn a tug before and after completing a stitch.
- To stop the Lang Yarns Opal yarn ends from unweaving, sew them down with a sharp-point sewing needle and thread. You may also want to use a little Fray Stop to keep the yarn from raveling.
- Although the washing instructions for Lang Yarns Opal indicate that it should not be machine dried, I found my swatch to be unharmed after numerous trips through the washer and dryer.
- The pink yarns must be dried immediately after they get wet, otherwise the colors may bleed. When blocking, cover with a dry cloth and steam lightly. Hold the iron about ⅛" (3 mm) over the cloth; do not press down. Don't wet-block and don't spray with water. Machine wash with like colors, using cool water and mild detergent. Machine dry on medium heat setting immediately.

LOWER BACK

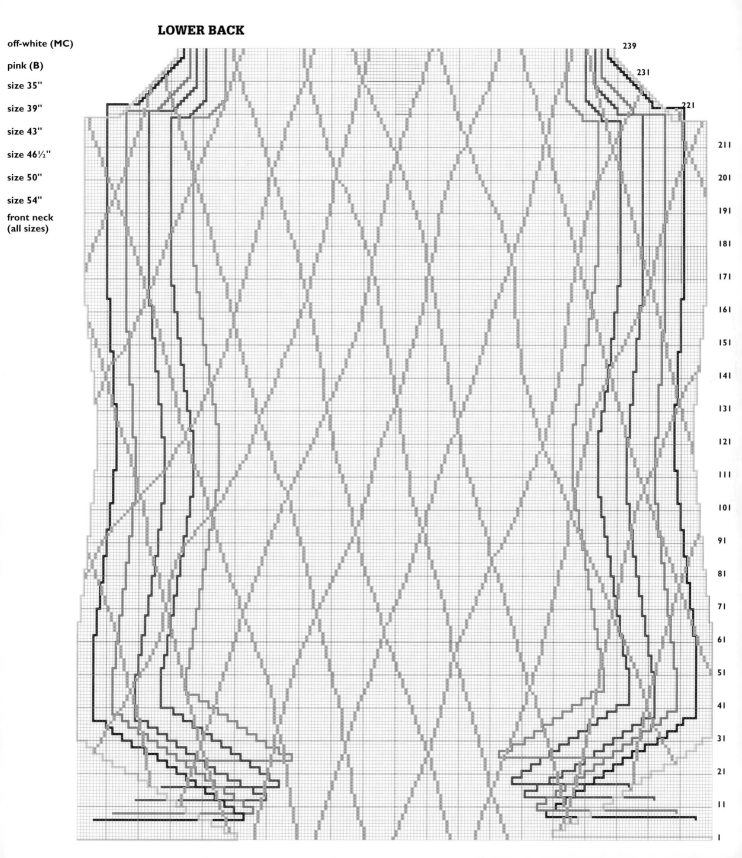

off-white (MC)

pink (B)

size 35"

size 39"

size 43"

size 46½"

size 50"

size 54"

front neck
(all sizes)

239

231

221

211

201

191

181

171

161

151

141

131

121

111

101

91

81

71

61

51

41

31

21

11

1

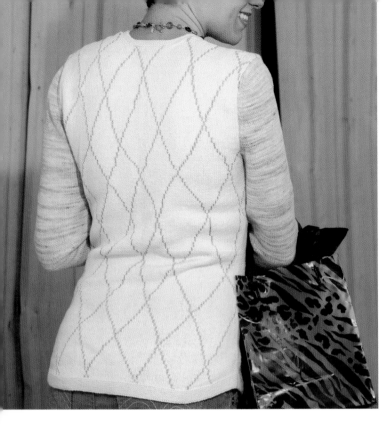

Back

With MC and larger needles, CO 131 (147, 163, 177, 189, 199) sts. Knit 14 rows.

Shape Hem

Change to St st and work Rows 25–46 (17–42, 13–38, 9–40, 7–38, 1–32) of Back Chart as indicated for your size, working short-rows (see Glossary, page 157) as foll:

Row 1: (RS) Work according to Row 25 (17, 13, 9, 7, 1) of chart, working first 33 (37, 41, 44, 47, 50) sts with MC only, then join B when needed and cont across next 65 (73, 81, 89, 95, 99) sts—98 (110, 122, 133, 142, 149) sts worked, turn work.

Row 2: Yo backwards (see Glossary, page 157), sl 1, p64 (72, 80, 88, 94, 98), turn.

Rows 3 and 5: Yo as usual, sl 1, knit to yo of previous row, k2tog (yo and next st from garter st hem), k3 (2, 3, 2, 2, 3), turn.

Rows 4 and 6: Yo backwards, sl 1, purl to yo of previous row, ssp (yo and next st from garter st hem; see Glossary, page 154), p3 (2, 3, 2, 2, 3), turn.

Rows 7 and 9: Yo as usual, sl 1, knit to yo of previous row, k2tog, k2 (2, 3, 2, 2, 3), turn.

Rows 8 and 10: Yo backwards, sl 1, purl to yo of previous row, ssp, p2 (2, 2, 3, 2, 3), turn.

Row 11: Yo as usual, sl 1, knit to yo of previous row, k2tog, k2, turn.

Row 12: Yo backwards, sl 1, purl to yo of previous row, ssp, p2, turn.

Rows 13–20: Rep Rows 11 and 12 four more times. Size 35" is complete—skip to Last 2 Hem Shaping Rows.

Sizes 39 (43, 46½, 50, 54)" only:

Rows 21 and 23: Yo as usual, sl 1, knit to yo of previous row, k2tog, k2 (2, 2, 3, 3), turn.

Rows 22 and 24: Yo backwards, sl 1, purl to yo of previous row, ssp, p2 (2, 2, 3, 3), turn. Sizes 39 and 43" are complete—skip to Last 2 Hem Shaping Rows.

Sizes 46½ (50, 54)" only:

Rows 25 and 27: Yo as usual, sl 1, knit to yo of previous row, k2tog, k2, turn.

Rows 26 and 28: Yo backwards, sl 1, purl to yo of previous row, ssp, p2, turn.

Row 29: Yo as usual, sl 1, knit to yo of previous row, k2tog, k1, turn.

Row 30: Yo backwards, sl 1, purl to yo of previous row, ssp, p1, turn. Sizes 46½ (50, 54)" are complete.

Last 2 Hem Shaping Rows (all sizes):

Row 1: (RS) Yo as usual, sl 1, knit to yo of previous row, k2tog, k3 (3, 3, 2, 3, 2), turn.

Row 2: (WS) Purl to yo of previous row, ssp, p3 (3, 3, 2, 3, 2)—still 131 (147, 163, 177, 189, 199) sts.

Work even in St st until WS Row 52 (52, 50, 52, 62, 66) of chart has been completed—piece should measure about 3¾ (4½, 4¾, 5¼, 6½, 7½)" (9.5 [11.5, 12, 13.5, 16.5, 19] cm) from CO at center back.

UPPER BACK

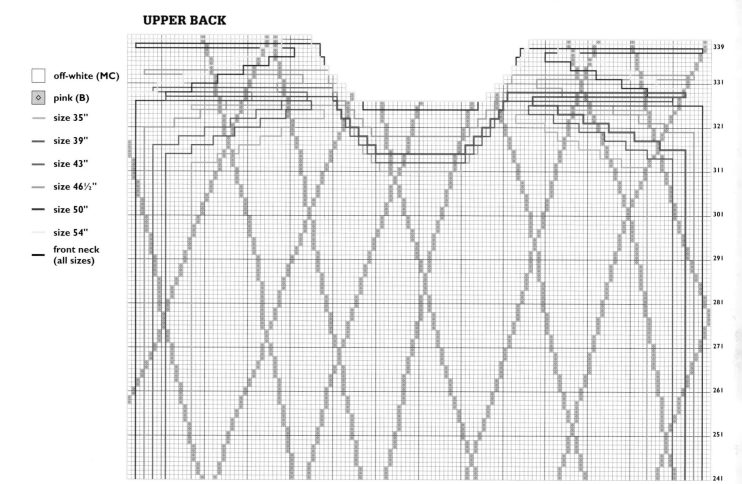

off-white (MC)

◇ pink (B)

— size 35"

— size 39"

— size 43"

— size 46½"

— size 50"

— size 54"

— front neck
(all sizes)

339
331
321
311
301
291
281
271
261
251
241

Shape Waist

Cont as charted and *at the same time,* beg with RS Row 53 (53, 51, 53, 63, 67) of chart, dec 1 st each end of needle as foll: K5, ssk, knit to last 7 sts, k2tog, k5—2 sts dec'd. Work 5 (3, 5, 7, 7, 7) rows even as charted. Dec 1 st each end of needle as before. Rep the last 6 (4, 6, 8, 8, 8) rows 8 (0, 5, 4, 4, 1) more time(s)—111 (143, 149, 165, 177, 193) sts rem. Dec 1 st each end of needle every foll 0 (6, 8, 10, 10, 10)th row 0 (8, 2, 1, 1, 3) time(s)—111 (127, 145, 163, 175, 187) sts rem; Row 107 (105, 103, 103, 113, 113) of chart has been completed. Work 19 rows even, ending with a WS row. Beg with RS Row 127 (125, 123, 123, 133, 133) of chart, inc 1 st each end of needle as foll: K5, right lifted inc (see Glossary, page 156), knit to last 5 sts, left lifted inc (see Glossary, page 156), k5—2 sts inc'd. Work 5 (5, 9, 15, 15, 9) rows even as charted. Inc 1 st each end of

needle as before. Rep the last 6 (6, 10, 16, 16, 10) rows 3 (1, 3, 1, 1, 2) more time(s)—121 (133, 155, 169, 181, 195) sts. Inc 1 st each end of needle every foll 8 (8, 0, 0, 0, 0)th row 3 (4, 0, 0, 0, 0) times—127 (141, 155, 169, 181, 195) sts; Row 175 (169, 163, 155, 165, 163) of chart has been completed. Work even through WS Row 218 (218, 220, 220, 222, 218) of chart—piece measures about 20 (20¾, 21¼, 21¾, 22, 22¼)" (51 [52.5, 54, 55, 56, 56.5] cm) from CO at center back.

Shape Armholes

Cont as charted, BO 5 (6, 8, 10, 10, 11) sts at beg of next 2 rows—117 (129, 139, 149, 161, 173) sts rem.

Dec row 1: (RS) K2, ssk, knit to last 4 sts, k2tog, k2—2 sts dec'd.

Dec row 2: (WS) P2, p2tog, purl to last 4 sts, ssp, p2—2 sts dec'd.

Dec 1 st each end of needle in this manner every row 3 (3, 5, 8, 12, 16) more times—107 (119, 125, 129, 133, 137) sts rem; Row 225 (225, 229, 232, 238, 238) of chart has been completed. Work even through WS Row 310 (312, 314, 318, 324, 326) of chart—armholes measure about 9 (9¼, 9¼, 9½, 10, 10½)" (23 [23.5, 23.5, 24, 25.5, 26.5] cm).

Shape Right Neck and Shoulder

Cont as charted and *at the same time,* beg with Row 311 (313, 315, 319, 325, 327) of chart, work short-rows as foll:

Row 1: (RS) K44 (49, 52, 53, 53, 53), place foll 63 (70, 73, 76, 80, 84) sts on holder.

Row 2: P38 (43, 46, 46, 46, 46), wrap next st, turn.

Rows 3 and 5: Knit to last 5 sts, k3tog, k2—2 sts dec'd each row.

Row 4: P31 (36, 38, 38, 38, 38), wrap next st, turn.

Row 6: P24 (29, 30, 30, 30, 30), wrap next st, turn.

Row 7: Knit to last 4 (5, 5, 5, 5, 5) sts, k2tog (k3tog, k3tog, k3tog, k3tog, k3tog), k2—1 (2, 2, 2, 2, 2) st(s) dec'd.

Row 8: P18 (21, 22, 22, 22, 22), wrap next st, turn.

Row 9: Knit to last 4 (4, 5, 5, 5, 5) sts, k2tog (k2tog, k3tog, k3tog, k3tog, k3tog), k2—1 (1, 2, 2, 2, 2) st(s) dec'd.

Row 10: P12 (14, 14, 14, 14, 14), wrap next st, turn.

Row 11: Knit to last 4 sts, k2tog, k2—1 st dec'd.

Row 12: P6 (7, 7, 7, 7, 7), wrap next st, turn.

Row 13: Knit to last 4 sts, k2tog, k2—1 st dec'd.

Purl 1 row, purling wrapped sts tog with their wraps—36 (40, 42, 43, 43, 43) sts rem. Place sts on holder.

Shape Left Neck and Shoulder

Place 63 (70, 73, 76, 80, 84) held sts on needle. With RS facing, rejoin yarn and cont as charted and *at the same time,* beg with Row 311 (313, 315, 319, 325, 327) of chart, work short-rows as foll:

Row 1: (RS) BO center 19 (21, 21, 23, 27, 31) sts, knit to end of row—44 (49, 52, 53, 53, 53) sts rem.

Row 2 and all WS rows: Purl.

Row 3: K2, sssk (see Glossary, page 154), k33 (38, 41, 41, 41, 41), wrap next st, turn—2 sts dec'd.

Row 5: K2, sssk, k26 (31, 33, 33, 33, 33), wrap next st, turn—2 sts dec'd.

Row 7: K2, ssk (sssk, sssk, sssk, sssk, sssk), k20 (24, 25, 25, 25, 25), wrap next st, turn—1 (2, 2, 2, 2, 2) st(s) dec'd.

Row 9: K2, ssk (ssk, sssk, sssk, sssk, sssk), k14 (17, 17, 17, 17, 17), wrap next st, turn—1 (1, 2, 2, 2, 2) st(s) dec'd.

Row 11: K2, ssk, k8 (10, 10, 10, 10, 10), wrap next st, turn—1 st dec'd.

Row 13: K2, ssk, k2 (3, 3, 3, 3, 3), wrap next st, turn—1 st dec'd.

Row 14: Purl.

Knit all sts, knitting wrapped sts tog with their wraps—36 (40, 42, 43, 43, 43) sts. Place sts on holder.

Front

Work as for back, working front chart in place of back chart, through WS Row 252 of chart—107 (119, 125, 129, 133, 137) sts rem; armholes measure about 3¼ (3¼, 3, 3, 3, 3¼)" (8.5 [8.5, 7.5, 7.5, 7.5, 8.5] cm).

Shape Left Side of Neck

Cont as charted, k53 (59, 62, 64, 66, 68), place foll 54 (60, 63, 65, 67, 69) sts on a holder to work later for right side of neck. Work 1 WS row. *Dec row:* (RS) Cont as charted, knit to last 4 sts, k2tog, k2—1 st dec'd. Work 1 WS row even. Rep the last 2 rows 16 (18, 19, 20, 22, 24) more times—36 (40, 42, 43, 43, 43) sts rem; Row 288 (292, 294, 296, 300, 304) of chart has been completed. Work even through RS Row 311 (313, 315, 319, 325, 327) of chart—armhole measures about 9 (9¼, 9¼, 9½, 10, 10½)" (23 [23.5, 23.5, 24, 25.5, 26.5] cm).

Shape Left Shoulder

Cont as charted and beg with Row 312 (314, 316, 320, 326, 328) of chart, work short-rows as foll:

Row 1: (WS) P30 (34, 36, 36, 36, 36), wrap next st, turn.

Row 2 and all RS rows: Knit.

Row 3: P25 (29, 30, 30, 30, 30), wrap next st, turn.

LOWER FRONT

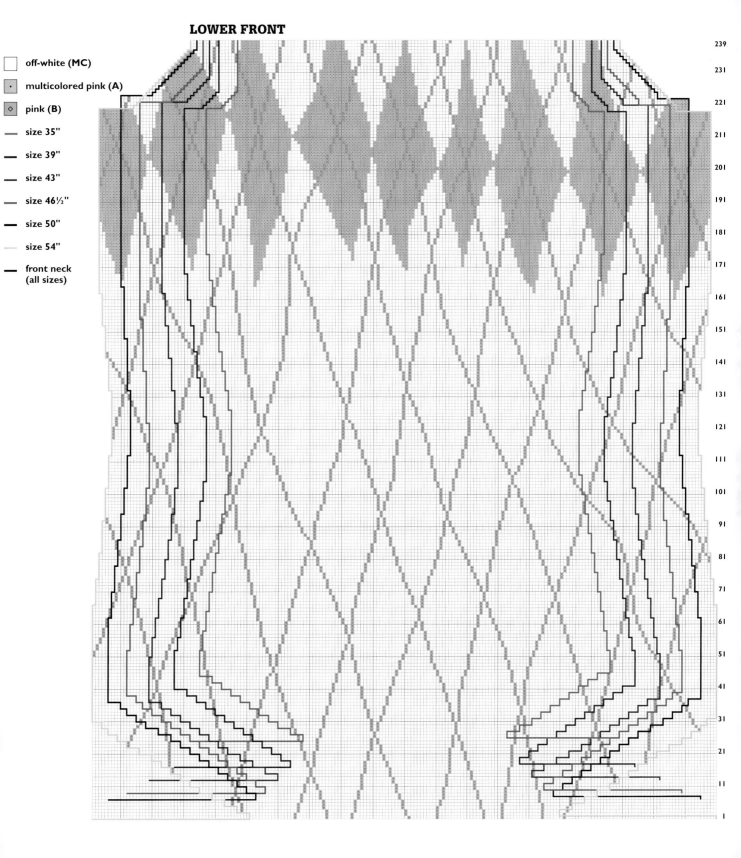

off-white (MC)

multicolored pink (A)

pink (B)

size 35"

size 39"

size 43"

size 46½"

size 50"

size 54"

front neck
(all sizes)

UPPER FRONT

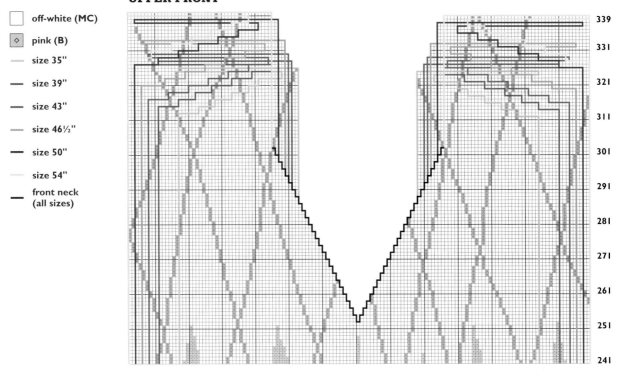

Legend:
- ☐ off-white (MC)
- ◇ pink (B)
- — size 35"
- — size 39"
- — size 43"
- — size 46½"
- — size 50"
- — size 54"
- — front neck (all sizes)

Chart row numbers: 339, 331, 321, 311, 301, 291, 281, 271, 261, 251, 241

Row 5: P20 (24, 24, 24, 24, 24), wrap next st, turn.

Row 7: P15 (18, 18, 18, 18, 18), wrap next st, turn.

Row 9: P10 (12, 12, 12, 12, 12), wrap next st, turn.

Row 11: P5 (6, 6, 6, 6, 6), wrap next st, turn.

Row 12: Knit.

Purl 1 row, working wrapped sts tog with their wraps—still 36 (40, 42, 43, 43, 43) sts. Place sts on holder.

Shape Right Side of Neck

Place center front st on waste yarn or small stitch holder. Replace 53 (59, 62, 64, 66, 68) held sts on needle. With RS facing, rejoin yarn and k53 (59, 62, 64, 66, 68) according to Row 253 of chart. Work 1 WS row. *Dec row:* (RS) K2, ssk, knit to end of row—1 st dec'd. Purl 1 row. Rep the last 2 rows 16 (18, 19, 20, 22, 24) more times—36 (40, 42, 43, 43, 43) sts rem; Row 288 (292, 294, 296, 300, 304) of chart has been completed. Work even through

WS Row 312 (314, 316, 320, 326, 328) of chart—armhole measures about 9 (9¼, 9¼, 9½, 10, 10½)" (23 [23.5, 23.5, 24, 25.5, 26.5] cm).

Shape Right Shoulder

Cont as charted and beg with RS Row 313 (315, 317, 321, 327, 329) of chart, work short-rows as foll:

Row 1: (RS) K30 (34, 36, 36, 36, 36), wrap next st, turn.

Row 2 and all WS rows: Purl.

Row 3: K25 (29, 30, 30, 30, 30), wrap next st, turn.

Row 5: K20 (24, 24, 24, 24, 24), wrap next st, turn.

Row 7: K15 (18, 18, 18, 18, 18), wrap next st, turn.

Row 9: K10 (12, 12, 12, 12, 12), wrap next st, turn.

Row 11: K5 (6, 6, 6, 6, 6), wrap next st, turn.

Row 12: Purl.

Knit 1 row, working wrapped sts tog with their wraps—still 36 (40, 42, 43, 43, 43) sts. Place sts on holder.

Sleeves

With A and cir needle, CO 60 (62, 64, 65, 66, 69) sts. Do not join; work back and forth in rows. Knit 10 rows. Change to larger needles. Work even St st until piece measures 9 (7¼, 4½, 4½, 4, 4)" (23 [18.5, 11.5, 11.5, 10, 10] cm) from CO, ending with a WS row. *Inc row:* (RS) K2, M1R (see Glossary, page 156), knit to last 2 sts, M1L (see Glossary, page 156), k2—2 sts inc'd. Work 3 rows even. Rep the last 4 rows 12 (13, 17, 26, 28, 29) more times—86 (90, 100, 119, 124, 129) sts. Rep Inc row. Work 5 rows even. Rep the last 6 rows 1 (4, 5, 1, 2, 3) more time(s)—90 (100, 112, 123, 130, 137) sts. Work even in St st until piece measures 19 (19, 19¾, 19¾, 20¾, 20½)" (48.5 [48.5, 50, 50, 52.5, 52] cm) from CO, ending with a WS row.

Shape Cap

BO 5 (6, 8, 10, 10, 11) sts at beg of next 2 rows—80 (88, 96, 103, 110, 115) sts rem. *Double dec row:* (RS) K2, sssk, knit to last 5 sts, k3tog, k2—4 sts dec'd. Work 1 row even. Rep the last 2 rows 0 (1, 0, 1, 1, 1) more time—76 (80, 92, 95, 102, 107) sts rem. *Dec row:* (RS) K2, ssk, knit to last 4 sts, k2tog, k2—2 sts dec'd. Work 1 row even. Rep the last 2 rows 5 (6, 9, 9, 11, 13) more times—64 (66, 72, 75, 78, 79) sts rem. Rep dec row, then work 3 rows even. Rep the last 4 rows 8 (5, 1, 2, 2, 1) more time(s)—6 (54, 68, 69, 72, 75) sts rem. Rep dec row, then work 1 row even. Rep the last 2 rows 4 (6, 9, 8, 10, 9) more times—36 (40, 48, 51, 50, 55) sts rem. Rep double dec row every RS row 2 (2, 3, 3, 2, 3) times—28 (32, 36, 39, 42, 43) sts rem. Purl 1 row. BO all sts.

Finishing

Block pieces to before-washing measurements (see special blocking and washing instructions, page 116).

Join Shoulders

Place 36 (40, 42, 43, 43, 43) shoulder sts on spare needles. Holding RS of garment tog, use the three-needle method (see Glossary, page 153) to BO shoulder sts tog, working from armhole edge towards neck edge.

Neckband

With MC, cir needle, RS facing, and beg at right shoulder seam, pick up and knit 35 (39, 41, 43, 47, 51) sts evenly spaced along back neck to shoulder, 49 (50, 52, 55, 58, 61) sts to center front, place marker (pm), k1 from holder, pick up and knit 49 (50, 52, 55, 58, 61) sts to end—134 (140, 146, 154, 164, 174) sts total. Place marker and join for working in the rnd.

Rnd 1: Purl.

Rnd 2: Knit to 2 sts before first marker, ssk, sl m, k1, k2tog, knit to end of rnd—2 sts dec'd.

Rep these 2 rnds 2 more times—128 (134, 140, 148, 158, 168) sts rem. Purl 1 rnd. BO as foll: *K2tog, sl st from right-hand needle to left-hand needle; rep from * to 3 sts before first marker (including slipped st), k3tog, sl st from right-hand needle to left-hand needle, k2tog, sl st from right-hand needle to left-hand needle, k3tog, sl st from right-hand needle to left-hand needle, **k2tog, sl st from right-hand needle to left-hand needle; rep from ** until all sts have been BO.

Duplicate Stitch

With the tails of B already attached to hem and shoulder edges of front and back, work duplicate stitches (see Glossary, page 155) to add missing B sts on the first and last rows of charts.

Seams

With RS tog, pin sleeve into armhole matching underarm side edges and center of BO edge of sleeve cap with shoulder seam. Ease in any fullness at top of sleeve cap. With yarn threaded on a tapestry needle, use a back-stitch (see Glossary, page 157) to sew sleeve caps into armholes. Sew sleeve and side seams.

Weave in loose ends.

Morrigan

design by Jenna Wilson

Ask knitters, "can you knit an aran without wool?" and they will probably deny it. They're mostly right, because a woolless Aran—in principle—defies physics. Arans require warmth, shape-holding texture, and a bit of loft and give to make cable twists pop, and wool provides that naturally. So, how do you get it wool-free? Designer Jenna Wilson knows cables very well. She's a legend on the Internet for designing the sleek, cabled Rogue (sheepy) sweater pattern and exquisite Shedir cabled (sheepless) cap. The Shedir cap was the key to making this sweater happen: knitted in the softest, stretchiest, cotton/acrylic microfiber blend yarn in 1/1 cables, it has warmth, shape-holding texture, and renders fine cable details beautifully. Just no baa. Bingo.

Says the online Encyclopedia Mythica, "The Morrigan is a goddess of battle, strife, and fertility." Why such a terrible name for this beautiful sweater? Well, making this pattern happen, to put it delicately, kicked Jenna's butt (in fact, our working title was *Ninja*). That's because she made sure that everything about this sweater reflected Aran tradition, while still being gorgeous to wear in a modern context and not threatening to droop to knee length as you walk. Mission accomplished. Jenna and Amy would like to thank Wannietta Prescod for doing battle with Morrigan—she knit the sweater you see photographed here.

Finished Size
36½ (41¼, 43¼, 47¼, 51¼, 55¼)" (92.5 [105, 110, 120, 130, 140.5] cm) bust circumference. Sweater shown measures 36½" (92.5 cm).

Yarn
DK-weight (CYCA #3 Light) yarn.
Shown here: Rowan Calmer (75% cotton, 25% microfiber; 175 yd [160 m]/50 g): #463 calmer (pale blue), 11 (13, 14, 15, 18, 20) balls.

Needles
Body and sleeves—size 3 (3.25 mm): straight and 24" (60 cm) circular (cir). Edging—size 2 (2.75 mm): straight and 24" (60 cm) cir. Adjust needle size if necessary to obtain the correct gauge.

Notions
Removable markers (m); 2 cable needles (cn); stitch holders or waste yarn; tapestry needle.

Gauge
40 stitches and 44 rows = 4" (10 cm) in lattice panel of Chart R3, worked either in rows or rounds, unstretched; Chart A measures about 2⅜" (6 cm) wide, worked either in rows or rounds.

Stitch Guide

Centered double decrease (ctr dbl dec)

RS rows: Sl 2 as if to k2tog, k1, p2sso—2 sts dec'd.

WS rows: [Sl 1 kwise] 2 times, return sl sts to left
needle, sl 2 as if to p2tog tbl, p1, p2sso—2 sts
dec'd.

Notes

- The body consists of a series of textured panels that are arranged symmetrically on the front and back. However, the back pattern is not a direct copy of the front.
- For the body, the beginning of the round is at the left side back, not at the midpoint of the underarm. Place a marker to indicate the beginning of the round, and if desired, place additional markers to indicate the beginning or end of each Chart panel.
- Minor length adjustments can be made at the hem and cuff by increasing the number of repeats of the first two rounds or rows.
- For all edge shaping, work all decreases at the edge and do not leave a selvedge stitch; the decrease sts will form the selvedge.

Body

With smaller cir needle, CO 306 (338, 380, 418, 456, 492) sts. Place marker (pm) and join for working in the rnd, being careful not to twist sts. Work Rnd 1 of the foll Charts (see pages 128–131 for Charts) as indicated for your size (the markers denote the back neck sts):

Size 36½" only: Side, *F, C, F, X, F, O, F, X*, D, B, D, A, E, B, E, **X, F, O, F, X, F, C, F**, Side, rep from * to * once, pm, F, O, F, X, F, C, F, X, F, O, F, pm, rep from ** to ** once.

Size 41¼" only: Side, O, *D, C, F, X, F, O, F, X*, D, B, D, A, E, B, E, **X, F, O, F, X, F, C, E**, O, Side, O, rep from * to * once, pm, F, O, F, X, F, C, F, X, F, O, F, pm, rep from ** to ** once, O.

Size 43¼" only: Side, F, O, F, X, *D, C, F, X, F, O, F, C*, D, B, D, A, E, B, E, **C, F, O, F, X, F, C, E**, X, F, O, F, Side, F, O, rep from * to * once, pm, F, O, F, X, F, C, F, X, F, O, F, pm, rep from ** to ** once, O, F.

Size 47¼" only: Side, F, O, F, X, F, O, *D, C, F, X, F, O, F, C*, D, B, D, A, E, B, E, **C, F, O, F, X, F, C, E**, O, F, X, F, O, F, Side, F, O, F, X, rep from * to * once, pm, F, O, F, X, F, C, F, X, F, O, F, pm, rep from ** to ** once, X, F, O, F.

Size 51¼" only: Side, F, O, F, X, F, O, F, X, *D, C, F, X, F, O, F, C*, D, B, D, A, E, B, E, **C, F, O, F, X, F, C, E**, X, F, O, F, X, F, O, F, Side, F, O, F, X, F, O, rep from * to * once, pm, F, O, F, X, F, C, F, X, F, O, F, pm, rep from ** to ** once, O, F, X, F, O, F.

Size 55¼" only: Side, F, X, F, O, F, X, F, O, F, X, *D, C, F, X, F, O, F, C*, D, B, D, A, E, B, E, **C, F, O, F, X, F, C, E**, X, F, O, F, X, F, O, F, X, F, Side, F, X, F, O, F, X, F, O, rep from * to * once, pm, F, O, F, X, F, C, F, X, F, O, F, pm, rep from ** to ** once, O, F, X, F, O, F, X, F.

All sizes: Work Rnd 2 of the Charts as established. Rep Rnd 1 and 2 of Charts 1 more time. Working 4 more rnds with smaller needle then changing to larger cir needle, cont as established until Rows 22–45 (22–45, 16–45, 16–45, 22–45, 22–45) of Chart A have been worked 4 (4, 4, 4, 5, 5) times, ending with Row 45 of Chart A— 119 (119, 137, 137, 143, 143) rows total from CO. Cont in patt as established, working Rows 46–66 (46–66, 46–64, 46–64, 46–66, 46–66) of Chart A (do not work last 2 rows of Chart A for sizes 43¼" and 47¼")—378 (418, 452, 494, 536, 580) sts; piece measures 12¾ (12¾, 14¼, 14¼, 15, 15)" (32.5 [32.5, 37, 37, 38, 38] cm) from CO.

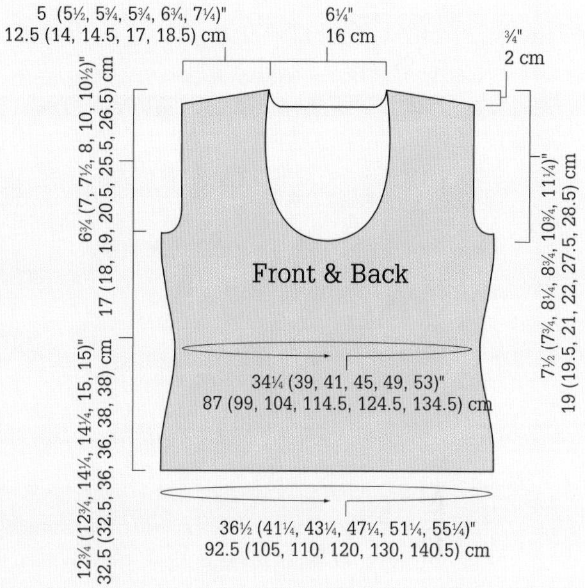

5 (5½, 5¾, 5¾, 6¾, 7¼)"
12.5 (14, 14.5, 17, 18.5) cm
6¼"
16 cm
¾"
2 cm
6¾ (7, 7½, 8, 10, 10½)"
17 (18, 19, 20.5, 25.5, 26.5) cm
Front & Back
7½ (7¾, 8¼, 8¾, 10¾, 11¼)"
19 (19.5, 21, 22, 27.5, 28.5) cm
34¼ (39, 41, 45, 49, 53)"
87 (99, 104, 114.5, 124.5, 134.5) cm
12¾ (12¾, 14¼, 14¼, 15, 15)"
32.5 (32.5, 36, 36, 38, 38) cm
36½ (41¼, 43¼, 47¼, 51¼, 55¼)"
92.5 (105, 110, 120, 130, 140.5) cm

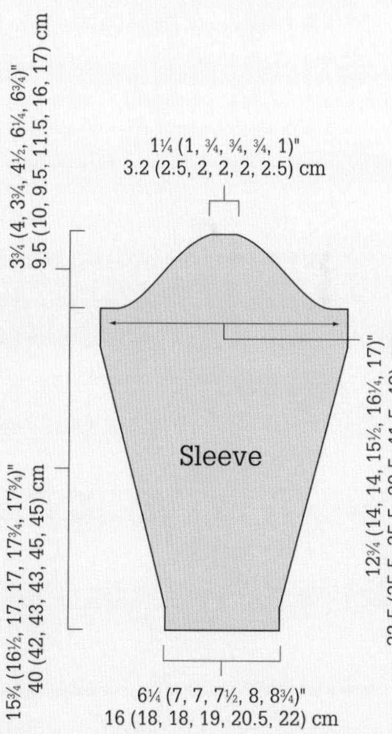

3¾ (4, 3¾, 4½, 6¼, 6¾)"
9.5 (10, 9.5, 11.5, 16, 17) cm
1¼ (1, ¾, ¾, ¾, 1)"
3.2 (2.5, 2, 2, 2, 2.5) cm
Sleeve
12¾ (14, 14, 15½, 16¼, 17)"
32.5 (35.5, 35.5, 39.5, 41.5, 43) cm
15¾ (16½, 17, 17, 17¾, 17¾)"
40 (42, 43, 43, 45, 45) cm
6¼ (7, 7, 7½, 8, 8¾)"
16 (18, 18, 19, 20.5, 22) cm

	k on RS; p on WS		ctr dbl dec (see Stitch Guide)

- ☐ k on RS; p on WS
- • p on RS; k on WS
- b k tbl on RS; p tbl on WS
- pb p tbl on RS; k tbl on WS
- ╱ k2tog on RS; p2tog on WS
- ╲ ssk on RS; ssp (see Glossary, page154) on WS
- ⊾ p2tog on RS; k2tog on WS
- ⊿ ssp on RS; ssk on WS
- ⋉ sssp (see Glossary, page 154) on RS; sssk on WS

- ⋏ ctr dbl dec (see Stitch Guide)
- ⋔ p5tog on RS; k5tog on WS
- M M1 kwise on RS; M1 pwise on WS
- MP M1 pwise on RS; M1 kwise on WS
- V k in st below st on left needle on RS, p in st 2 rows below st on right needle on WS
- V k in st 2 rows below st on right needle on RS, p in st below st on left needle on WS
- ▨ no stitch
- ☐ pattern repeat

1/1 RTC: on RS, sl 1 st onto cn and hold in back, k1tbl, k1tbl from cn; on WS, sl 1 st onto cn and hold in back, p1tbl, p1tbl from cn

1/1 LTC: on RS, sl 1 st onto cn and hold in front, k1tbl, k1tbl from cn; on WS, sl 1 st onto cn and hold in front, p1tbl, p1tbl from cn

1/1 RTPC: on RS, sl 1 st onto cn and hold in back, k1tbl, p1 from cn; on WS, sl 1 st onto cn and hold in back, k1, p1tbl from cn

1/1 LTPC: on RS, sl 1 st onto cn and hold in front, p1, k1tbl from cn; on WS, sl 1 st onto cn and hold in front, p1tbl, k1 from cn

2/1 RPC: on RS, sl 1 st onto cn and hold in back, k2, p1 from cn; on WS, sl 2 sts onto cn and hold in back, k1, p2 from cn

2/1 LPC: on RS, sl 2 sts onto cn and hold in front, p1, k2 from cn; on WS, sl 1 st onto cn and hold in front, p2, k1 from cn

1/1/1 RTPC: on RS, sl 1 st onto first cn and hold in back, sl 1 st onto 2nd cn and hold in back, k1tbl, p1 from 2nd cn, k1tbl from first cn; on WS, sl 1 st onto first cn and hold in back, sl 1 st onto 2nd cn and hold in front, p1tbl, k1 from 2nd cn, p1tbl from first cn

1/1/1 LTPC: on RS, sl 1 st onto first cn and hold in front, sl 1 st onto 2nd cn and hold in back, k1tbl, p1 from 2nd cn, k1tbl from first cn; on WS, sl 1 st onto first cn and hold in front, sl 1 st onto 2nd cn and hold in front, p1tbl, k1 from 2nd cn, p1tbl from first cn

2/1 RTC: on RS, sl 2 sts onto cn and hold in back, k1tbl, k2tbl from cn; on WS, sl 1 st onto cn and hold in back, p2tbl, p1tbl from cn

2/2 RC: on RS, sl 2 sts onto cn and hold in back, k2, k2 from cn; on WS, sl 2 sts onto cn and hold in back, p2, p2 from cn

2/2 LC: on RS, sl 2 sts onto cn and hold in front, k2, k2 from cn; on WS, sl 2 sts onto cn and hold in front, p2, p2 from cn

2/1 RIC: on RS, sl 1 st onto cn and hold in back, k2, M1, k1 from cn; on WS, sl 2 sts onto cn and hold in back, p1, M1 pwise, p2 from cn

2/1 LIC: on RS, sl 2 sts onto cn and hold in front, k1, M1, k2 from cn; on WS, sl 1 st onto cn and hold in front, p2, M1 pwise, p1 from cn

2/1/2 RPC: on RS, sl 2 sts onto first cn and hold in back, sl 1 st onto 2nd cn and hold in back, k2, p1 from 2nd cn, k2 from first cn; on WS, sl 2 sts onto first cn and hold in back, sl 1 st onto 2nd cn and hold in front, p2, k1 from 2nd cn, p2 from first cn

2/1/2 LPC: on RS, sl 2 sts onto first cn and hold in front, sl 1 st onto 2nd cn and hold in back, k2, p1 from 2nd cn, k2 from first cn; on WS, sl 2 sts onto first cn and hold in front, sl 1 st onto 2nd cn and hold in front, p2, k1 from 2nd cn, p2 from first cn

Chart A

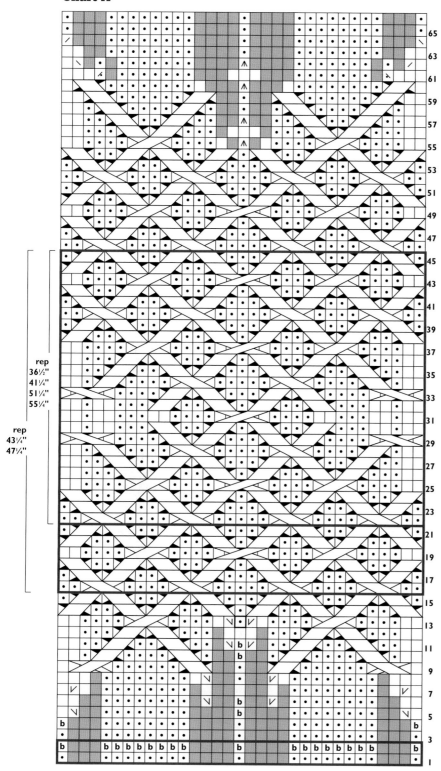

Chart B-Left

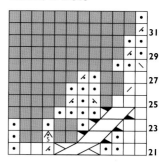

Chart B-Right

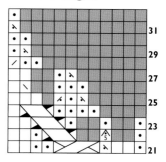

Chart B

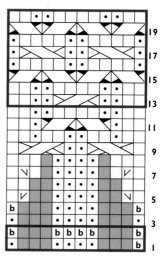

129

Chart C

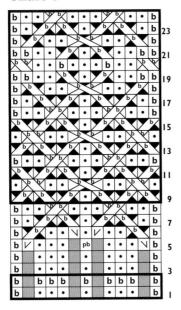

Side Chart, Rows 53–66

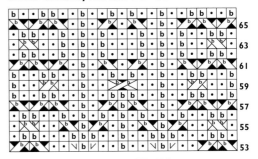

Side Chart, Rows 35–52

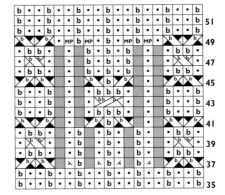

Side Chart, Rows 67–92

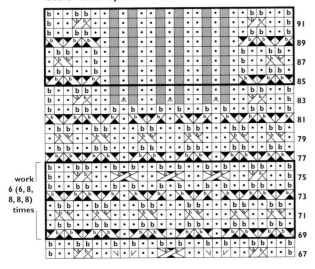

work
6 (6, 8,
8, 8, 8)
times

Side Chart, Rows 1–34

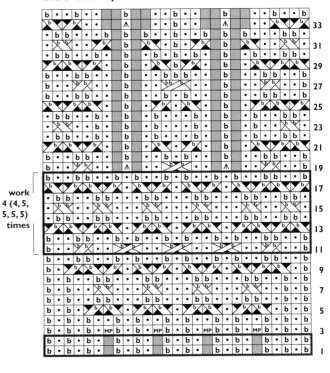

work
4 (4, 5,
5, 5, 5)
times

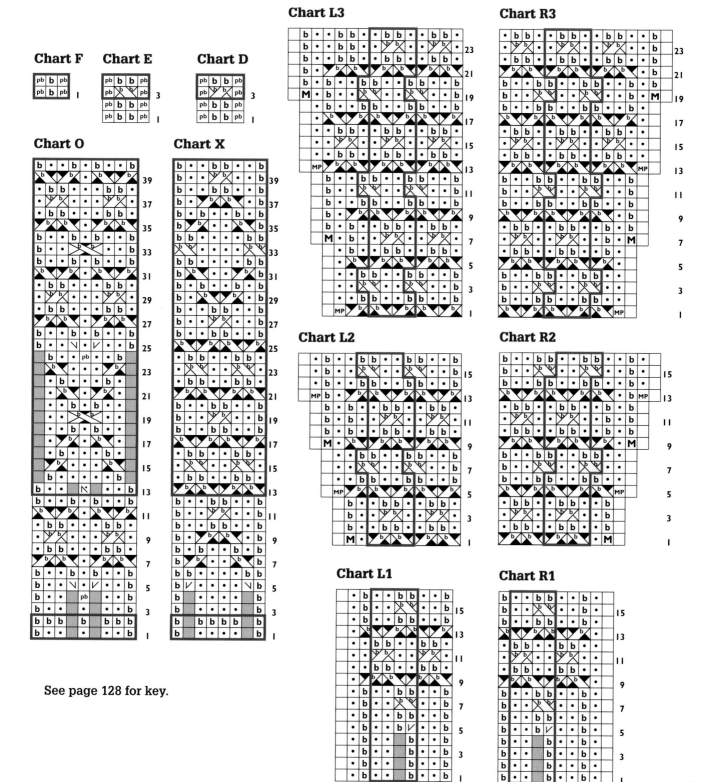

See page 128 for key.

Divide for Back and Front

Note: In the foll sections, the charts gain and lose sts at the same time as shaping occurs; therefore the stitch counts may appear inconsistent. Cont in patt and beg with Side Chart, BO center 9 (15, 15, 15, 23, 23) sts of Side Chart, work across front to beg of Chart A sts, BO all Chart A sts, work across front to Side Chart, BO center 9 (15, 15, 15, 23, 23) sts of Side Chart; work across back, work rem sts of Side Chart, remove marker—183 (197, 201, 223, 235, 257) sts rem for back; 79 (86, 101, 111, 118, 129) sts rem for each front.

Back

Working 183 (197, 201, 223, 235, 257) back sts back and forth in rows, cont in patt and BO 2 (3, 3, 6, 6, 6) sts at beg of next 2 (2, 4, 2, 2, 2) rows, then BO 0 (0, 0, 2, 2, 2) sts at beg of foll 0 (0, 0, 2, 2, 2) rows—179 (191, 189, 207, 235, 257) sts rem. Dec 1 st each end of needle every row 4 (6, 6, 10, 10, 14) times, then every other row 2 (3, 3, 8, 8, 10) times—167 (165, 183, 171, 199, 209) sts rem. Working the first and last st in rev St st (purl RS rows; knit WS rows), cont even in patt until armholes measure about 6¾ (7, 7½, 8, 10, 10½)" (17 [18, 19, 20.5, 25.5, 26.5] cm), ending with Row 16 (20, 40, 18, 20, 26) of Chart X.

Shape Shoulders

With RS facing and cont in patt, work to first marker (neck edge), turn work. Work short-rows (see Glossary, page 157) as foll:

Short-row 1: Work in patt to last 13 (15, 16, 14, 22, 17) sts, wrap next st, turn, work to neck edge.

Short-row 2: Work in patt to 13 (12, 15, 13, 11, 19) sts before previous wrapped st, wrap next st, turn, work to neck edge.

Short-row 3: Work in patt to 9 (14, 12, 15, 14, 18) sts before previous wrapped st, wrap next st, turn, work to neck edge.

Cont in patt, work across all sts, working wraps tog with wrapped sts and dec 1 st at any points at or near any cable crossings to eliminate flaring as foll:

Size 36½" only: Dec 2 sts over first Chart X, 2 sts over Chart O, 1 st over next Chart X, and 3 sts over Chart C—8 sts dec'd.

Size 41¼" only: Dec 1 st over first Chart X, 4 sts over second Chart X, 5 sts over Chart C, and 2 sts over second Chart O—12 sts dec'd.

Size 43¼" only: Dec 2 sts over first Chart C, 2 sts over first Chart O, 2 sts over Chart X, and 6 sts over second Chart C—12 sts dec'd.

Size 47¼" only: Dec 6 sts over first Chart C, 2 sts over Chart O, 3 sts over Chart X, and 2 sts over second Chart C—13 sts dec'd.

Size 51¼" only: Dec 4 sts over first Chart C, 1 st over first Chart O, 3 sts over Chart X, 4 sts over second Chart C, and 2 sts over second Chart O—14 sts dec'd.

Size 55¼" only: Dec 6 sts over first Chart C, 3 sts over first Chart O, 2 sts over Chart X, 6 sts over second Chart C, and 4 sts over second Chart O—21 sts dec'd.

All sizes: 41 (44, 45, 44, 51, 51) shoulder sts rem. Place these sts on holder. With RS facing, join yarn at right neck edge and BO all sts to next marker (left neck edge), dec 1 st at or near any cable crossings to eliminate flaring as foll: dec 2 (1, 4, 2, 1, 0) st(s) over each Chart O, 2 (1, 1, 4, 1, 4) st(s) over each Chart X, and 2 (2, 2, 2, 2, 3) sts over Chart C—10 (6, 12, 14, 6, 11) sts dec'd. Remove neck markers. Cont in patt, work to left armhole edge. Turn and work back to left neck edge. Beg with Short-row 1, work shoulder shaping as before. Place sts on holder.

Left Front

Place 79 (86, 101, 111, 118, 129) held left front sts on needle. With WS facing, rejoin yarn at neck edge and cont in patt (Row 20 of Chart B), BO 3 sts, work to end—76 (83, 98, 108, 115, 126) sts rem. *Next row:* (RS) BO 2 (3, 6, 6, 6, 6) sts at armhole edge, work to beg of Chart B sts, work Row 21 of Chart B-Left. Cont in patt, and *at the same time* shape armhole (beg of RS rows) as foll: **BO 0 (0, 3, 4, 4, 4) sts 0 (0, 2, 3, 3, 4) times, then dec 1 st every row 4 (6, 6, 13, 11, 14) times, then dec 1 st every other row 2 (3, 6, 5, 6, 7) times**, and *also at the same time,* when Chart B-Left is completed, cont to dec 1 st at neck edge every 4th row 2 more times, working the last st at neck edge in rev St st (purl on RS; knit on WS). At neck edge, work Chart F in place of Chart D—54 (55, 62, 58, 70, 75) sts rem after all shaping is complete. Working the first and last st in rev St st, cont in patt until armhole measures same as back, ending with Row 16 (20, 40, 18, 20, 26) of Chart X.

Shape Shoulder

With RS facing and cont in patt, work across all sts. Beg with Short-row 1, shape shoulder as for back. Cont in patt, work across all sts, working wraps tog with wrapped sts, dec 1 st at any points at or near any cable crossings to eliminate flaring, and dec 3 extra sts at neck edge, as foll:

Size 36½" only: Sssk (see Glossary, page 154), dec 3 sts over first Chart X, 2 sts over Chart O, 1 st over next Chart X, and 3 sts over Chart C—11 sts dec'd.
Size 41¼" only: Sssk, dec 2 sts over first Chart X, 4 sts over second Chart X, 5 sts over Chart C, and 2 sts over second Chart O—15 sts dec'd.
Size 43¼" only: Sssk, dec 3 sts over first Chart C, 2 sts over first Chart O, 2 sts over Chart X, and 6 sts over second Chart C—15 sts dec'd.
Size 47¼" only: Sssk, dec 7 sts over first Chart C (the first dec will be a double dec), 2 sts over Chart O, 3 sts over Chart X, and 2 sts over second Chart C—16 sts dec'd.
Size 51¼" only: Sssk, dec 5 sts over first Chart C, 1 st over first Chart O, 3 sts over Chart X, 4 sts over second Chart C, and 2 sts over second Chart O—17 sts dec'd.
Size 55¼" only: Sssk, dec 7 sts over first Chart C (the first dec will be a double dec), 3 sts over first Chart O, 2 sts over Chart X, 6 sts over second Chart C, and 4 sts over second Chart O—24 sts dec'd.
All sizes: 41 (44, 45, 44, 51, 51) sts rem. Place sts on holder.

Right Front

Place 79 (86, 101, 111, 118, 129) held right front sts on needle. With WS facing, rejoin yarn at right armhole edge and cont in patt (Row 20 of Chart B), BO 2 (3, 6, 6, 6, 6) sts at beg of row, work to end—77 (83, 95, 105, 112, 123) sts rem. *Next row:* (RS) BO 3 sts at neck edge, work Row 21 of Chart B-Right, work to end of row in patt. Cont in patt, work armhole shaping as indicated for left front from ** to ** and *at the same time,* when Chart B–Right is completed, cont to dec 1 st at neck edge every 4th row 2 more times, keeping first st at neck edge in rev St st. At neck edge, work Chart F in place of Chart E—54 (55, 62, 58, 70, 75) sts rem after all

shaping is complete. Working the first and last st in rev St st, cont in patt until armhole measures same as back, ending with Row 16 (20, 40, 18, 20, 26) of Chart X (yarn is at neck edge).

Shape Right Shoulder
Cont in patt, and beg with Short-row 1, shape shoulder as for back, then work final dec row as for left front—41 (44, 45, 44, 51, 51) sts rem. Place sts on holder.

Sleeves

With smaller straight needles, CO 63 (69, 69, 75, 81, 87) sts. Work row 1 of the following Charts in this order: R1 working patt rep a total of 3 (4, 4, 5, 6, 7) times, F, X, F, C, F, X, F, L1 working patt rep a total of 3 (4, 4, 5, 6, 7) times. Work Row 2 of the Charts as established. Rep Row 1 and 2 of Charts 1 more time. Cont in patt until Charts R1 and L1 are complete, changing to larger needles on row 7 of Chart. Cont in patt, switching from Charts R1 and L1 to R2 and L2, working patt rep 3 (4, 4, 5, 6, 7) times total. Rep Charts R2 and L2, working patt rep 4 (5, 5, 6, 7, 8) times total. Rep Charts R2 and L2, working patt rep 5 (6, 6, 7, 8, 9) times total—101 (109, 109, 117, 125, 133) sts; piece measures 6" (15 cm) from CO.
Sizes 47¼ (51¼, 55¼)" only: Rep Charts R2 and L2, working 4-st rep 8 (9, 10) times total.
All sizes: Rep Rows 1–4 of Charts R2 and L2 once more, working 4-st rep 6 (7, 7, 9, 10, 11) times total—70 (70, 70, 86, 86, 86) rows total. Cont in patt, changing from Charts R2 and L2 to Charts R3 and L3, work 4-st rep 6 (7, 7, 9, 10, 11) times total. Rep Charts R3 and L3, working 4-st rep 7 (8, 8, 10, 11, 12) times total. Rep Charts R3 and L3, working 4-st rep 8 (9, 9, 11, 12, 13) times total. Work Rows 0 (1, 1, 1, 1, 1)

to 0 (12, 12, 12, 12, 12) of Charts R3 and L3 once more, working 4-st rep 0 (10, 10, 12, 13, 14) times total—142 (154, 154, 170, 170, 170) rows total; 127 (139, 139, 155, 163, 171) sts. Cont in patt, rep Rows 19 (7, 7, 7, 7, 7) to 24 (12, 12, 12, 12, 12) of Charts R3 and L3 without inc, by working M1 as k1tbl, until piece measures 15¾ (16½, 17, 17, 17¾, 17¾)" (40 [42, 43, 43, 45, 45] cm) from CO, ending with a WS row.

Shape Cap

Keeping in patt, BO 7 (10, 10, 10, 10, 10) sts at beg of next 2 rows, then BO 3 (4, 4, 4, 4, 4) sts at beg of foll 2 (2, 4, 4, 4, 4) rows, then BO 0 (0, 2, 2, 2, 2) sts at beg of foll 0 (0, 2, 2, 2, 2) rows—107 (111, 99, 115, 123, 131) sts rem. *Note:* Work the foll decs on the edge sts; the decs will form the selvedge edges. Dec 1 st each end of needle every row 14 (32, 26, 15, 13, 13) times—79 (47, 47, 85, 97, 105) sts rem. Work 1 (0, 0, 0, 0, 0) row even. For sizes 47¼ (51¼, 55¼)" only, dec 1 st each end of needle every other row 2 (13, 16) times. For all sizes, dec 1 st each end of needle every row 15 (0, 0, 15, 13, 13) times, ending with a WS row—49 (47, 47, 51, 45, 47) sts rem. Work short-rows as foll:

Short-row 1: Keeping in patt, work to last 2 (2, 3, 3, 2, 2) sts, wrap next st, turn, work to last 2 (2, 3, 3, 2, 2) sts, wrap next st, turn.

Short-row 2: Work to 3 (4, 4, 6, 4, 4) sts before previous wrapped st, wrap next st, turn, work to 3 (4, 4, 6, 4, 4) sts before previous wrapped st, wrap next st, turn.

Short-row 3: Work to 6 sts before previous wrapped st, wrap next st, turn, work to 6 sts before previous wrapped st, wrap next st, turn.

Short-row 4: Work to 7 sts before previous wrapped st, wrap next st, turn, work to 7 sts before previous wrapped st, wrap next st, turn.

BO all sts loosely, hiding wraps as you go.

Finishing

Using the three-needle bind-off (see Glossary, page 153), join fronts to back at shoulders.

Neckband

With smaller cir needle, RS facing, and beg at left shoulder seam, pick up and knit 67 (68, 70, 72, 85, 89) sts along left front, 19 sts across front neck, 67 (68, 70, 72, 85, 89) sts along right front, 7 sts along right back neck, mark last st with a removable marker, pick up and knit 48 sts across back neck, 1 st along left back neck, mark last st with a removable marker, pick up and knit 6 more sts along left back neck—215 (217, 221, 225, 251, 259) sts total. Pm and join for working in the rnd. Knit to 1 st before marked st, work ctr dbl dec (see Stitch Guide), knit to 1 st before next marked st, work ctr dbl dec, knit to end—211 (213, 217, 221, 247, 255) sts rem. Purl 1 rnd. Rep last 2 rnds once more—207 (209, 213, 217, 243, 251) sts rem. BO all sts kwise, working ctr dbl decs as before.

With yarn threaded on a tapestry needle, sew sleeve seams. Sew sleeve caps into armholes, making sure that Chart C is centered at shoulder seam for sizes 43¼", 47¼", 51¼", and 55¼" (underarm seam will be off-center). Weave in loose ends. Block to measurements.

Tomato

design by Wendy Bernard

As comfy as a bowl of tomato soup, but exponentially sexier. This sweater is knitted in Blue Sky Cotton, which is soft, soft, soft, but at a tighter gauge than the ball band suggests to improve the drape and wearability. It's designed to be close fitting, with waist shaping and a seriously flattering deep scoopy neck. (Too deep for you? Slip a camisole underneath, or shorten the neckline.) And for a little spice, designer Wendy Bernard has knitted in a simplified houndstooth pattern.

Notes

- This sweater is worked in stockinette stitch—when working back and forth in rows, knit all RS rows and purl all WS rows; when working in rounds, knit all rounds.

- If you desire a less dramatic neckline, hold the garment up to your body as you knit—making note that the neckline ribbing will add 1½" (3.8 cm)—and, when the neckline is the desired length, cast on the 22 (22, 26, 30, 36, 42) center front neck stitches and join for working in the round (the sleeve and body increases will not be completed). Work until you have 70 (76, 84, 92, 100, 110) back stitches before dividing for armholes. Divide for armholes and continue working the pattern as instructed (without casting on any more stitches at center front, of course).

Finished Size
About 31 (35½, 40, 44½, 48¾, 53¼)" (78.5 [90, 101.5, 113, 124, 135.5] cm) bust circumference. Sweater shown measures 35½" (90 cm).

Yarn
Worsted-weight (CYCA #4 Medium) yarn.
Shown here: Blue Sky Alpacas Dyed Cotton (100% cotton; 150 yd [137 m]/100 g): #619 tomato (MC), 4 (5, 5, 6, 6, 7) skeins. Blue Sky Alpacas Organic Cotton (100% organic cotton; 150 yd [137 m]/100 g): #82 nut (CC), 1 skein (all sizes).

Needles
Body and sleeves—size 7 (4.5 mm): 29" (70 cm) circular (cir). Edging—size 6 (4 mm): 16" or 24" (40 or 60 cm) cir or set of 4 double-pointed (dpn). Adjust needle size if necessary to obtain the correct gauge.

Notions
Markers (m); tapestry needle; a few yards (meters) of waste yarn.

Gauge
18 stitches and 25 rows = 4" (10 cm) in stockinette stitch on larger needle.

Upper Body

With MC and larger size cir needle, CO 1 st for right front, place marker (pm), CO 6 (7, 8, 8, 8, 10) sts for right sleeve, pm, CO 24 (24, 28, 32, 38, 44) sts for back, pm, CO 6 (7, 8, 8, 8, 10) sts for left sleeve, pm, CO 1 st for left front—38 (40, 46, 50, 56, 66) sts total; 4 markers placed. Work upper body back and forth in rows as foll:

Row 1: (RS) K1f&b (see Glossary, page 156), slip marker (sl m), k1f&b, knit to 1 st before next m, k1f&b, sl m, k1f&b, knit to 1 st before next m, k1f&b, sl m, k1f&b, knit to 1 st before next m, k1f&b, sl m, k1f&b—8 sts inc'd; 46 (48, 54, 58, 64, 74) sts total.

Row 2: (WS) Purl.

Row 3: Knit to 1 st before first m, k1f&b, sl m, k1f&b, knit to 1 st before second m, k1f&b, sl m, k1f&b, knit to 1 st before third m, k1f&b, sl m, k1f&b, knit to 1 st before last marker, k1f&b, sl m, k1f&b, knit to end—8 sts inc'd.

Rep the last 2 rows 21 (24, 26, 28, 29, 31) more times—222 (248, 270, 290, 304, 330) sts total; 24 (27, 29, 31, 32, 34) sts for each front; 52 (59, 64, 68, 70, 76) sts for each sleeve; 70 (76, 84, 92, 100, 110) sts for back. Work Row 2 once more—piece measures about 7¼ (8¼, 9, 9½, 10, 10½)" (18.5 [21, 23, 24, 25.5, 26.5] cm) from CO.

Divide for Armholes

With RS facing, work across left front sts, place 52 (59, 64, 68, 70, 76) sleeve sts on waste yarn, removing markers, use the backward loop method (see Glossary, page 153) to CO 0 (2, 3, 4, 5, 5) sts for underarm, pm for beg of rnd (it's helpful to use a different colored marker here), CO 0 (2, 3, 4, 5, 5) more sts as before, k70 (76, 84, 92, 100, 110) back sts, place next 52 (59, 64, 68, 70, 76) sts on waste yarn for other sleeve,

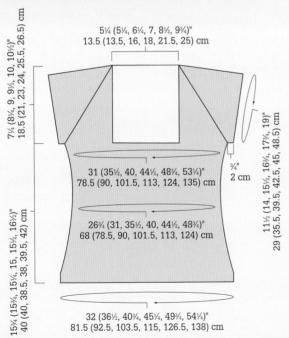

5¼ (5¼, 6¼, 7, 8½, 9¾)"
13.5 (13.5, 16, 18, 21.5, 25) cm

7¼ (8¼, 9, 9¼, 10, 10½)"
18.5 (21, 23, 24, 25.5, 26.5) cm

31 (35½, 40, 44½, 48¾, 53¼)"
78.5 (90, 101.5, 113, 124, 135) cm

¾"
2 cm

26¾ (31, 35½, 40, 44½, 48¾)"
68 (78.5, 90, 101.5, 113, 124) cm

11½ (14, 15½, 16¾, 17¾, 19)"
29 (35.5, 39.5, 42.5, 45, 48.5) cm

15¾ (15¾, 15, 15¼, 16½)"
40 (40, 38.5, 38, 39.5, 42) cm

32 (36½, 40¾, 45¼, 49¾, 54¼)"
81.5 (92.5, 103.5, 115, 126.5, 138) cm

removing markers, CO 0 (2, 3, 4, 5, 5) sts as before, pm, CO 0 (2, 3, 4, 5, 5) more sts as before, k24 (27, 29, 31, 32, 34) front sts, CO 22 (22, 26, 30, 36, 42) sts for center front, join for working in the rnd, knit to end of rnd—140 (160, 180, 200, 220, 240) sts total.

Lower Body

Knit 3 rnds. Change to CC and knit 1 rnd. *Next rnd:* Change to MC and dec 4 sts as foll: k1, k2tog, knit to 3 sts before next m, ssk, k1, sl m, k1, k2tog, knit to 3 sts before end-of-rnd m, ssk, k1—136 (156, 176, 196, 216, 236) sts rem. Work check patt as foll (note that it is not necessary to cut yarn when changing colors):

Rnd 1: K1 with MC, *k1 with CC, k3 with MC; rep from * to last 3 sts, k1 with CC, k2 with MC.

Rnd 2: *K1 with MC, k3 with CC; rep from * to end.

Rnd 3: *K3 with CC, k1 with MC; rep from * to end.

Rnd 4: K2 with MC, *k1 with CC, k3 with MC; rep from * to last 2 sts, k1 with CC, k1 with MC.

Rep Rnds 1–4 two more times—12 rnds total. Knit 1 rnd with MC. Knit 1 rnd with CC. Cont with MC until piece measures 4¾ (4, 3½, 3, 3, 3)" (12 [10, 9, 7.5, 7.5, 7.5] cm) from underarm.

Shape Waist

Dec at each side "seam" as foll: K1, k2tog, knit to 3 sts before next m, ssk, k1, sl m, k1, k2tog, knit to last 3 sts, ssk, k1—4 sts dec'd. Knit 4 rnds even. Rep the last 5 rnds 3 more times—120 (140, 160, 180, 200, 220) sts rem. Cont even until piece measures 9¼ (8½, 8, 7¾, 8, 7½)" (23.5 [21.5, 20.5, 19.5, 20.5, 19] cm) from underarm. Inc at each side "seam" as foll: K1, M1 (see Glossary, page 156), knit to 1 st before next m, M1, k1, sl m, k1, M1, knit to last st, M1, k1—4 sts inc'd. Knit 4 rnds even. Rep the last 5 rnds 5 more times—144 (164, 184, 204, 224, 244) sts. Cont even until piece measures 14¼ (14¼, 13¾, 13½, 14, 15)" (36 [36, 35, 34.5, 35.5, 38] cm) from underarm, or about 1½" (3.8 cm) less than desired total length.

Ribbing

*K2, p2; rep from * to end of rnd. Rep this rnd until a total of 1½" (3.8 cm) of rib have been worked. Knit 2 rnds. Loosely BO all sts.

Finishing

Neck Edging

With MC, smaller cir needle or dpn, RS facing, and beg at the upper right back, pick up and knit 24 (24, 28, 32, 38, 44) sts along back neck, 5 (6, 7, 7, 7, 9) sts along top of left sleeve, 29 (31, 37, 40, 41, 43) sts along left front edge, pm, pick up and knit 16 (18, 20, 22, 26, 32) sts across center front neck, pm, pick up and knit 29 (31, 37, 40, 41, 43) sts along right front neck, and 5 (6, 7, 7, 7, 9) sts along top of right sleeve—108 (116, 136, 148, 160, 180) sts total. (*Note:* The number of sts you need to pick up for the neck edging may vary from this number, as long as it is a multiple of 4 sts; adjust your numbers as necessary to prevent the garment from puckering or gaping.) Pm and join for working in the rnd. Work in k2, p2 rib for 8 rnds. *Next rnd:* Work in patt to first front neck m, sl m, work to first k2 pair and knit these 2 sts tog, cont to work each k2 pair tog to next neck m, sl m, work in patt to end of rnd. Work 1 rnd even, working the sts as they present themselves. Loosely BO all sts.

Sleeve Edging

With MC and RS facing, place 52 (59, 64, 68, 70, 76) held sleeve sts on smaller cir needle or dpn, pick up and knit 0 (2, 3, 4, 5, 5) sts at underarm, pm, pick up and knit 0 (2, 3, 4, 5, 5) sts at underarm—0 (4, 6, 8, 10, 10) sts total picked up (this will close the hole between the body and the sleeves so you won't have to seam the area later); 52 (63, 70, 76, 80, 86) sts total. *Next rnd:* Dec 4 (7, 10, 12, 12, 14) sts evenly spaced—48 (56, 60, 64, 68, 72) sts rem. Work in k2, p2 rib for 4 rnds. Knit 1 rnd. Loosely BO all sts.

Weave in loose ends. Block to measurements.

Peerie Fleur

design by Zoe Valette

This cardigan is knitted in yummy chocolate brown accented with fleur-de-lis–inspired motifs in strong pink and an indefinable color Rowan calls "ghost." It's knitted in the round and then . . . steeked. What? You can't do that without wool. Or can you? Will the steeks unravel and the stranded-color patterning gape where the colors cross? They might, if you don't choose your yarn wisely.

      Designer Zoe Valette's secret here is the almost-sticky yarn: Rowan Summer Tweed. This mostly silk yarn has more grab than most nonwools; it sticks to itself much like wool does. Zoe recommends you machine-sew your steeks so there's no chance of the yarn escaping.

Notes

- To minimize tangles in the balls of yarn, place each ball of yarn in a zippered sandwich bag, cut a small hole in one of the corners, and pull the yarn through the hole.
- Because this yarn is very inelastic and will relax only slightly after blocking, be careful to strand unused yarns loosely across the wrong side when working the stranded-color pattern.
- For all areas of stranded-color pattern, you may want to weave in the floats on the back of the work if they are longer than 4–5 stitches, for neatness and to help keep an even tension.
- Purl all steek stitches every round so that they will fold neatly to the wrong side when cut apart.
- To minimize the number of ends to weave in, change colors and balls of yarn in the center of the steek stitches.
- The Yoke chart increases at regular intervals as marked on the chart. You may want to place markers between each pattern repeat to help you keep your place.
- This pattern is designed with short-rows at the back neck to allow the back neck to be higher than the front. You can omit these short-rows if you prefer.

Finished Size

36½ (42¼, 47¼, 52¾, 55¾, 59½)" (92.5 [107.5, 120, 134, 141.5, 151] cm) bust circumference. Sweater shown measures 36½" (92.5 cm).

Yarn

Worsted-weight (CYCA #4 Medium) yarn.

Shown here: Rowan Summer Tweed (70% silk, 30% cotton; 118 yd [108 m]/ 50 g): #531 chocolate fudge (MC), 9 (11, 13, 14, 15, 16) skeins; #528 brilliant (fuchsia; CC1) and #506 ghost (off-white; CC2), 2 (2, 2, 2, 2, 2) skeins each.

Needles

Body and sleeves—size 6 (4 mm): 32" (80 cm) circular (cir), 16" (40 cm) cir, and set of 4 or 5 double-pointed (dpn); size 8 (5 mm): 32" (80 cm) cir and set of 4 or 5 dpn. Ribbing—size 5 (3.75 mm): 16" (40 cm) cir and set of 4 or 5 dpn. Adjust needle size if necessary to obtain the correct gauge.

Notions

Markers (m); safety pins; sewing needle and thread to match MC; sewing machine (optional but recommended) and thread to contrast with MC; 1¾ yd (1.6 m) of ⅞" (2.2 cm) wide double-fold bias binding (available at fabric stores; optional); six ¾" (2 cm) buttons.

Gauge

19 stitches and 28 rounds = 4" (10 cm) in stockinette stitch worked in a single color on middle-size needle; 22 stitches and 22 rounds = 4" (10 cm) in stranded color pattern on largest needle; 19 stitches and 28 rounds = 4" (10 cm) in k2, p2 ribbing on smallest needle.

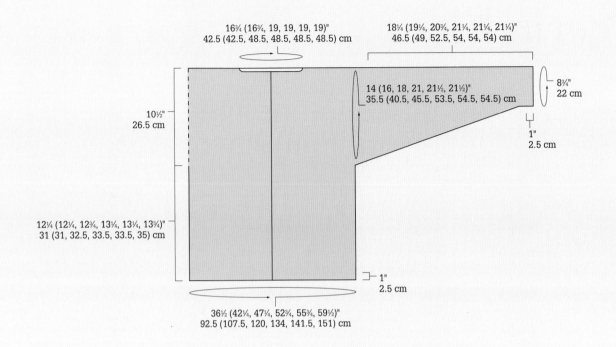

16¾ (16¾, 19, 19, 19, 19)"
42.5 (42.5, 48.5, 48.5, 48.5, 48.5) cm

18¼ (19¼, 20¾, 21¼, 21¼, 21¼)"
46.5 (49, 52.5, 54, 54, 54) cm

14 (16, 18, 21, 21½, 21½)"
35.5 (40.5, 45.5, 53.5, 54.5, 54.5) cm

8¾"
22 cm

10½"
26.5 cm

1"
2.5 cm

12¼ (12¼, 12¾, 13¼, 13¼, 13¾)"
31 (31, 32.5, 33.5, 33.5, 35) cm

1"
2.5 cm

36½ (42¼, 47¼, 52¾, 55¾, 59½)"
92.5 (107.5, 120, 134, 141.5, 151) cm

Body

With MC and smallest cir needle or dpn, CO 86 (86, 96, 96, 96, 96) sts. Place marker (pm) and join for working in the rnd, being careful not to twist sts.

Neckband

Set-up rnd: P3 (steek sts), [k1, p2] 1 (1, 0, 0, 0, 0) time, *k2, p2; rep from * to last 4 (4, 5, 5, 5, 5) sts, k1 (1, 2, 2, 2, 2), p3 (rem steek sts). Purling all steek sts, work center 80 (80, 90, 90, 90, 90) sts in rib as established (knit the knits and purl the purls) until piece measures 1" (2.5 cm) from CO. Change to middle-size needle and work 1 rnd in St st, purling all steek sts, and working short-rows (see Glossary, page 157) if desired (see Notes) as foll:

Row 1: P3, k27 (27, 30, 30, 30, 30), pm, k26 (26, 30, 30, 30, 30), wrap next st, turn work.

Row 2: Purl to m, remove m, wrap next st, turn.

Row 3: Knit to wrapped st, knit wrap tog with wrapped st, k2, wrap next st, turn.

Row 4: Purl to wrapped st, purl wrap tog with wrapped st, p2, wrap next st, turn.

Row 5: Knit to wrapped st, knit wrap tog with wrapped st, knit to last 3 sts, p3.

Work 1 rnd, working rem wrap tog with wrapped st.

Next rnd: P3, k40 (40, 45, 45, 45, 45), M1, knit to last 3 sts, p3—81 (81, 91, 91, 91, 91) body sts and 6 steek sts.

Yoke

Work Rnds 1–3 of Yoke chart on center 81 (81, 91, 91, 91, 91) sts, beg and end as indicated on chart. Change to largest needle and work Rnds 4–29 of Yoke chart, then work Rnds 30–45 as specified for your size—305 (353, 397, 451, 469, 487) yoke sts and 6 steek sts. *Next rnd:* Change to middle-size needle and work Rnd 46 of chart.

Key:

- ■ chocolate fudge (MC)
- × fuchsia (CC1)
- ◇ off-white (CC2)
- Ⅿ M1 using MC
- ▨ no stitch
- ☐ pattern repeat

Peerie

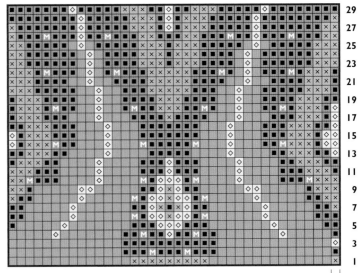

end
sleeve

end
body

beg
body
and
sleeve

Yoke, Rows 1–29

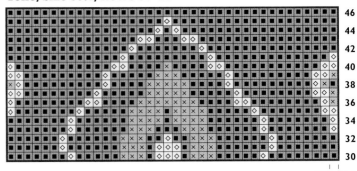

29
27
25
23
21
19
17
15
13
11
9
7
5
3
1

end beg

Yoke, size 36½, Rows 30–46

46
44
42
40
38
36
34
32
30

end beg

Yoke, sizes 42½" and 47¼", Rows 30–46

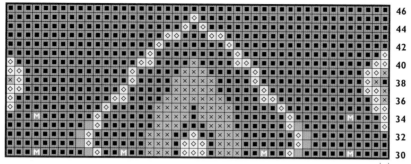

Yoke, size 52¾", Rows 30–46

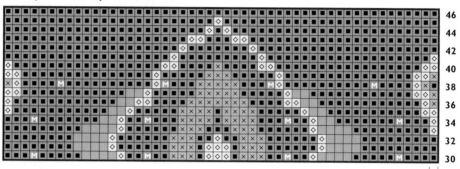

Yoke, size 55¾", Rows 30–46

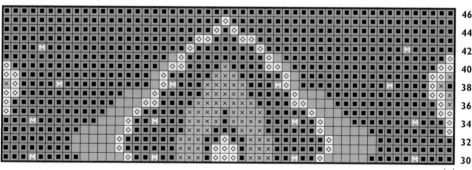

Yoke, size 59½", Rows 30–46

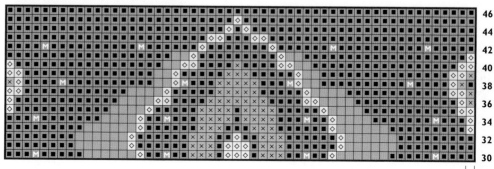

145

Divide for Armholes

P3 steek sts, k43 (51, 56, 61, 66, 71) for left front, pm, k66 (76, 86, 100, 102, 102) for left sleeve and place these sts on waste yarn, k87 (99, 113, 129, 133, 141) for back, pm, k66 (76, 86, 100, 102, 102) for right sleeve and place these sts on waste yarn, k43 (51, 56, 61, 66, 71) for right front, p3 steek sts—173 (201, 225, 251, 265, 283) sts plus 6 steek sts rem for body.

Body

Work body even in St st, purling all steek sts as established, until center front measures 18 (18, 18½, 19, 19, 19½)" (45.5 [45.5, 47, 48.5, 48.5, 49.5] cm) from CO. Inc 1 st at each side "seam" marker every rnd 4 (2, 2, 1, 0, 3) time(s)—181 (205, 229, 253, 265, 289) sts plus 6 steek sts. Cont even in patt until center front measures 19 (19, 19½, 20, 20, 20½)" (48.5 [48.5, 49.5, 51, 51, 52] cm) from CO. Change to largest needle. Work Rnds 1–9 of Peerie chart on center 181 (205, 229, 253, 265, 289) sts, beg and end as indicated for body. Change to middle-size needle and work Rnds 10–12 of chart.

Ribbing

Change to smallest needle and work rib as foll: P3, *k2, p2; rep from * to last 4 sts, k1, p3. Purling all steek sts, cont in rib as established for 1" (2.5 cm). Loosely BO all sts.

Sleeves

Place 66 (76, 86, 100, 102, 102) held sleeve sts on middle-size needle, pm to denote underarm "seam" and join for working in the rnd. Knit 1 rnd. *Dec rnd:* K2tog, knit to last 2 sts, ssk—2 sts dec'd. Dec 1 st each end of needle in this manner every 10 (8, 6, 6, 4, 4)th rnd 4 (2, 2, 3, 2, 2) more times, then every 6 (5, 4, 4, 4, 4)th rnd 4 (11, 16, 22, 24, 24) times—48 sts rem. Work even until piece measures 15 (16, 17½, 18, 18, 18)" (38 [40.5, 44.5, 45.5, 45.5, 45.5] cm) from underarm.

Change to largest needles. Work Rnds 1–9 of Peerie chart, beg and end as indicated for sleeve. Change to middle-size needles and work Rnds 10–12 of chart. Change to smallest needles and work in k2, p2 rib for 1" (2.5 cm). Loosely BO all sts.

Finish Steeks

Pick up and knit sts for the button and buttonhole bands, machine stitch along the center front between the bands, then cut the front open between the lines of sts as described in box at right. The machine stitching will prevent the sts from raveling and the button and buttonhole bands will be exactly the right length.

Buttonband

With smallest needle, MC, and RS facing, pick up and knit 134 (134, 138, 138, 138, 142) sts evenly spaced along left front center edge between steek and first body st (see Figure 1 at right). Work in k2, p2 rib for 1" (2.5 cm). Firmly BO all sts. Beg and end about ½–¾" (1.3–2 cm) down from neck and up from lower hem, mark placement of 6 buttons evenly spaced.

Buttonhole Band

With smallest needle, MC, and RS facing, pick up and knit 134 (134, 138, 138, 138, 142) sts evenly spaced along right front center edge between steek and first body st.

Row 1: Work in k2, p2 rib as for buttonband.

Row 2: Make a 2-st vertical buttonhole opposite each button marker as foll: *Work in rib to buttonhole marker, BO 2 sts; rep from * 5 more times, work in rib to end of row.

Row 3: *Work in rib to gap made by BO on previous row, use the backward loop method (see Glossary, page 153) to CO 2 sts over gap to complete buttonhole; rep from * 5 more times, work in rib to end of row.

Incorporating new sts into established rib, cont in rib until band measures 1" (2.5 cm). Firmly BO all sts.

Bias Binding

If desired, apply bias binding to the cut edges of the steek. (This makes for a pretty finish on the inside of the sweater, concealing all of the ends, but is not mandatory.) Unfold one side of the binding and sew along the fold line as close as possible to the bands on the steek sts. Fold the steek sts to the inside and fold the bias binding over them. With matching thread and sewing needle, tack down the edge of the bias binding invisibly to the inside of the sweater, taking care not to pull or distort the sweater.

If not using bias binding, tack steeks to WS of sweater. Sew buttons to buttonband, opposite button-holes. Weave in loose ends. With iron set on "cotton" and maximum steam, press the sweater flat.

Finishing Steeks

Pick up stitches for front bands between steek and first body stitches (Figure 1). With contrasting thread on a sewing machine set for a straight stitch, mark a cutting line by sewing a straight line of stitches along the center of the steek sts. Machine stitch another line along the steek, as close as possible to the buttonband. Machine stitch another line along the steek, this time as close as possible to the buttonhole band—3 lines of machine stitching from neck to hem along steek sts (Figure 2). Change to a zigzag stitch and sew a line of zigzag sts each side of the center cutting line (Figure 3). With sharp scissors, carefully cut along the center cutting line between the 2 rows of zigzag sts.

Figure 1

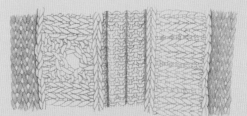

Figure 2

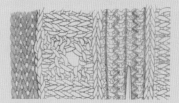

Figure 3

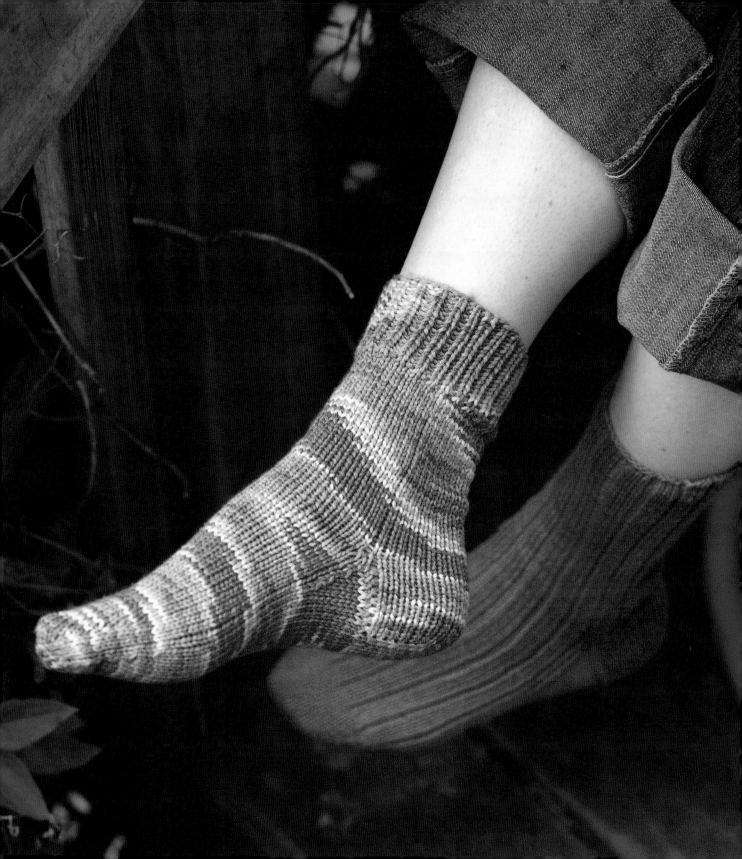

No-Wool Socks

design by Kate Atherley

Don't be fooled into thinking that socks have to be knitted out of wool. Designer Kate Atherley has your feet covered sheeplessly. The Cheeky Ribbed socks (pink) are knitted from pure cotton but without the droop. To balance the lack of elasticity in pure cotton yarn, she's ribbed this sock all over. But Kate's no knitting masochist; she's specified a k3, p1 ribbing, which she finds sufficiently stretchy and much less tedious to knit on double-pointed needles than the typical (and slightly more stretchy) k1, p1 rib.

The No Sweat Socks (multicolored) are mostly unribbed for two good reasons. The first is that the yarn—a marvelous blend of soy and polypropylene—has a good degree of elasticity so will stretch to fit and bounce back on its own. The second is that the variegated colorway looks better in plain old stockinette stitch than in a rib pattern (but you do need a little bit of ribbing at the top to help the sock stay up, and to stop the top from curling). The polypropylene—often found in sports and outdoor gear—wicks moisture away from the skin, making it ideal for socks.

Cheeky Ribbed Socks
Leg

CO 60 sts. Distribute sts evenly on 3 dpn (20 sts each needle), place marker (pm), and join for working in the rnd, being careful not to twist sts. Work 3/1 rib as foll: *K3, p1; rep from * to end of rnd. Cont in rib as established until piece measures 6" (15 cm) from CO, or desired length to top of heel.

Finished Size

Cheeky Ribbed Socks: About 6" (15 cm) foot circumference, unstretched, and 7¾" (19.5 cm) foot length. To fit women's U.S. shoe sizes 5–7.
No Sweat Socks: About 7¼ (8)" (18.5 [20.5] cm) foot circumference and 7½ (8½)" (19 [21.5] cm) foot length. To fit women's U.S. shoe sizes 5–7 (8–10). Socks shown measure 7¼" (18.5 cm).

Yarn

Cheeky Ribbed Socks: Fingering-weight (CYCA #1 Super Fine) yarn.
Shown here: Rowan 4-Ply Cotton (100% cotton; 186 yd [170 m]/50 g); #133 cheeky, 2 balls.
No Sweat Socks: Worsted-weight (CYCA #4 Medium) yarn.
Shown here: Knit One Crochet Too Wick (53% soy, 47% polypropylene; 120 yd [110 m]/50 g): #467 columbine, 3 balls.

Needles

Cheeky Ribbed socks—size 2.5 mm (or, for a U.S. size, size 2 [2.75 mm]): set of 4 double-pointed (dpn). No Sweat Socks—size 3 mm (or, for a U.S. size, size 2 [2.75 mm]): set of 4 double-pointed (dpn). Adjust needle size if necessary to obtain the correct gauge.

Notions

Marker (m); stitch holder; tapestry needle.

Gauge

Cheeky Ribbed socks: 40 stitches and 44 rounds = 4" (10 cm) in k3, p1 rib worked in the round, unstretched. No Sweat Socks: 25 stitches and 41 rounds = 4" (10 cm) in stockinette stitch, worked in the round.

Heel

K27, place rem 33 sts on holder to work later for instep (instep sts begin and end with a purl st).

Heel Flap

Beg with a WS (purl) row and slipping the first st of every row, work 27 heel sts back and forth in St st (knit RS rows; purl WS rows) for 25 rows, ending with a WS row.

Turn Heel

Work short-rows to shape the heel as foll:

Row 1: (RS) K18, ssk (see Glossary, page 154), turn work.

Row 2: (WS) Sl 1, p9, p2tog, turn.

Row 3: Sl 1, k9, ssk, turn.

Rep Rows 2 and 3 until all sts have been worked, ending with a WS row—11 heel sts rem.

Shape Gussets

Pick up sts each side of heel flap and rejoin for working in the rnd as foll:

Rnd 1: With Needle 1, k11 heel sts, then pick up and knit 15 sts along selvedge edge of heel flap (pick up 1 st in each slipped edge st and additional sts above and below slipped sts as necessary); with Needle 2, work 33 held instep sts in patt as established; with Needle 3, pick up and knit 15 sts along other selvedge edge of heel flap, then work first 6 sts from Needle 1 again—74 sts total; 20 sts on Needle 1, 33 sts on Needle 2, and 21 sts on Needle 3. Rnd begins at back of heel.

Rnd 2: Work even as established (work instep sts in patt; work gusset and sole sts in St st), working all picked-up sts through their back loops (tbl).

Rnd 3: On Needle 1, knit to last 3 sts, k2tog, k1; on Needle 2, work all sts in patt; on Needle 3, k1, ssk, knit to end—2 sts dec'd.

Rnd 4: Work even as established.

Rep Rnds 3 and 4 until 60 sts rem—13 sts on Needle 1, 33 sts on Needle 2, 14 sts on Needle 3.

Foot

Work until foot measures about 5¾" (14.5 cm) from back of heel, or 2" (5 cm) less than desired total length.

Toe

If necessary, rearrange sts so that there are 15 sts each on Needle 1 and Needle 3, 30 sts on Needle 2, and rnd begins at center of sole (beg of Needle 1). *Dec rnd:* On Needle 1, knit to last 3 sts, k2tog, k1; on Needle 2, k1, ssk, knit to last 3 sts, k2tog, k1; on Needle 3, k1, ssk, knit to end—4 sts dec'd. Work 3 rnds even. [Rep Dec rnd, then work 2 rnds even] 2 times. [Rep Dec rnd, then work 1 rnd even] 3 times—36 sts rem; 9 sts each on Needle 1 and Needle 3, 18 sts on Needle 2. Rep Dec rnd every rnd 7 times—8 sts rem; 2 sts each on Needle 1 and Needle 3, 4 sts on Needle 2.

Finishing

Cut yarn, leaving a 12" (30.5 cm) tail. Thread tail through rem sts, pull tight to close toe, and fasten off to WS. Weave in loose ends. Block lightly if desired.

No Sweat Socks
Leg

CO 46 (50) sts. Distribute sts as evenly as possible on 3 dpn, place marker (pm), and join for working in the rnd, being careful not to twist sts. *K1, p1; rep from * to end of rnd. Rep this rnd until piece measures 2" (5 cm) from CO. Work even in St st until piece measures 5½ (6½)" (14 [16.5] cm) from CO, or desired length to top of heel.

Heel

K23 (25), place rem 23 (25) sts on holder to work later for instep.

Heel Flap

Beg with a WS (purl) row and slipping the first st of every row, work 23 (25) heel sts back and forth in St st (knit RS rows; purl WS rows) for 17 (19) rows, ending with a WS row.

Turn Heel

Work short-rows to shape heel as foll:

Row 1: (RS) K15 (17), ssk (see Glossary, page 154), turn work.

Row 2: (WS) Sl 1, p7 (9), p2tog, turn.

Row 3: Sl 1, k7 (9), ssk, turn.

Rep Rows 2 and 3 until all sts have been worked, ending with a WS row—9 (11) heel sts rem.

Shape Gussets

Pick up sts each side of heel flap and rejoin for working in the rnd as foll:

Rnd 1: With Needle 1, k9 (11) heel sts, then pick up and knit 12 (13) sts along selvedge edge of heel flap (pick up 1 st in each slipped selvedge st and additional sts above and below slipped sts as necessary); with Needle 2, work 23 (25) held instep sts; with Needle 3, pick up and knit 12 (13) sts along other selvedge edge of heel flap, then knit the first 4 (5) heel sts again—56 (62) sts total; 17 (19) sts on Needle 1, 23 (25) sts on Needle 2, 16 (18) sts on Needle 3. Rnd begins at back of heel.

Rnd 2: Knit, working all picked-up sts through back loops (tbl).

Rnd 3: On Needle 1, knit to last 3 sts, k2tog, k1; on Needle 2, work even in patt; on Needle 3, k1, ssk, knit to end—2 sts dec'd.

Rnd 4: Work even in patt.

Rep Rnds 3 and 4 until 46 (50) sts rem; 12 (13) sts on Needle 1, 23 (25) sts on Needle 2, 11 (12) sts on Needle 3.

Foot

Cont even in patt until piece measures about 5¾ (6½)" (14.5 [16.5] cm) from back of heel, or 1¾ (2)" (4.5 [5] cm) less than desired finished length.

Toe

Dec rnd: On Needle 1, knit to last 3 sts, k2tog, k1; on Needle 2, k1, ssk, knit to last 3 sts, k2tog, k1; on Needle 3, k1, ssk, knit to end—4 sts dec'd; 42 (46) sts rem. Work 3 rnds even. [Work Dec rnd, work 2 rnds even] 2 times—34 (38) sts rem. [Work Dec rnd, work 1 rnd even] 3 times—22 (26) sts rem. Work Dec rnd every rnd 3 (4) times—10 sts rem.

Finish as for Cheeky Ribbed Socks.

Abbreviations

beg	beginning; begin(s)		**rem**	remain(s); remaining
bet	between		**rep**	repeat(s)
BO	bind off		**rev St st**	reverse stockinette stitch
CC	contrast color		**rnd(s)**	round(s)
cm	centimeter(s)		**RS**	right side
cn	cable needle		**sl**	slip
CO	cast on		**sl st**	slip st (slip 1 st pwise unless otherwise indicated)
dec(s)	decrease(s); decreasing		**ssk**	slip , slip, knit (decrease)
dpn	double-pointed needles		**st(s)**	stitch(es)
g	gram(s)		**St st**	stockinette stitch
inc(s)	increase(s); increasing		**tbl**	through back loop
k	knit		**tog**	together
k1f&b	knit into the front and back of same st		**WS**	wrong side
kwise	knitwise, as if to knit		**wyb**	with yarn in back
m	marker(s)		**wyf**	with yarn in front
MC	main color		**yd**	yard(s)
mm	millimeter(s)		**yo**	yarnover
M1	make one (increase)		*****	repeat starting point
p	purl		*** ***	repeat all instructions between asterisks
p1f&b	purl into front and back of same st		**( )**	alternate measurements and/or instructions
patt(s)	pattern(s)		**[ ]**	work instructions as a group a specified number of times
psso	pass slipped st over			
pwise	purlwise, as if to purl			

Glossary

BIND-OFFS

Standard Bind-Off

Knit the first stitch, *knit the next stitch (2 stitches on right needle), insert left needle tip into first stitch on right needle (Figure 1) and lift this stitch up and over the second stitch (Figure 2) and off the needle (Figure 3). Repeat from * for the desired number of stitches.

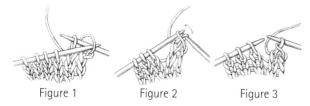

Figure 1   Figure 2   Figure 3

Three-Needle Bind-Off

Place the stitches to be joined onto two separate needles and hold the needles parallel so that the right sides of knitting face together. Insert a third needle into the first stitch on each of two needles (Figure 1) and knit them together as one stitch (Figure 2), *knit the next stitch on each needle the same way, then use the left needle tip to lift the first stitch over the second and off the needle (Figure 3). Repeat from * until no stitches remain on left needles. Cut yarn and pull tail through last stitch to secure.

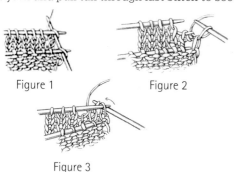

Figure 1   Figure 2

Figure 3

CAST-ONS

Backward Loop Cast-On

*Loop working yarn and place it on needle backward so that it doesn't unwind. Repeat from *.

Knitted Cast-On

Make a slipknot of working yarn and place on the left needle if there are no stitches already there. *Use the right needle to knit the first stitch (or slipknot) on left needle (Figure 1) and place new loop onto left needle to form a new stitch (Figure 2). Repeat from * for the desired number of stitches, always knitting into the last stitch made.

Figure 1

Figure 2

Long-Tail Cast-On

Leaving a long tail (about ½" [1.3 cm] for each stitch to be cast on), make a slipknot and place on right needle. Place thumb and index finger of your left hand between the yarn ends so that working yarn is around your index finger and tail end is around your thumb, and secure the yarn ends with your other fingers. Hold your palm upwards, making a V of yarn (Figure 1). *Bring needle up through loop on thumb (Figure 2), catch first strand around index finger, and go back down through loop on thumb (Figure 3). Drop loop off thumb and, placing thumb back in V configuration, tighten resulting stitch on needle (Figure 4). Repeat from * for the desired number of stitches.

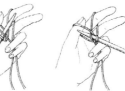

Figure 1   Figure 2   Figure 3   Figure 4

Provisional Cast-On

Make a loose slipknot of working yarn and place it on the right needle. Hold a length of waste yarn next to the slipknot and around your left thumb; hold working yarn over your left index finger. *Bring right needle forward under waste yarn, over working yarn to grab a loop and come forward under waste yarn (Figure 1), then bring needle to the back behind working yarn and grab a second loop (Figure 2). Repeat from * for the desired number of stitches. When you're ready to work in the opposite direction, place the exposed loops on a knitting needle as you pull out the waste yarn.

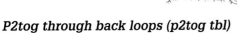

Figure 1   Figure 2

DECREASES

K2tog

Knit 2 stitches together as if they were a single stitch.

K2tog through back loops (k2tog tbl)

Knit 2 stitches together through the loops on the back of the needle.

P2tog

Purl 2 stitches together as if they were a single stitch.

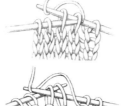

P2tog through back loops (p2tog tbl)

Bring right needle tip behind 2 stitches on left needle, enter through the back loop of the second stitch, then the first stitch, then purl them together.

Ssk

Slip 2 stitches individually knitwise (Figure 1), insert left needle tip into the front of these 2 slipped stitches, and use the right needle to knit them together through their back loops (Figure 2).

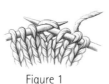

Figure 1   Figure 2

Sssk

Slip 3 stitches individually knitwise (Figure 1), insert left needle tip into the front of these 3 slipped stitches, and use the right needle to knit them together through their back loops (Figure 2).

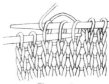

Figure 1   Figure 2

Ssp

Holding yarn in front, slip 2 stitches individually knitwise (Figure 1), then slip these 2 stitches back onto left needle (they will be turned on the needle) and purl them together through their back loops (Figure 2).

Figure 1   Figure 2

EMBROIDERY

Buttonhole Stitch

Working into the edge
half-stitch of the knitted
piece, *bring tip of threaded
needle in and out of a
knitted stitch, place
working yarn under needle
tip, then bring threaded needle through the stitch
and tighten. Repeat from *, always bringing
threaded needle on top of working yarn.

Duplicate Stitch

Horizontal

Bring threaded needle out from back to front at the
base of the V of the knitted stitch you want to cover.
*Working right to left, pass needle in and out under the
stitch in the row above it and back into the base of the
same stitch. Bring needle back out at the base of the V
of the next stitch to the left. Repeat from * for desired
number of stitches.

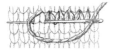

Vertical

Beginning at lowest point, work as for horizontal duplicate stitch, ending by bringing the needle back out at the
base of the stitch directly above the stitch just worked.

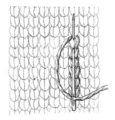

GRAFTING

Kitchener Stitch

Arrange stitches on two needles so that there is the
same number of stitches on each needle. Hold the
needles parallel to each other with right sides of the
knitting facing up. Allowing about ½" (1.3 cm) per
stitch to be grafted, thread matching yarn on a tapestry
needle. Work from right to left as follows:

Step 1. Bring tapestry needle through the first stitch on
the front needle as if to purl and leave the stitch on
the needle (Figure 1).

Step 2. Bring tapestry needle through the first stitch on
the back needle as if to knit and leave that stitch
on the needle (Figure 2).

Step 3. Bring tapestry needle through the first front
stitch as if to knit and slip this stitch off the needle,
then bring tapestry needle through the next front
stitch as if to purl and leave this stitch on the needle
(Figure 3).

Step 4. Bring tapestry needle through the first back
stitch as if to purl and slip this stitch off the needle,
then bring tapestry needle through the next back
stitch as if to knit and leave this stitch on the needle
(Figure 4).

Repeat Steps 3 and 4 until no stitches remain on the
needles, adjusting the tension to match the rest of
the knitting as you go.

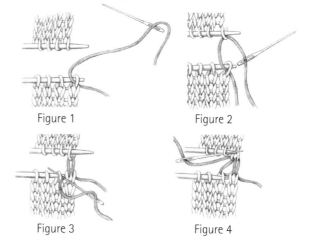

Figure 1   Figure 2

Figure 3   Figure 4

INCREASES

K1f&b

Knit into a stitch but leave it on the left needle
(Figure 1), then knit through the back
loop of the same stitch (Figure 2) and slip
the original stitch off the needle.

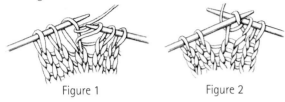

Figure 1   Figure 2

Lifted Increase

Note: If no direction of slant is specified, use the
right slant.

Right Slant

Knit into the back of the stitch (in the "purl bump")
in the row directly below the stitch on the needle
(Figure 1). Knit into the stitch on the needle,
then slip the original stitch off the needle.

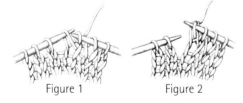

Figure 1   Figure 2

Left Slant

Insert left needle tip into the back of
the stitch below the stitch just knitted
(Figure 1), then knit this stitch (Figure 2).

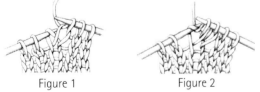

Figure 1   Figure 2

Raised (M1) Increase

Note: If no direction of slant is specified, use the left slant.

Left Slant (M1L)

With left needle tip, lift the strand between
last knitted stitch and first stitch on left needle
from front to back (Figure 1), then knit the
lifted loop through the back (Figure 2).

Figure 1   Figure 2

Right Slant (M1R)

With left needle tip, lift the strand between
the needles from back to front (Figure 1). Knit
the lifted loop through the front (Figure 2).

Figure 1   Figure 2

Make One Purlwise (M1pwise)

Note: If no direction of slant is specified, use the left slant.

Right Slant (M1L pwise)

With left needle tip, lift the strand between the needles
from back to front (Figure 1), then purl the lifted loop
through the front (Figure 2).

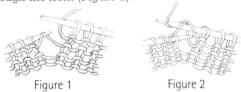

Figure 1   Figure 2

Left Slant (M1R pwise)

With left needle tip, lift the strand between the needles
from front to back (Figure 1), then purl the lifted loop
through the back (Figure 2).

Figure 1   Figure 2

Yo (yarnover)

Wrap the working yarn around the needle from front to back, then bring yarn into position to work the next stitch (leave it in back if a knit stitch follows; bring it under the needle to the front if a purl stitch follows).

Yarnover backwards (backward yo)

Bring the yarn to the back under the needle, then over the top to the front so that the leading leg of the loop is at the back of the needle.

PICK UP AND KNIT

With right side facing and working from right to left, insert tip of needle under the front half (Figure 1) or both halves (Figure 2) of stitch along selvedge edge, wrap yarn around needle, and pull it through to form a stitch on the needle. For a tighter join, pick up the stitches and knit them through the back loop (Figure 3).

Figure 1   Figure 2   Figure 3

SEAMING

Backstitch Seam

Hold pieces to be seamed so that their right sides face each other and so that the edges to be seamed are even with each other. Thread seaming yarn on a tapestry needle and join the pieces as follows: *Insert threaded needle through both layers, from back to front, two stitches to the left (Figure 1), then from front to back one stitch to the right (Figure 2). Repeat from *, working right to left so that seaming yarn follows a circular path.

Figure 1

Figure 2

Invisible Seam (Mattress Stitch) for Stockinette Stitch

Hold pieces to be seamed side by side with their right sides facing upward. Thread seaming yarn on a tapestry needle and join the pieces as follows: *Insert threaded needle under two horizontal bars between the two edge stitches on one piece (Figure 1), then under two bars between the corresponding stitches on the other piece (Figure 2), pulling the seaming yarn firmly to bring the pieces together. Repeat from *, alternating a stitch from one piece and a stitch from the other piece.

Figure 1   Figure 2

SHORT-ROWS

Work to turning point, slip next stitch purlwise to right needle, then bring the yarn to the front (Figure 1). Slip the same stitch back to the left needle (Figure 2), turn the work around and bring the yarn in position for the next stitch, wrapping the slipped stitch with working yarn as you do so. When you come to a wrapped stitch on a subsequent row, hide the wrap by working it together with the wrapped stitch as follows: insert right needle tip under the wrap (from the front if wrapped stitch is a knit stitch; from the back if wrapped stitch is a purl stitch), then into the stitch on the needle, and work the stitch and its wrap together as a single stitch.

Figure 1   Figure 2

Contributors

Kate Atherley knits and lives in Toronto, Ontario.

Libby Baker hasn't been able to let go of her needles since her first stitch in 2001. She keeps track of all of the resulting projects on her blog, Creazativity (creazativity.typepad.com), and tries to sort out the resulting yarn entanglements at her home in Englewood, Colorado.

Wendy Bernard is convinced that she's always known how to knit, but admits that she didn't pick up the needles until about four years ago. She's intrigued by top-down construction and anything that can be worked in one piece or in the round. Wendy lives in Southern California with her daughter and husband. Read about her on her blog, Knit and Tonic.

Celeste Culpepper has been knitting for decades and lives in Nelson, British Columbia. To see more of her hemp designs, visit www.hempforknitting.com and look for the Lacy Little Top and the Leaf Lace Skirt.

Barbara Gregory knits and illustrates in Toronto, Ontario. She likes to use many colors in both of these pursuits. Her husband of many years watches in bemused silence. You can see examples of Barbara's efforts at www.barbaragregory.com.

Sivia Harding is a designer with a growing following who dabbles in lace, beads, and most recently, socks. Her work can be seen in Knitty.com and the books *Knitgrrl 2* and *Big Girl Knits*. Someday Sivia is going to start a blog.

Karin Maag-Tanchak grew up in Germany and learned how to knit in school at age eight. She has an MA in English, writes poetry, and just closed her yarn shop to devote more time to actual knitting! She lives in Albany, New York, with her husband, son, and daughter, all of whom know how to knit.

Jillian Moreno is co-author of *Big Girl Knits* and editor of Knittyspin.com magazine. Her brain is filled with so many fibery ideas that sometimes she has to lie down and nap. Jillian lives in Ann Arbor, Michigan, with her family and a room full of fiber.

Kristi Porter is a knitwear designer, technical editor, teacher, and author whose work has been featured in *Knit Wit*, the *Knitgrrl* series, *Big Girl Knits,* and her own book, *Knitting for Dogs*. Kristi contributes features, patterns, and the column Frankenknits, which celebrates recycling, reknitting, and refashioning old garments, to Knitty.com. Kristi lives with her husband, two daughters, and lots of yarn in La Jolla, California.

Stephannie Roy likes creating and knitting small, portable projects. Her designs have appeared on Knitty.com, and in *Knit Wit* and *Big Girl Knits*. She lives in Toronto with her husband and two children where she works as a sociologist and advertising manager for Knitty.com. Read about Stephannie on her blog at acunningplan.typepad.com.

Jeannine Sims has been knitting for more than twenty-five years and has a broad background in traditional knitting and handspinning. Jeannine has participated in several New York Sheep-to-Shawl contests and has test knitted patterns for Cottage Creations' Babies & Bears Sweater for Grownups. She teaches sweater and sock classes, specialty workshops, and knits every chance she gets.

Brooke Snow lives on an island in Florida where wool is reserved for the cold month and other plant fibers are used all year. Brooke divides her time between chasing her son on the beach and knitting while he naps. She dreams of a support group for mothers who can't stop knitting.

Amy Swenson, together with her partner Sandra, owns and operates Make One Yarn Studio (www.make1yarns.com) in Calgary, Alberta. Amy is author of *Not Your Mama's Crochet*, and has contributed designs for *Knit Wit, Big Girl Knits, Stitch 'N Bitch Nation, Get Hooked 2, Knitgrrl,* and *Knitting for Dogs*. More of her designs can be found on Knitty.com and in yarn shops under the pattern line IndiKnits (www.indiknits.com).

Zoe Valette taught herself to knit in high school because she loved textiles and couldn't find the sweaters she wanted to wear. She studied fashion design at the Fashion Institute of Technology and Istituto Marangoni in Milan, and interned with several design houses in New York.

Deb White is a wife, mother, teacher, writer, and artist, as well as a knitter. Her recent work can be found on Knitty.com, as well as in *New Knits on the Block* and *Big Girl Knits*. Deb records her current designs, as well as various ramblings, on her blog, notprettytowatch.blogspot.com.

Jenna Wilson lives and knits in Toronto. By day, she's a mild-mannered intellectual property lawyer, and by night she dabbles in knitwear design. Jenna taught herself to knit and sells original patterns through her website, girlfromauntie.com. Jenna's patterns appear on Knitty.com and in *Stitch 'N Bitch: The Knitter's Handbook, Knit Wit,* and *Knitgrrl 2*.

Wendy Wonnacott lives in Sicily, Italy, with her husband and daughter. She finds inspiration in the local markets, shop windows, and from people watching. You can find more of Wendy's work on The Garter Belt (www.thegarterbelt.com).

Holli Yeoh lives in beautiful Vancouver, British Columbia, where she likes to design knitwear and knit while watching her son at playgrounds. Visit her website www.beesneesknits.ca for more designs.

Sources of Supplies

Alchemy Yarns
PO Box 1080
Sebastopol, CA 95473
www.alchemyyarns.com
Bamboo

Artyarns
39 Westmoreland Ave.
White Plains, NY 10606
www.artyarns.com
Regal Silk

Berroco Inc./Lang Yarns
14 Elmdale Rd.
PO Box 367
Uxbridge, MA 01569
www.berroco.com, and

Estelle Designs
2220 Midland Ave., Unit 65
Scarborough, ON
Canada M1P 3E6
www.estelleyarns.com
Lang Opal

Blue Heron Yarns
29532 Canvasback Dr. #6
Easton, MD 21601
www.blueheronyarns.com
Cotton Rayon Seed

Blue Moon Fiber Arts
56587 Mollenhour Rd.
Scappoose, OR 97056
www.bluemoonfiberarts.com
Sock Candy

Blue Sky Alpacas
PO Box 88
Cedar, MN 55011
www.blueskyalpacas.com
Organic Cotton
Dyed Cotton

Classic Elite Yarns
300 Jackson St.
Lowell, MA 01852
www.classiceliteyarns.com
Temptation

Curious Creek Fibers
3070 Palm St.
San Diego, CA 92104
www.curiouscreek.com
Isalo

Furryarns
www.furryarns.com
Tussah Silk Roving

Hand Maiden Fine Yarn
www.handmaiden.ca
Silken

JCA Inc./Artful Yarns
35 Scales Ln.
Townsend, MA 01469
www.jcacrafts.com
Artful Candy

Knit One Crochet Too
7 Commons Ave., Ste. 2
Windham, ME 01469
www.knitonecrochettoo.com
Wick

Muench Yarns Inc./GGH
1323 Scott St.
Petaluma, CA 94954
www.muenchyarns.com
GGH Linova

Lanaknits Designs
320 Vernon St.
Nelson, BC
Canada V1L 4E4
www.lanaknits.com
Hemp for Knitting Allhemp6

Louet Sales/Euroflax
808 Commerce Park Dr.
Ogdensburg, NY 13669, *and*
RR 4, Prescott, ON
Canada K0E 1T0
www.louet.com
Euroflax Geneva

Knitting Fever Inc./Euro Yarns
35 Debevoise Ave.
Roosevelt, NY 11575
www.knittingfever.com
Euro Yarns Cotolino

S. R. Kertzer Ltd.
50 Trowers Rd.
Woodbridge, ON
Canada L4L 7K6
www.kertzer.com
Butterfly Super 10

Skacel Collection
PO Box 88110
Seattle, WA 98138
www.skacelknitting.com
Schulana Supercotton

Westminster Fibers/Rowan
4 Townsend West, Unit 8
Nashua, NH 03063
www.knitrowan.com
Rowan 4-Ply Cotton
Rowan Summer Tweed
Rowan Calmer

Bibliography and Further Reading

Aspin, Chris. *The Cotton Industry.* Buckinghamshire, U.K.: Shire Publications Limited, 2004.

—. *The Woollen Industry.* Buckinghamshire, U.K.: Shire Publications Limited, 1994.

Baines, Patricia. *Flax and Linen.* Buckinghamshire, U.K.: Shire Publications Limited, 2003.

Bourrie, Mark. *Hemp: a short history of the most misunderstood plant and its uses and abuses.* Buffalo, New York: Firefly Books, 2003.

Bush, Sarah. *The Silk Industry.* Buckinghamshire, U.K.: Shire Publications Limited, 2000.

Cook, J. Gordon. *Handbook of Textile Fibres.* England: Merrow Publishing Co. Ltd, 1960.

Feltwell, Dr. John. *The Story of Silk.* New York: St. Martin's Press, 1990.

Hochberg, Bette. *Fiber Facts.* Santa Cruz, California: Bette and Bernard Hochberg, 1993.

—. *Spin Span Spun.* Santa Cruz, California: Bette and Bernard Hochberg, 1998.

The Viscose Company. *The Story of Rayon.* New York: Rogers & Company, 1929.

Zimmermann, Elizabeth. *Knitter's Almanac.* Dover Publications, October 1, 1981.

Yafa, Stephen. *Big Cotton: how a humble fiber created fortunes, wrecked civilizations, and put America on the map.* New York: Viking Penguin, 2005.

Online Reading

http://www.euroflax.com
http://www.industrialhemp.net
http://Knitty.com
http://www.naihc.org (North American Industrial Hemp Council)
http://www.seacell.com
http://www.wormspit.com
http://www.vreseis.com (Home of Fox Fibre cotton)

Index